# POPULAR MUSIC AND THE MYTHS OF MADNESS

*To Stan, Jake and Mia*

# Popular Music and the Myths of Madness

NICOLA SPELMAN
*University of Salford, UK*

ASHGATE

Published by
Ashgate Publishing Limited
Wey Court East
Union Road
Farnham
Surrey, GU9 7PT
England

Ashgate Publishing Company
Suite 420
101 Cherry Street
Burlington
VT 05401-4405
USA

www.ashgate.com

**British Library Cataloguing in Publication Data**
Spelman, Nicola.
Popular music and the myths of madness. – (Ashgate popular and folk music series)
1. Psychoanalysis and music – History – 20th century.
2. Psychotherapy and music – History – 20th century.
3. Popular music – 1961–1970 – History and criticism.
4. Popular music – 1971–1980 – History and criticism.
I. Title II. Series
781.6'4'09046–dc23

**Library of Congress Cataloging-in-Publication Data**
Spelman, Nicola.
Popular music and the myths of madness / Nicola Spelman.
    p. cm. — (Ashgate popular and folk music series)
Includes bibliographical references and index.
ISBN 978-1-4094-1831-3 (hardcover : alk. paper) — ISBN 978-1-4094-4476-3 (ebook) 1. Mental illness in music. 2. Popular music—1961–1970—History and criticism. 3. Popular music—1971–1980—History and criticism. I. Title.
    ML3470.S646 2012
    781.64'159—dc23

2011041529

ISBN 9781409418313 (hbk)
ISBN 9781409444763 (ebk)

Printed and bound in Great Britain by the MPG Books Group, UK.

# Contents

# General Editor's Preface

The upheaval that occurred in musicology during the last two decades of the twentieth century has created a new urgency for the study of popular music alongside the development of new critical and theoretical models. A relativistic outlook has replaced the universal perspective of modernism (the international ambitions of the 12-note style); the grand narrative of the evolution and dissolution of tonality has been challenged, and emphasis has shifted to cultural context, reception and subject position. Together, these have conspired to eat away at the status of canonical composers and categories of high and low in music. A need has arisen, also, to recognize and address the emergence of crossovers, mixed and new genres, to engage in debates concerning the vexed problem of what constitutes authenticity in music and to offer a critique of musical practice as the product of free, individual expression.

Popular musicology is now a vital and exciting area of scholarship, and the *Ashgate Popular and Folk Music Series* presents some of the best research in the field. Authors are concerned with locating musical practices, values and meanings in cultural context, and draw upon methodologies and theories developed in cultural studies, semiotics, poststructuralism, psychology and sociology. The series focuses on popular musics of the twentieth and twenty-first centuries. It is designed to embrace the world's popular musics from Acid Jazz to Zydeco, whether high tech or low tech, commercial or non-commercial, contemporary or traditional.

Professor Derek B. Scott
Professor of Critical Musicology
University of Leeds

# List of Music Examples

# Acknowledgements

I would first like to thank Derek Scott whose good humour, encouragement and critical guidance played a vital role in the completion of this book. I am also grateful to Sheila Whiteley for her unremitting faith in my work and much valued friendship. Thanks to George McKay and Tim Wise for proof-reading parts of the book, and to those individuals who have assisted with its publication. I am also grateful to my University of Salford colleagues, both past and present, who have offered comment and advice along the way. A special word of thanks goes to my loving family for their invaluable support and good cheer.

# Introduction

Portrayals of madness in popular music have shown it to be a wide-ranging and powerful medium for facilitating and communicating extremes of emotion. Songs that utilize madness and its associated themes as little more than a means to generate irreverent humour exist alongside those of a more sombre nature which delve further into the psychological and social implications of its many forms and treatments. All so-called 'mad' songs capitalize on our seemingly inherent fascination and fear of the abnormal and irrational, and most offer depictions of madness which place it as the antithesis of rationalism and mental coherence.

A comprehensive investigation of popular music's assorted representations of madness reveals the potential for identifying specific trends where ideas about its definition and treatment appear, for a time, to coalesce and resonate with radical medical opinion and artistic works from other cultural idioms. This book concentrates on one such instance in popular music's history where, in the late 1960s and 1970s, there was an apparent proclivity for portrayals of madness centred on a critique of mainstream psychiatry. Songs emerged that had the potential to challenge common beliefs and problematize conceptions of madness in ways that were equally visible in contemporary film and literature. Many prominent and influential songwriters at this time employed a sympathetic yet provocative treatment of the subject, and I assert that the principal reason for this may be found once the music is related to the dissemination of the innovative and often extreme theories of the anti-psychiatry movement. To demonstrate this premise, the following chapters present close readings of representative songs by David Bowie, Lou Reed, Pink Floyd, Alice Cooper, the Beatles and Elton John, exploring their indebtedness to anti-psychiatric ideas and analysing the ways in which those ideas are embodied both verbally and musically. The concluding discussion reveals the uniqueness of the period in question through cross-referencing and analysis of comparable songs drawn from a variety of styles and eras, assessing their correspondence to the anti-psychiatric frame of reference.

## Anti-Psychiatry

The defiant and multifaceted nature of popular songs engaging with the topic of madness during the late 1960s and 1970s necessitates an exploration of contemporaneous texts offering a critique of mainstream psychiatry; and here lies an abundance of materials. As Ann Claytor observes: 'Psychiatry has been subject to suspicion and challenge throughout its history [...] However, anti-psychiatry does constitute a particularly extreme and widespread opposition to psychiatry emerging at a time when psychiatry appeared to be increasingly accepted as a bona fide branch of twentieth century medicine.'[1] In fact, sufficient questions were being asked at this time in relation to not only the appropriateness of specific psychiatric diagnoses and treatments but also the very existence of mental illness itself, to warrant commentators referring to an anti-psychiatry 'movement'[2] – and this despite numerous differences of opinion existing between its foremost figures.

The term 'anti-psychiatry' was conceived by David Cooper in 1967 when, in relation to the psychiatric establishment, he admitted that: 'A more profound questioning has led some of us to propose conceptions and procedures that seem quite antithetic to the conventional ones – in fact what may be regarded as a germinal anti-psychiatry.'[3] The individuals most commonly associated with anti-psychiatry are R.D. Laing, David Cooper, Thomas Szasz, Thomas Scheff, Erving Goffman and, to a lesser extent, Michel Foucault. Their ideas are undeniably diverse yet demonstrate a mutual objection to the medical model of psychiatry[4] – meaning they take issue with the medicalization of mental disorder, critiquing to various degrees, and with a variety of approaches, the processes, methods and treatments which constitute it. It is worth noting that none were attempting to eradicate psychiatry per se, but their theories advocated a need for essential

---

[1]     Ann Claytor, *A Changing Faith: A History of Developments in Radical Critiques of Psychiatry Since the 1960s* (Sheffield, 1993), pp. 3–4. Jane Ussher makes a similar point regarding the prevalence of opposition at this time: 'Dissention and revolt, resulting in attempts to overthrow the dominant discourse of madness, have been endemic in every society where the concept of madness has existed. Latterly it was the archetypal sixties radicals, the "anti-psychiatrists," who popularized the critiques of madness, placing them firmly in the public arena and declaring openly that "the emperor has no clothes".' Jane Ussher, *Women's Madness: Misogyny or Mental Illness* (Hemel Hempstead, 1991), p. 130.

[2]     Both David Ingleby and Marijke Gijswijt-Hofstra, for example, refer to anti-psychiatry as a 'movement' – in Gijswijt-Hofstra's case it is a termed a 'kaleidoscopic movement' (implying a frequently changing pressure group). Marijke Gijswijt-Hofstra and Roy Porter (eds), *Cultures of Psychiatry and Mental Health Care in Postwar Britain and the Netherlands* (Amsterdam and Atlanta, 1998), pp. 1 and 296 respectively.

[3]     David Cooper, *Psychiatry and Anti-Psychiatry* [1967] (London, 2001), p. ix. It should be noted, however, that of those figures most associated with a critique of psychiatry at this time, the majority voiced their dissatisfaction with the term 'anti-psychiatry', as Ussher highlights: 'Called such in the face of their own ardent disclaimers that they were not to be categorized together, each claiming that their work certainly could not be subsumed under such an ignominious label'. Ussher, p. 157.

[4]     Stephen Snelders has identified this common ground between anti-psychiatrists, defining the medical model of mental illness as follows: 'In this model a person who arrives (in whatever way) at a doctor is diagnosed by him and can be classified as a patient, suffering from certain phenomena which constitute an illness. He or she is then treated according to the medical system, i.e. further diagnosis, prognosis and therapy.' Stephen Snelders, 'LSD and the Dualism between Medical and Social Theories of Mental Illness', in Gijswijt-Hofstra and Porter, p. 104.

change that, as will be discussed in my concluding chapter, struck a chord with the radical stance of the 1960s counter-culture.

Before identifying each key figure's output and its potential value to an understanding of representations of madness within popular music, I will provide a brief summary of anti-psychiatry ideas, one of the foremost being an objection to the involuntary 'treatment' of a person deemed mentally disordered. Here the issue of enforced hospitalization is often used to imply that psychiatry is a form of social control wherein the applied medication (drugs) or physical treatment – such as electroconvulsive therapy (ECT) – is intended to eradicate deviant behaviour. Such a view requires some form of alignment with an equally prominent anti-psychiatry idea – that which questions the existence of mental illness itself, believing it to be a fictitious concept where diagnosis amounts to little more than labelling those who fail to conform to societal norms. The basis for such an idea comes from an unwillingness to accept biological failings as the root cause of mental problems; instead such problems are the product of social circumstances wherein the role of the family comes under particular scrutiny. The condemnation of invasive physical and medicinal treatments (electroshock, psychosurgery and psychotropic drugs) is widespread, and somewhat less common is the notion that the form of mental disturbance commonly identified as schizophrenia has the potential to initiate a form of mental regeneration – a process whereby the individual concerned is reunited with their 'true' self.

The fact that the main arguments of the anti-psychiatrists are relatively diverse is reflected in my choice of songs for analysis, as each one appears to beam in on a different combination of anti-psychiatric ideas. For this reason, each of the subsequent chapters draws upon the theories of individual figures from the anti-psychiatry movement, interweaving analyses of the songs and relevant theoretical discussions in a way that aims to demonstrate the extent of their influence. According to David Ingleby, anti-psychiatry was 'just as much an American invention as a British one',[5] and this is borne out by the fact that, of all the so-called anti-psychiatrists, the works of American psychiatrist Thomas Szasz and British psychiatrist R.D. Laing have been of greatest value to my investigations.

Szasz's first book, *The Myth of Mental Illness* (1961), was responsible for propagating the idea that, contrary to popular and medical belief, mental illness does not actually exist. Citing clear differences between physical, organic defects of the body and so-called mental deficiencies, he claimed that what psychiatrists term 'mental illnesses' are, in fact, 'problems in living', with no biological basis.[6] In his later book, *Insanity: The Idea and Its Consequences* (1987), Szasz returned to this, his principal argument, likening mental illness to a theatrical impersonation which a person is encouraged to adopt once they have been diagnosed mentally

[5]    David Ingleby, 'The View from the North Sea', in Gijswijt-Hofstra and Porter, p. 295.

[6]    Thomas Szasz, *The Myth of Mental Illness: Foundations of a Theory of Personal Conduct* [1961] (London, 1972), p. 269.

deficient.[7] Such a theory is of relevance to popular musicology because it highlights the potential for popular music artists to critique psychiatry and its diagnostic criteria through the use of role play, where the shift between portrayals of behaviour commonly associated with madness and those believed to constitute normality implies the invented nature of mental illness. Chapters 1 and 4 both elaborate on this premise.

Szasz's contention that 'mad' behaviour is diagnosed as such because it contravenes social rules provides the basis for some of his principal arguments. Of particular relevance to the way in which 'mad' protagonists in popular song may be recognized as deviant is his claim concerning psychiatry's potential for policing the sane – that the 'symbolic offender' is used as a means to legitimize the beliefs of the majority and 'strengthen group cohesion'. Szasz's work *The Manufacture of Madness* (1970) is especially useful for explaining the identification of 'mad' characters as Other; the role they have in confirming the virtue of those in positions of power and authority; and their potential threat to recognized order. Works such as *Ideology and Insanity: Essays on the Psychiatric Dehumanization of Man* (1970) equally demonstrate ways in which those considered mentally sick may be thought of as victims of an oppressive social regime as opposed to sufferers of their own internal biology.[8] While Szasz in no way romanticizes the plight of 'mad' men and women, his arguments nevertheless elucidate the potential for 'mad' protagonists to occupy positions of resistance; and, as such, further discussion of the aforementioned theories may be found throughout this book.

Szasz's premise that involuntary mental hospitalization is morally wrong is also applicable to an understanding of the ways in which popular songs question psychiatric practice. Indeed his propensity to draw the most ruthless of comparisons in this regard – comparing such treatment in *The Manufacture of Madness* to the witch-hunts of the Spanish Inquisition – is analogous to those songs which portray the confinement of the 'mad' as a harmful and interminable act of incarceration. In addition, Szasz's repeated assertion that the role of the mental hospital patient is more like that of a prison inmate than a medical patient[9] is useful for interpreting songs that focus on the act of involuntary internment as an act of chastisement as opposed to cure; see, for example, references to *Ideology and Insanity, Insanity: The Idea and Its Consequences* and *Cruel Compassion* (1994) in Chapter 4. His reluctance to criticize psychiatric treatments for fear that such discussion may inadvertently imply the actual existence of 'biological' mental illness means that his works are less pertinent to analyses of songs critical of procedures such as ECT and drug therapy, but his stance is nevertheless comparable with songs that mock – as opposed to question – such procedures.

While Szasz maintains the same essential arguments throughout his prolific body of work, the same is not true of Laing, whose abounding critique of psychiatry

7      Thomas Szasz, *Insanity: The Idea and Its Consequences* (New York, 1987), p. 212.
8      Thomas Szasz, *The Manufacture of Madness* [1970] (London, 1973), p. 86.
9      Szasz, *Insanity*, p. 112.

took time to develop and then subside. As such, only two of Laing's works – *Sanity, Madness and the Family* (1964) and *The Politics of Experience* (1967) – are of real relevance to the central concern of this book. Laing's well-known work *The Divided Self* (1960), for example, offers an insight into his early attempts to offer some understanding of why madness occurs and the progression it may take, but there is no questioning of the medical model itself. It is also worth noting that, while at times Laing shares Szasz's contention that mental illness is purely a social construction, his political standpoint is very different.[10] In particular, his involvement with the 1960s counter-culture informed not only the way in which he articulated his arguments but also the extent of his cultural impact – a factor that is especially pertinent to my concluding discussion of why anti-psychiatry ideas should appear within popular songs during the period in question.

The research that Laing and co-author Aaron Esterson conducted in their work *Sanity, Madness and the Family* seeks to demonstrate that the behaviour of identified schizophrenics is understandable in relation to their family situations. It insinuates that supposedly unintelligible behaviour diagnosed as mental illness is either a direct result of problematic family relations or a consequence of some form of family conspiracy. As John Henzell notes: 'Laing and Esterson were concerned with a radically alternative account of "crazy" experience, and also with a critical examination of the often oppressive social norms embedded in the family, medical practice and our "official consciousness".'[11] Its stance thus has a bearing on the significant number of popular songs that situate their 'mad' protagonists within a family setting, either as sons or daughters bound by excessive parental control or as fathers, mothers and spouses incapable of fulfilling the traditional roles society expects of them. Laing's criticism of the family became more patent within his later work, *The Politics of Experience*, where its function is regarded as a principal tool in the reproduction of 'one-dimensional man'.[12] As such, its content helps to illuminate songs that exhibit negative representations of parents incapable of relating to their progeny, where desire for compliance appears excessive, even menacing.

Published at the height of Laing's popularity, the aforementioned work also contains a number of theories relevant to an understanding of popular songs that construct a positive, seemingly heroic, identity for their 'mad' protagonists. Specifically, Laing suggests that psychotic experience can be potentially enlightening, part of a natural healing process in which a person might relinquish

---

[10] For a discussion of differences between the politics and theories of Szasz and Laing, see Zbigniew Kotowicz, *R.D. Laing and the Paths of Anti-Psychiatry* (London, 1997), pp. 90–93.

[11] John Henzell, 'Art, Madness and Anti-Psychiatry: A Memoir', in Katherine Killick and Joy Schaverien (eds), *Art, Psychotherapy and Psychosis* (London, 1997), p. 180.

[12] Ronald D. Laing, *The Politics of Experience* [1967] (Harmondsworth, 1978), p. 26. Note the reference is to Herbert Marcuse's work *One-Dimensional Man: Studies in the Ideology of Advanced Industrial Society* (1964).

their 'false' self and be reunited with their 'true' self.[13] He eulogizes over the innocent sensibilities of childhood, and claims that a rediscovery of inner space and time is essential to the process of being spiritually re-born. Moreover, his assertion that schizophrenics can teach psychiatrists about the inner world[14] suggests an identification with the mythology of enlightened madness where those labelled 'mad' possess the gift of uncanny insight. Songs representing madness in terms of a mystical virtuousness thus possess a certain affinity with Laing's work, and Chapters 3 and 5 discuss these ideas in greater depth.

Laing's encouragement to acknowledge the dangers of a 'false' existence is buoyed by his theory of man's estranged state which provides a useful reference point from which to identify songs advocating that normality is simply a façade. In particular, Laing's repeated criticism in *The Politics of Experience* of so-called 'normal' existence – alongside his premise that those with a diagnosis of mental illness had the potential to demonstrate a greater level of sanity than those without – is also pertinent to an investigation of songs that adopt a reversal strategy, advocating the sanity of 'madness' over the irrational behaviour of the supposed 'sane'.

Evident similarities exist between the work of Laing and Cooper, although Cooper's writings are more political and, while questioning contemporary notions of madness and sanity, he does not share Laing's view regarding the self-healing potential of psychosis. His works *Psychiatry and Anti-Psychiatry* (1967) and *The Death of the Family* (1971) are both of value to an exploration of popular music and madness – the former arguing that, rather than existing inside the individual, madness exists within a 'system of relationships' the so-called patient happens to participate in.[15] His criticism of the family unit begins with the claim that unwanted adolescent behaviour is invalidated by the family via the label of illness. His escalation of such theories is then exemplified in the title of his later work, *The Death of the Family*, which reaffirms Laing's call for a reawakening of the human being's true potential, equating sanity and normality with an absence of experience, while vilifying the family by arguing that it effectively conspires with the institution of psychiatry to rid its members of their desire for individual autonomy.[16] Cooper's work is thus pertinent to an investigation of 'mad' songs in many of the ways outlined above with respect to Laing; but the fact that his critique is applied more widely – requesting a 'revolution from all the mechanizations of capitalist society'[17] – and, in relation to the family, more harshly, means his works are particularly applicable to those songs harbouring a more extreme form of resistance. As Claytor explains: 'For Cooper, sanity could never be the product of simple individual transformation. The whole of society

---

[13]   See Laing, *The Politics of Experience*, pp. 105–7.

[14]   Ibid., p. 91.

[15]   Cooper, *Psychiatry and Anti-Psychiatry*, p. 148.

[16]   David Cooper, *The Death of the Family* (London, 1971), p. 11.

[17]   Ibid., p. 139.

must be transformed.'[18] Cooper's criticism of physical psychiatric treatments designed to alter an individual's behaviour – which he regards as further evidence of underhand social conditioning – means that his work also provides valuable evidence of condemnation from within the psychiatric profession that is comparable to popular songs demonstrating a similar stance with respect to electroshock and lobotomy.

The fact that Cooper provided an introduction to the translated version of Foucault's *Histoire de la Folie* (1961), retitled *Madness and Civilization* (1964), implies that it too contains ideas of an anti-psychiatric nature. However, unlike Szasz, Laing and Cooper, Foucault was not a trained psychiatrist but a critical social historian. As such, his work is of relevance to the concerns of this book because of its ability to problematize traditional histories of psychiatry. As Pilgrim and Rogers attest, such works 'challenge self-regulatory versions of history, which tend to mask the interests of powerful sections of society, such as the psychiatric profession and the central capitalist State'.[19] Foucault's arguments regarding a perceived loss of dialogue between reason and madness, its cause and consequences, are of particular relevance to songs which explore the social exclusion of the identified 'mad'. Furthermore, his contention that the confinement of madness resulted in its medicalization, and that the 'mad' came to be viewed and treated as children, provides a useful framework from which to interpret songs exhibiting social control theories. Like Laing and Cooper, there is also the suggestion that madness came to be linked with notions of the family, and his observations regarding the voyeuristic appeal of madness are pertinent to songs that critique madness as spectacle. By referencing numerous examples of art and literature Foucault also demonstrates how conceptions of madness have changed throughout history. Of particular value are his insights into the potential origins of various myths – such as the metaphorical connection between madness and water – that maintain a presence within more current popular texts.

The final two anti-psychiatry figures of significance to the premise of this book, Goffman and Scheff, represent a sociological perspective that aims to discredit the medical model of madness by highlighting its lack of scientific objectivity. Their basic assertion is that mental illness is a social construct that is thus mutable – it is identified via the process of labelling behaviour society deems undesirable as deviant, and what is considered 'normal' at one point in time has the potential to be considered 'mad' at another. Goffman's work *Asylums: Essays on the Social Situation of Mental Patients and Other Inmates* (1961) criticizes 'total institutions', claiming that, in the case of mental hospitals, behaviour exhibited by patients considered symptomatic of their 'illness' is actually an understandable reaction to the treatment they receive and the social roles they are assigned. In general terms, *Asylums* offers ideas relevant to an understanding of songs that seek

---

[18]   Claytor, p. 85.

[19]   David Pilgrim and Anne Rogers, *A Sociology of Mental Health and Illness* (Buckingham and Philadelphia, 1999), p. 145.

to question definitions of madness and sanity, but it is of specific relevance to those works that suggest the negative impact of involuntary confinement on a person's sanity. Goffman's examination of inmates' behaviour also provides information pertinent to an understanding of popular texts that exhibit an apparent sense of solidarity amongst those identified as 'mad'.

Arising from a similar tenet, Scheff's work *Being Mentally Ill: A Sociological Theory* (1966) concentrates on the existence and reiteration of 'stereotypes of insanity', claiming that the concept of mental illness, through its identification of unacceptable behaviour, serves to 'preserve the current mores' of society.[20] His argument that stigmatizing labels are meted out as a means of condemning conduct at variance with what the majority consider correct and rational offers a useful basis from which to explore songs that problematize stereotypical 'mad' behaviour. Such songs typically highlight society's predilection for understanding deviancy in terms of illness, and Chapters 2 and 4 discuss this in relation to the artist's construction of a deviant persona. As Simon Cross points out, stereotypical notions of madness 'make it clear how madness is seen: visible differences of appearance and behaviour that demarcate a symbolic boundary between "us" and "them"'.[21] With this in mind, my alignment of select musical examples to the aforementioned anti-psychiatry texts makes it possible to demonstrate how they convey an unexpected sense of reversal, promoting the weaknesses of 'us' while simultaneously advocating the potential benefits of being one of 'them'.

Having briefly detailed the problematic nature of the term 'anti-psychiatry', it is important to observe that the terms 'mental illness' and 'madness' are also not straightforward in definition and application. In this regard, I have adopted the terminological choices of Stephen Harper who, in his article 'Media, Madness and Misrepresentation', refers to the term 'mental illness' as being 'appropriate in descriptions of madness in psychiatric or institutional contexts', while the term 'madness' is used 'in other contexts, where the meaning of the term exceeds psychiatric discourse'.[22] Thus in this book I refer predominantly to 'madness' for, as Harper concludes: 'the term allows cultural critics to shift their critical focus from marginalized individuals to questions of institutional and social madness' – an approach that is clearly applicable to my own analyses. Furthermore, in acknowledgement of the stigmatizing potential of the unofficial term 'mad', and in an effort to stress its equivocal nature (where its use presupposes the abnormal when this may not be the case), it appears within scare quotes throughout.

---

[20]     Thomas Scheff, *Being Mentally Ill: A Sociological Theory* (London, 1966), p. 79.

[21]     Simon Cross, 'Visualizing Madness: Mental illness and Public Representation', *Television New Media*, 5/3 (2004), p. 199.

[22]     Stephen Harper, 'Media, Madness and Misrepresentation: Critical Reflections on Anti-Stigma Discourse', *European Journal of Communication*, 20/4 (2005), p. 462.

## Music and Madness Criticism

To date, very little research has been conducted with respect to representations of madness in popular music; and, considering the first academic works to display an interest in the subject appeared in the 1990s, this paucity is quite surprising. Sheila Whiteley's analysis of Pink Floyd's *The Dark Side of the Moon* (1973) was one of the first to make specific reference to the way in which certain musical gestures work alongside lyrics to inflect meaning: the songs 'Speak to Me' and 'Brain Damage', for example, are examined in terms of their ability to create an impression of the 'threat of madness' wherein the 'montage of bizarre sound images' and melodic details such as narrow range and displaced accents are regarded as significant.[23] While devoid of explicit reference to anti-psychiatry or its commentators, Whiteley's work nevertheless identifies a number of ideas that are analogous to those espoused by Laing and Cooper. Society's expedient manipulation of the individual and accusations of material insanity are two such examples that appear in her analyses of 'Breathe', 'Time' and 'Money', but of greatest significance is her proposition that 'Brain Damage' reveals how 'ultimately, society has the say in who is sane, who is the lunatic'.[24] Alongside Whiteley's summing up of the album's principal theme as 'contemporary society's threats and disillusionment, its pressures and hypercritical values which can ultimately lead to madness',[25] this insight reveals the music's potential to challenge the disease model of madness. Her observations thus provide a useful starting point from which to conduct analysis intent on demonstrating an identifiable anti-psychiatric stance.

Pink Floyd's *The Dark Side of the Moon* engendered a further work of relevance in the 1990s in the form of Phil Rose's *Which One's Pink?* (1998). Like Whiteley, there is an attempt to offer insights regarding the impact of the musical text with respect to meanings surrounding issues of madness and alienation, although these are not as subtly nuanced. The work is important, however, for its perceptive references to social climate wherein Rose draws attention to 'a serious social concern current with the album's release: the general distrust of psychiatry and its questionable therapeutics, and the confused nature of what constitutes its views of mental illness'.[26] While identifying a potential anti-psychiatric stance, Rose looks to contemporary works such as Valenstein's *Brain Control* (1973)[27] rather than tracing the influence back to the anti-psychiatry movement of the 1960s, claiming that 'studies of this phenomenon began to appear with some

---

[23]     Sheila Whiteley, *The Space Between the Notes: Rock and the Counter-Culture* (London, 1992), pp. 105 and 115 respectively.

[24]     Ibid., p. 116.

[25]     Ibid., p. 110.

[26]     Philip Rose, *Which One's Pink? An Analysis of Concept Albums of Roger Waters and 'Pink Floyd'* (Burlington, Ontario, 1998), p. 33.

[27]     Elliot Valenstein, *Brain Control: A Critical Examination of Brain Stimulation and Psychosurgery* (New York, 1973).

regularity almost simultaneously with the release of the album'.[28] His work thus falls short of acknowledging the impact of figures such as Laing and Cooper, but does highlight the music's ability to provide constructions of madness that both reflect and inform society's conceptions of mental illness.

Both Whiteley and Rose offer a distinctly pessimistic interpretation concerning *The Dark Side of the Moon's* overriding message – Whiteley concluding that 'The final track points to the fallacy of escape from madness',[29] Rose claiming that the album principally emphasizes 'a concern for our failure to build on Freud's postulations, or come any closer to illuminating a remedy for the human condition'.[30] And, in this respect, their readings differ from my own, for it is only by taking into consideration the notion of enlightened madness – and in particular Laing's theory of spiritual rebirth – that a more positive, even hopeful, interpretation becomes possible. As such, Chapter 3 explains this standpoint in greater depth.

The first work to identify a link between anti-psychiatry and popular music actually pre-dates both of the aforementioned texts, although being a piece of rock criticism written by Albert Goldman and published in *Life* magazine in 1971, it focuses on the lives and influences of its featured artists and their fans as opposed to analysing the potential meanings proffered by their music. In it Goldman claims, with erudite cynicism, that both the rock press and rock fans are switching their attention away from the music to an interest in their icons' 'neuroses and psychoses'.[31] Most significantly, he cites the influence of radical psychiatrists R.D. Laing and Arthur Janov claiming that: 'The reason the ravaged lives of Lennon and the Taylors loom larger at this moment than their buoyant music is because so many people are now in the mood for a harsh new trip which they label "The Return to Reality".'[32] Summing up Laing's and Janov's impact, he states that:

> Both advocate radical solutions: in the one case blowing your mind with a regressive trip to the primal scene/scream; in the other a schizophrenic withdrawal that may remain a permanent condition of alienation (virtually endorsed by Laing as a state of being no less 'crazy' than the lives of uptight 'normal' men and women).[33]

---

[28]     Rose, p. 33.

[29]     Whiteley, p. 116.

[30]     Rose, p. 39.

[31]     Albert Goldman, *Sound Bites* (New York, 1992), p. 196.

[32]     Ibid., p. 198. Here Goldman is referring to John Lennon, James Taylor and his younger brother, Livingston Taylor. With respect to the latter two, he writes that 'no listener to their songs could have guessed that these young men were drug addicts, patients in mental institutions, and potential suicides', p. 197.

[33]     Ibid.

In particular, Goldman condemns what he regards as a trend for identifying evidence of artists' mental abnormalities within their songs, alleging that rock fans 'hold up the incongruity between [James] Taylor's occasionally disquieting lyrics and his rather conventional tunes as evidence of deep-seated schizophrenia'.[34] While clearly resentful of this new intrusion upon his perceived direction of rock culture – concluding that 'The promises of cure from the curse of contemporary consciousness [...] are just replays of the siren song of LSD'[35] – Goldman is one of the first writers to acknowledge the impact that anti-psychiatrists such as Laing were capable of exerting on popular music. His caution regarding attempts to identify evidence of artists' mental anguish within their music also informs my own methodology which, as will be elucidated presently, remains firmly rooted within issues of musical representation where intention and the artists' own state of mind are considered largely inconsequential.

With regard to academic texts that identify a link between anti-psychiatry and popular music, Philip Auslander's *Performing Glam Rock: Gender and Theatricality in Popular Music* (2006) makes a connection between R.D. Laing's ideas of madness being a social construct and the sentiment expressed within a short spoken section of David Bowie's song 'All the Madmen' (1971). Auslander employs this linkage in an attempt to demonstrate Bowie's continued allegiance to the 'counterculture's social perspective' which, he claims, is in total contrast to Alice Cooper's 'theatrical, sensationalistic, and apolitical depiction of madness' witnessed in his song 'The Ballad of Dwight Fry' (1971).[36] Given that these two songs form the basis of two lengthy chapters within this book, it is worth briefly pointing out the extent to which I agree with his brief assessment of them.

Auslander's conclusions are based primarily on lyric analysis, with the exception of his reference to Bowie's use of a consistent verse/chorus structure which, alongside 'the lyric's adherence to varied but regular time schemes', is used to suggest 'the actual clarity and orderliness of the protagonist's mind'.[37] While I agree with this assessment of the protagonist, I believe that it requires further evidence drawn from the musical text in order to make it plausible; and my own analysis aims to demonstrate the way in which a variety of musical gestures convey a positive representation of madness set against an opposing, negative representation of so-called 'normality'. Auslander's claim that madness is a choice for Bowie's protagonist is likewise based solely on analysis of the chorus lyric 'I'd rather stay here with all the madmen'; and again, while I share his assertion, a more detailed examination of the music reveals more substantial evidence in support of the protagonist's ability to simply 'play' the role of the 'madman'. Furthermore, with respect to his analysis of Alice Cooper, Auslander finds no

---

[34]   Ibid., p. 196.

[35]   Ibid., p. 199.

[36]   Philip Auslander, *Performing Glam Rock: Gender and Theatricality in Popular Music* (Ann Arbor, MI, 2006), p. 37.

[37]   Ibid.

evidence of an anti-psychiatric stance, writing that he 'implicated his audience in his staged incarceration without implying the superiority of madness to sanity or criticizing society's treatment of the insane'.[38] In this respect, I offer a conflicting interpretation, identifying numerous aspects of the song which encourage a questioning of psychiatry's methods, in particular its recourse to involuntary confinement. Despite such disagreements, Auslander's contrasting interpretation of the two 'mad' protagonists – which he relates to differences in the stylistic direction of the artists concerned – is interesting and will doubtless encourage others to consider the ways in which representations of madness in music are shaped, in part, by matters of musical style and social outlook.

Szasz, Laing and Cooper are also referred to in Annette Hames and Ian Inglis's overview of mental illness in their work 'And I Will Lose My Mind ... Images of Mental Illness in the Songs of the Beatles' (1999). Explaining the intangible nature of mental illness in terms of its capacity to encompass seemingly arbitrary definitions of normality and abnormality, the aforementioned psychiatrists are mentioned as proof of those who have challenged its legitimacy. While there is no attempt to uncover links between anti-psychiatry and popular music, Hames and Inglis's research is the first to examine how song lyrics make reference to 'states or conditions associated with forms of mental illness'.[39] Interpretations of meaning are not provided, for there is no musicological analysis, and Hames and Inglis make clear that their study concentrates solely on discussions of the theme or subject of a song. Nonetheless, their work offers valuable insights concerning the possible function that representations of mental illness have in the songs of the Beatles, and highlights the importance of such engagement to 'the assumed knowledge of mental illness in contemporary popular culture'.[40]

A further text worthy of note in terms of its illuminating discoveries concerning musical depictions of madness is Susan McClary's *Feminine Endings: Music, Gender and Sexuality* (1991). Focusing predominantly on the classical idiom, her chapter 'Excess and Frame: The Musical Representation of Madwomen' is the first to consider historical context crucial to an understanding of the way in which madness is described in musical terms. Specifically, her exploration of dominant cultural beliefs surrounding madness and endeavour to apply such knowledge to interpretations of famous musical portrayals of madwomen offer a methodology that is potentially applicable to different time periods and genres. That said, McClary's aim is different from my own in that she seeks to demonstrate the ways in which her chosen musical examples helped to communicate and reinforce perceived differences between reason and unreason that were effectively created and disseminated by 'official institutions (law and medicine) and also cultural

---

[38]     Ibid., p. 36.

[39]     Annette Hames and Ian Inglis, 'And I Will Lose My Mind ... Images of Mental Illness in the Songs of the Beatles', *International Review of the Aesthetics and Sociology of Music* (*IRASM*), 30/2 (1999), p. 174.

[40]     Ibid., p. 175.

enterprises', claiming 'music likewise participated in this process',[41] while I intend to demonstrate how music may serve an opposing function, effectively challenging such dominant assumptions.

The final significant work to engage in debates surrounding music and madness is Robert Walser's *Running with the Devil: Power, Gender and Madness in Heavy Metal Music* (1993). Specifically, his astute construal of Iron Maiden's song 'Can I Play with Madness' – which he claims is 'less about literal madness than about madness as a trope for unconventional thought'[42] – points to the hidden complexities and multiple meanings often present within such cultural expressions. While there is less exploration of musical representations of madness than the title of the book might suggest, Walser's defence of heavy metal's more extreme subject matter – in particular his claim that its musicians 'explore images of horror and madness in order to comprehend and critique the world as they see it'[43] – provides an essential standpoint from which to investigate references to madness within more current death and doom metal bands.[44]

In addition to the aforementioned works, texts such as Lionel Trilling's *The Liberal Imagination* (1950) and Anthony Storr's *The Dynamics of Creation* (1972) seek to address questions concerning the much purported link between creativity and mental illness. Storr's work, for example, offers some valuable insights into the arguments surrounding madness and genius, but his investigation is clearly focused on an assessment of the creative mind as opposed to an examination of cultural representations of madness. It is also the case that articles exploring the link between pop stardom and mental illness in the music press routinely reinforce stereotypical conceptions of madness, alluding to famous cases of suicide and breakdown with telling headlines such as 'Rock'n'Roll Drives You Mad'[45] and 'The 50 Craziest Pop Stars Ever!'[46] Their content, while demonstrating the

---

[41] Susan McClary, *Feminine Endings: Music, Gender, and Sexuality* (Minneapolis, 1991), p. 81.

[42] Robert Walser, *Running with the Devil: Power, Gender and Madness in Heavy Metal Music* (Hanover, NH, 1993), p. 155.

[43] Ibid., p. 170.

[44] In reference to thrash metal band Megadeth, Walser offers a further, relevant explanation: 'If their imagery is horrible, it is intended – and understood by fans – as an honest reflection and critique of a brutal world,' Walser, p. 158.

[45] *Q* Magazine, 147 (December 1998). Above the start of this article is a double-page, cropped photograph of Kurt Cobain's eyes exhibiting a wide, intense stare. The accompanying caption reads 'the eyes have (lost) it', and below this appears the headline 'Rock and Roll Drives You Mad'.

[46] *Blender* Magazine, 10 (January 2008). On this list, Michael Jackson appears in the number one position, with David Bowie placed at number 47 and Elton John positioned at 50. For each star there is a section detailing their 'case history' and key 'crazy moment', retrieved 1 September 2008 from: http://www.blender.com/guide/arfticles.aspx?ID=2516.

resilience of such stereotypical conceptions, is thus relatively unhelpful to any serious examination of popular music's engagement with the subject of madness.

Despite the important insights offered by the previously listed texts, it is fair to say that none have made representations of madness within popular music their central concern. For this reason, I have found it useful to explore comparative studies of film, television and literature because many of these have already demonstrated how constructions of madness may be referenced in order to stigmatize but also liberate protagonists in ways that reinforce or challenge contemporaneous notions of normality. Fleming and Manvell's *Images of Madness* (1985), for example, relates artistic depictions of madness to contemporary popular and clinical opinion, stressing the importance of social context and the shifting perceptions of madness throughout history. Otto Wahl's *Media Madness: Public Images of Mental Illness* (1995) similarly discusses a wide range of media representations of mental illness, but with the express aim of demonstrating their erroneous, stereotypical and hence detrimental nature. It thus provides a background from which to identify specific musical texts likewise guilty of such ignoble referencing, but also those possessing a more progressive make-up.[47]

The work most akin to this book in terms of overall theme, however, is Barbara Tepa Lupack's *Insanity as Redemption in Contemporary American Fiction* (1995). In particular, her analysis of literary works that offer revolutionary depictions of madness with the potential to challenge societal norms is comparable to my own choice of songs for the purpose of analysis. But while Tepa Lupack defines her case studies as novels that 'explore precisely the illogic (and, at times, the outright insanity) of contemporary existence. Each portrays a protagonist who is mad or is considered by others to be mad – a protagonist who, however, possesses or reveals a special insight into the dangers of the institution's demand for social, political, and cultural conformity.'[48] My book is more resolute in its concentration on texts which specifically criticize the psychiatric establishment. They too exhibit the aforementioned trait of exposing the insanity of the supposed 'sane'; but the depiction of characters either labelled or driven 'mad' by others facilitates various scenarios from which to convey a distinctly anti-psychiatry as opposed to purely anti-Establishment stance.

A more current work that further relates to the objectives of subsequent chapters is Stephen Harper's 'Media, Madness and Misrepresentation: Critical Reflections on Anti-Stigma Discourse' (2005), which evaluates the achievements of earlier studies and makes suggestions regarding the potential direction for future analyses. His identification of some of the problems with past anti-stigma

---

[47]     Other works such as Lillian Feder's *Madness in Literature* (Princeton, 1980) and Derek Russell Davis's *Scenes of Madness: A Psychiatrist at the Theatre* (London, 1995) are also important for their consideration of social context and insistence that literal depictions of madness differ from real-life experiences of mental illness.

[48]     Barbara Tepa Lupack, *Insanity as Redemption in Contemporary American Fiction* (Gainesville, FL, 1995), p. 2.

works such as Wahl's *Media Madness* – their inclination to overgeneralize and 'tendency to reinforce conservative notions about the cultural value of popular texts'[49] – leads him to call for 'more tightly focused studies of media texts that seek to reveal their narrative, generic and formal complexities'.[50] This is effectively what the following chapters strive to accomplish. Harper also argues that, rather than attempting to gauge the extent to which fictional depictions of madness are faithful to true experiences of mental illness, more concentrated studies should contemplate 'the *function* of madness in particular texts';[51] and, again, this is an important concern within this book.

## Investigating Popular Music and Madness

Texts such as Lindsay Prior's *The Social Organization of Mental Illness* (1993) and Roy Porter's *Madness: A Brief History* (2002) provide information concerning the different ways in which madness has been defined, explained and treated throughout history. As well as helping to determine the context within which my selected songs were produced, such works also point to the origins of particular ideas about madness that continue to resonate within contemporary popular culture. Works of a less general nature – such as David Jones's *Myths, Madness and the Family* (2002) and Joan Busfield's *Men, Women and Madness* (1996) – equally contribute to an understanding of the way in which popular music's dealings with madness, alongside our interpretations of such, are shaped by its frequently complex links to issues of the family, sexuality and gender.

Additional texts critical of the psychiatric establishment – including more recent examples such as Lucy Johnstone's *Users and Abusers of Psychiatry: A Critical Look at Psychiatric Practice* (2000) – alongside works offering an overview of anti-psychiatry writings illuminate the principal arguments and continued relevance of such figures as Laing and Szasz. As David Brackett notes: 'While musical texts may retain a "relative autonomy" – music is a medium with specific properties, practices, limitations, and possibilities – they gain their meaning by circulating with other texts from other media which may include mass media publications, videos, films, industry publications, and "historical" documents';[52] and, as such, I have also endeavoured to identify and examine a number of secondary sources that adopt a comparable anti-psychiatric position. On occasion, such texts from other cultural fields are referenced from many years previous and, while this is not intended to infer that such works had a direct influence on my chosen songs

---

[49]    Harper, p. 465.

[50]    Ibid., p. 478.

[51]    Ibid.

[52]    David Brackett, *Interpreting Popular Music* (Berkeley and Los Angeles, 2000), p. 18.

for analysis, they nevertheless reveal running themes and motifs present within artistic representations of madness.

My contention that the songs examined in the subsequent chapters fit within an anti-psychiatric frame of reference involves a concentration on meanings that may be made at the point of reception as a consequence of ideas about madness that were circulating at the time. These ideas are then linked to contemporary conventions of musical expression in order to illustrate certain interpretative possibilities. In this regard, I am influenced by the writings of eminent musicologists Susan McClary, Robert Walser and Derek Scott, whose works are enlightened by a belief that musical conventions, ideals and meanings are linked to specific social and cultural contexts.[53] I make no judgements about how faithfully the musical texts duplicate supposed 'truths' about mental illness and psychiatric practice as extolled in contemporary medical discourse, but I am certainly interested in the influence these have on my selected songs and how the music in turn functions in the way McClary identifies: 'as a public forum' where different ideas on the subject of madness may be 'asserted, adopted, contested, and negotiated'.[54]

In demonstrating the relationship of anti-psychiatry theory to the range of ideas about madness embodied within my selected songs, I refrain from any detailed discussion of artistic intention. Where appropriate, occasional suggestions are provided regarding specific biographical details that may have prompted a particular artist's interest in the subject matter, but, like Scott, I contend that representations occur aside from an artist's stipulated objective; particular images may consequently be conjured up involuntarily and unintentionally.[55] Like the aforementioned musicologists, I attempt to explain the existence of specific meanings by incorporating social semiotics, agreeing with Eric Clarke and Nicola Dibben that 'musical materials have a "history of use," one consequence of which is that sounds are heard as cultural references and associations'.[56] I have therefore found it useful to investigate how musical depictions of madness work against the listener's awareness of stylistic conventions. In particular, my analysis is informed by arguments that there is no inherent connotation within isolated musical gestures, but that the combination of, and relationship between, multiple gestures and their effects provides the possibility of identifying 'chains of signifiers' that point towards potential meanings. As Walser explains: 'a C major chord has no intrinsic meaning; rather, it can signify in different ways in different discourses, where it is contextualized by other signifiers, its own history as a signifier, and the social activities in which the discourse participates'.[57]

---

[53]     See, for example, Derek Scott, *From the Erotic to the Demonic: On Critical Musicology* (Oxford, 2003), p. 4.

[54]     McClary, p. 8.

[55]     Scott, p. 8.

[56]     Eric Clarke and Nicola Dibben, 'Sex, Pulp and Critique', *Popular Music*, 19/2 (2000), p. 233.

[57]     Walser, p. 27.

While supporting evidence for my reading of the musical texts comes from popular musicological analysis – incorporating discourse analysis and social semiotics – and investigation of socio-historical context, I do not presume mine to be the only interpretations possible. The following chapters exhibit my strong commitment to detailing the various ways in which both music and lyric combine to result in an overall questioning of the psychiatric establishment, and the gestures I identify are those I find most conspicuous and interesting. My analysis is based on sound and vocality (not vocality and gesture or psychology) and involves discussion of the potential effects of specific musical details with respect to the articulation of tension and release, perceived direction, structural norms, listener expectation and so forth. Where appropriate, I also include transcription to help illustrate the content of particular gestures.

In conclusion to this introduction, I feel it important to offer a brief explanation regarding my choice of artists and songs for analysis – particularly the lack of women singer-songwriters featured. I wish to make clear that this imbalance was merely a product of the sources available, and not due to any personal oversight or prejudice. Following a general survey of commercially successful albums – believing these would likely contain material that resonates most with contemporary opinions about madness – I discovered numerous songs that were critical of psychiatry and problematized conceptions of madness, all released within an eight-year time span (1967–74). Six songs and one album in particular offered the richest ideas in terms of their verbal and musical contents, and all happened to be written and performed by male artists. Initially, I knew very little about anti-psychiatry but, following an investigation of prominent works by Laing, Cooper, Szasz and Goffman, I realized the pattern of critique I had discovered within the music might best be theorized with reference to their arguments.

I was surprised to discover how few women artists had engaged with issues of madness during the period in question. Indeed, I located only three songs written and/or performed by women in the early 1970s that contain traces of an anti-psychiatric standpoint, and it is fair to say that none of these demonstrate the acute concentration of ideas (both musical and verbal) witnessed in the songs of their male counterparts. Dory Previn's 'Mr Whisper' (1970) would be better served by an analysis intent on revealing the ways in which artists engage with issues of personal mental illness, while Melanie Safka's 'Psychotherapy' (1970) – whose lyrics are sung to the melody of 'Battle Hymn of the Republic' – offers a humorous parody of Freud's psychoanalysis but lacks real scrutiny of the medical model of psychiatry.[58] Joni Mitchell's 'Twisted' (1974) further illustrates the widespread interest in the subject of madness at this time, but is actually a cover of a song

---

[58]    Safka's better-known 'What Have They Done to My Song, Ma' (1970) had already touched on the topic of madness, with its second verse incorporating an unexpected allusion to brain damage and insanity: 'Look what they've done to my brain, Ma. Look what they've done to my brain. Well they picked it like a chicken bone, and I think I'm half insane, Ma. Look what they've done to my song.'

originally released in 1960 by jazz vocalese group Lambert, Hendricks and Ross. The lyric text (written by Annie Ross and applied to tenor saxophonist Wardell Gray's melody) aligns to an anti-psychiatry frame of reference through its central preoccupation with questioning the analyst's diagnosis; but, again, the musical text is not as fertile as those selected for detailed analysis in subsequent chapters.

Since the late 1970s there has undoubtedly been a greater occurrence of women artists exploring concepts of madness, with songs such as 'Medication' by Garbage (1998), 'Opheliac' by Emilie Autumn (2006) and 'Runs in the Family' by Amanda Palmer (2008) demonstrating a questioning of psychiatry and its methods similar to that identified in the ensuing case studies. This is a topic I intend to return to in the future. Many more songs that engage with the theme of madness in a variety of ways appear in the concluding chapter of this book in order to substantiate claims regarding the uniqueness of the period in question, although the majority are again by male artists, and the potential reasons for this imbalance are explored to some extent within my concluding discussion.

Chapter 1

# 'All the Madmen': Denouncing the Psychiatric Establishment and Supposedly 'Sane' Through the Art of Role Play

'All the Madmen' is the second track from *The Man Who Sold the World*,[1] the album generally regarded as marking the beginning of David Bowie's hard rock period.[2] The song's incorporation of role play, alongside its apparent veneration for the identified 'mad', make it a prime example of the way in which musical and verbal gestures can function to invoke an effective reversal of traditional concepts of madness and sanity.

Due to the quick succession of albums released, and Bowie's previous interest in narrative forms, it is likely his audience throughout the early 1970s would have been accustomed to his use of characterization. As Allan Moore reveals: 'Bowie forced attention upon the notion that a performer can inhabit a persona, rather than that persona being an aspect of the performer.'[3] In the song 'All the Madmen' Bowie is playing the character of the labelled madman while still projecting the persona of the rock star. Our reading of Bowie's character is thus shaped by our knowledge of his star status and vice versa; the distancing between them is what Frith refers to when he compares the act to that of a film star playing a role: 'In one respect, then, a pop star is like a film star, taking on many parts but retaining an essential "personality" that is common to all of them and is the basis of their popular appeal.'[4] While this observation regarding characterization may seem

---

[1]   David Bowie, *The Man Who Sold the World* (Mercury, 1971).

[2]   In his review for the *All Music Guide* (http://allmusic.com), Stephen Erlewine cites the album as 'the beginning of David Bowie's classic period' (retrieved 8 January 2002) and, according to Kate Lynch, 'this is where "Rock Bowie" really begins'; see Kate Lynch, *David Bowie: A Rock'n'Roll Odyssey* (London, 1984), p. 47. Despite spending a total of 31 weeks in the UK charts and reaching the position of 23, it is fair to assume that most fans would have become acquainted with *The Man Who Sold the World* after the success of later albums such as *The Rise and Fall of Ziggy Stardust and the Spiders from Mars* (RCA, 1972).

[3]   Allan F. Moore, *Rock – The Primary Text: Developing a Musicology of Rock* (Buckingham, 1993), p. 171.

[4]   Simon Frith, *Performing Rites: On the Value of Popular Music* (Oxford, 1996), p. 199.

obvious, it has a greater relevance within this particular song for it enables a reading based on what has been termed the conspiratorial model of madness.

In *The Myth of Mental Illness* (1961), Szasz argues that what the majority of society and the psychiatric establishment refer to as mental illness is fundamentally separate and distinct from organic brain disease: 'Strictly speaking, disease or illness can affect only the body; hence, there can be no mental illness. "Mental illness" is a metaphor. Minds can be "sick" only in the sense that jokes are "sick" or economies are "sick".'[5] In Szasz's opinion, so-called 'mental illness' should therefore lose its mythical identity and be correctly defined as 'personal, social, and ethical problems in living'.[6] He offers a number of persuasive arguments in an attempt to elucidate the creation and perpetuation of this myth. The most crucial of these concerns the way in which mental illness serves as justification for the authority of the psychiatric profession while providing society with a means of labelling and hence scapegoating individuals whose behaviour is deemed undesirable:

> Institutional Psychiatry is largely medical ceremony and magic. This explains why the labelling of persons – as mentally healthy or diseased – is so crucial a part of psychiatric practice. It constitutes the initial act of social validation and invalidation, pronounced by the high priest of modern, scientific religion, the psychiatrist; it justifies the expulsion of the sacrificial scapegoat, the mental patient, from the community.[7]

What is of particular relevance here is Szasz's insistence that 'mental illness is not something a person *has*, but is something he *does* or *is*'.[8] In this sense once someone is, for whatever reason, labelled 'mad', they are, as a consequence, encouraged to take on the role of the insane person, as Szasz explains: 'mental illness is an action not a legion. As Shakespeare showed [...] it is also an act, in the sense of a theatrical impersonation.'[9] Within my analysis of 'All The Madmen' one of my aims will therefore be to illustrate the ways in which Bowie's characterization of madness represents Szasz's myth of mental illness, for it exposes the myth for what it is – a role, a form of game play and a performance.

The theme emphasized initially in the song is that of alienation, or more specifically the alienation inherent within society itself. In the introduction and first two verses the listener is encouraged to feel empathy for Bowie's character, who is left behind while his friends are taken away to 'mansions cold and grey'. The imagery here draws upon eighteenth- and early nineteenth-century depictions

---

5    Thomas Szasz, *The Myth of Mental Illness: Foundations of a Theory of Personal Conduct* [1961] (London, 1972), p. 275.

6    Ibid., p. 269.

7    Szasz, *The Manufacture of Madness* [1970] (London, 1973), p. 296.

8    Szasz, *The Myth of Mental Illness*, p. 275.

9    Thomas Szasz, *Insanity: The Idea and Its Consequences* (New York, 1987), p. 212.

of madhouses that were criticized for their inhumane methods of treatment and wrongful confinement. In her unfinished book *The Wrongs Of Woman* (1797) Mary Wollstonecraft's protagonist, Maria, is incarcerated in a 'mansion of despair';[10] Henry Mackenzie describes the living quarters of Bedlam in his classic *The Man of Feeling* (1771) in terms of 'dismal mansions';[11] and John Conolly, a Victorian physician and head of Hanwell Asylum in Middlesex, told of the dreadful conditions prior to the licensing and inspection of asylums, referring to 'gloomy mansions in which hands and feet were daily bound with straps or chains'.[12] While the act of incarcerating people presumably against their will is called into question here, it is not, however, the source of Bowie's character's sadness. Rather, it is the isolation of the world in which he remains that proves undesirable.

The sparse accompanying texture, comprising plectrum-strummed, steel-strung acoustic guitar and a lone synth call (which fades in and out a minor 6th above the tonic E), provides a suggestively bleak backdrop that is heightened by stark 4th and 5th intervals between two recorder sounds in verse two. The use of strummed acoustic guitar creates a sense of intimacy, being associated as it is with an accompanying role in songs with a more personal message, and this contrasts with the distancing of the vocal itself achieved through the use of panning and artificial reverb. The reverb seems excessive and effectively evokes the isolation of Bowie's character, while the spatial dimension is significant in that the guitar shifts from far left to far right to make way for the voice entering alone, far left. This effect is further enhanced through the melodic line which, despite its use of an ascending major scale, appears confined and non-directed during the first two bars. Rhythmically dislocated, there are few obvious points of phrase repetition and the rhythms are sometimes clipped, sometimes lengthened to accentuate particular aspects of the lyric content (for example, 'send', 'friend', 'mansions' and 'far'). The unhappy separation of Bowie's character from his 'friends' is also emphasized through a leap up to the minor 7th and a 6–5 appoggiatura which stresses the word 'far' before descending back to its starting point via E Phrygian. The contour of the melodic line during the verse thus resembles a sigh; it grows in pitch and complexity, incorporating more non-harmony notes, before finally resolving back to the tonic (see Example 1.1).

The fact that the harmony resists change during the first three bars of the verse also offers little comfort, for the major identity is repeatedly challenged by the shift to E7sus4 in the beginning of bars two and three. The eventual move up a semitone to the F chord in bar four does offer some sense of release, but the progression to E Phrygian denies any reassurance of diatonic closure. The choice of Phrygian mode

---

[10] Mary Wollstonecraft, *Maria; or The Wrongs of Woman* (New York: Norton, 1975), pp. 21, 23, 27. Quoted in Elaine Showalter, *The Female Malady: Women, Madness, and English Culture, 1830–1980* (New York, 1985), p. 1.

[11] Henry Mackenzie, *The Man of Feeling* [1771] (Oxford, 1987), p. 23.

[12] John Conolly, *Treatment of the Insane without Mechanical Restraints* [1856] (reprint edn, London: Dawsons, 1973), pp. 32–3. Quoted in Showalter, p. 25.

is in itself significant, having traditionally been used in western musical idioms to symbolize the unfamiliar with its characteristic minor 2nd interval carrying, according to Robert Walser, a 'frantic, claustrophobic effect'.[13] While the tonic E remains a recognized point of stability during the verse, the harmonic language and modal melodic inflections are uncertain and this in turn represents the feelings of unease that surround Bowie's character.

Example 1.1 'All the Madmen' verse 1 (vocal and chords)

The sense of isolation and restlessness evoked in the opening musical and lyrical gestures is, I would argue, crucial to the overall message of the song. If Bowie's protagonist is to convince us of his desire to stay with 'all the madmen', then we must have a point of comparison – his feelings in the opening represent the alternative, a life of loneliness among the supposed 'sane'. While not an original concept, it does appear to reflect the thinking of R.D. Laing and his theory of man's estranged state which he first articulated in *The Politics of Experience* (1967). Laing wrote: 'The condition of alienation, of being asleep, of being unconscious, of being out of one's mind, is the condition of the normal man'[14] and he supported his belief by claiming that, for many people, their 'true self' is lost behind a 'false self' acquired to deal with a society that is profoundly estranged from reality.[15] Such

---

[13]     Robert Walser, *Running with the Devil: Power, Gender and Madness in Heavy Metal Music* (Hanover, NH, 1993), p.156. Walser's suggestion that the minor 2nd relationship between the first and second degrees of the mode produces a sense of instability is equally relevant: 'the second degree hangs precariously over the tonic, making the mode seem claustrophobic and unstable' (Walser, p. 47). Phrygian has also been used to signify the culturally alien (see for example Verdi's most popular opera, *Aida* (1871), where the Priestesses of Mighty Phtah sing in the Phrygian mode). In Anglo-American popular music, it remains one of the least commonly used of the seven modes derived from a parent major scale (along with the Locrian mode) and this has arguably strengthened its aptitude for signifying Otherness.

[14]     Ronald D. Laing, *The Politics of Experience* [1967] (Harmondsworth, 1978), p. 24.

[15]     Laing's development of this theory may be best illustrated if one compares his reference to 'masks' in the first publication of *The Divided Self* with his additional preface provided four years later: 'A man without a mask is indeed very rare. One even doubts the possibility of such a man. Everyone in some measure wears a mask [...] In "ordinary"

views had, in fact, become commonplace in the New Left's attempts to highlight the necessity for social change, a change that would require involvement on a personal level to overcome what Theodore Roszak referred to as 'the deadening of man's sensitivity to man'.[16] The suggestion that humanity's 'true self' had been lost behind a mask adopted to succeed within a fake social reality was equally appealing to those who had chosen to 'drop out' of society – the Bohemian fringe of the counter-culture. Unsurprisingly, Laing became associated with the aforementioned groups and, indeed, similarities in his use of language are revealed if one compares arguments posed within *The Politics of Experience* with an extract from the SDS Port Huron Statement of 1962:[17] 'we regard man as infinitely precious and possessed of unfulfilled capacities for reason, freedom and love […] Loneliness, estrangement, isolation describe the vast distance between man and man today.'[18] One can, of course, only postulate that such thinking had an impact on Bowie, although biographical writers such as Kate Lynch have pointed to his creation of a Bohemian lifestyle during his time at Haddon Hall (the setting for the original and controversial cover to *The Man Who Sold the World*)[19] and his interest in Tibetan Buddhism ('One must question one's existence and when you do it leaves you with an incredible loneliness … Buddhism made me very keen on creativity').[20] Accompanied by statements in which he criticized 'the whole idea of Western life',[21] these suggest a certain identification with contemporary radical opinion.

The notion that labelled madmen were, in fact, enlightened, honest, artistic individuals wrongly scapegoated by a sick society seems to have become more common during the late 1960s and early 1970s when through literature, film

---

life it seems hardly possible for it to be otherwise.' Ronald D. Laing, *The Divided Self: An Existential Study in Sanity and Madness* [1960] (Harmondsworth, 1964), p. 101. With the new preface, Laing appears far more certain of the detrimental effect such 'masks' have on a person's ability to fulfil his or her potential: 'Thus I would wish to emphasize that our "normal," "adjusted" state is too often the abdication of ecstasy, the betrayal of our true potentialities, that many of us are only too successful in acquiring a false self to adapt to false realities.' Laing, *The Divided Self*, p. 12.

[16]     Theodore Roszak, *The Making of a Counter Culture: Reflections on the Technocratic Society and Its Youthful Opposition* (London, 1970), p. 58.

[17]     SDS refers to the radical youth group 'Students for a Democratic Society', established in America in 1959. The Port Huron Statement was their political manifesto, the majority of which was written by Tom Hayden.

[18]     From the statement as it appears in Mitchell Cohen and Dennis Hale (eds), *The New Student Left* (revised edn, Boston, MA: Beacon Press, 1967), pp. 12–13. Quoted in Roszak, p. 58.

[19]     Lynch, pp. 31, 40.

[20]     *Rave*, January 1970. Quoted in George Tremlett, *David Bowie: Living on the Brink* (London, 1996), p. 21.

[21]     Bowie actually stated: 'As far as I'm concerned, the whole idea of Western life, that's the life we live now, is wrong.' *Melody Maker*, 26 February 1966. Quoted in Barry Miles, *David Bowie Black Book* (London, 1980), p. 13.

and music a number of artists set out to challenge conventional notions of 'mad' behaviour. In a similar affront to the Establishment, labels of insanity were used by certain theorists to criticize a society that continued to sanction acts of greed and war; and Michael Fleming's research into portrayals of madness is valuable here, for he claims: 'The production of such films [by which he is referring to a number of works cited such as *Marat-Sade* (1967), *King of Hearts* (1966) and *The Ruling Class* (1972)],[22] which markedly increased in the late sixties and early seventies, clearly emerged from a particular social, political, and psychological zeitgeist.'[23] For examples of such influential rhetoric, Szasz himself quotes Herbert Marcuse's attack upon the wastefulness of western society in which he declared 'I call this society insane!'[24] And R.D. Laing's warning that 'social adaption to a dysfunctional society may be very dangerous' was given further poignancy when he added: 'The perfectly adjusted bomber pilot may be a greater threat to species survival than the hospitalized schizophrenic deluded that the Bomb is inside him.'[25]

When one considers the success of such works as Ken Kesey's *One Flew Over the Cuckoo's Nest*[26] and Philippe de Broca's *King of Hearts*,[27] Bowie's adoption of the madman character and the attraction this might hold for both him and his fans becomes clearer. In his investigation of fictional images of mental illness during the 1960s, Charles Winick suggests that 'the mentally ill are seen as heroic and intelligent' and that in Kesey's book are 'almost Christ-like, crushed by a capricious society'.[28] I suggest that similar positive associations may be possible with Bowie's character if one considers the way in which the musical gestures of the chorus support such a reading. In contrast to the sombre quality of the verse and bridge sections, the chorus appears unabashedly victorious, utilizing a V–I pivot junction into A major, an ascending bass arpeggiation in the first two bars spanning an interval of an eleventh and a higher melodic pitch range emphasizing harmony tones. The strength of this albeit brief spell of functional harmony, melodic consonance and wide-ranging ascent allows a release from the previous uncertainty of the Phrygian mode and conveys a more lucid and determined message in support of the lyric 'I'd rather stay here with all the madmen'. While the guitar retains a minimal approach to sounding the accompanying harmony,

---

[22]     The films referred to were directed by Peter Brook, Philippe de Broca, and Peter Medak respectively.

[23]     Michael Fleming and Roger Manvell, *Images of Madness: The Portrayal of Insanity in the Feature Film* (London, 1985), p. 169.

[24]     Herbert Marcuse, quoted in 'Democracy Has/Hasn't a Future ... a Present', *New York Times Magazine* (26 May 1968), pp. 30–31, 98–104; p. 102. Quoted in Szasz, *The Manufacture of Madness*, p. 136.

[25]     Laing, *The Politics of Experience*, p. 99.

[26]     Ken Kesey, *One Flew Over the Cuckoo's Nest* (New York, 1962).

[27]     *King of Hearts* (1966) directed by Philippe de Broca, MGM United Artists.

[28]     Charles Winick, 'The Image of Mental Illness in the Mass Media', in Walter R. Gove (ed.), *Deviance and Mental Illness* (London, 1982), p. 230.

the drum kit and bass are used to intensify the chorus dynamic, filling the space between vocal phrases with rhythmically active interjections at the half bar.[29]

Bowie's character indicates that he would rather give up his liberty than 'perish with the sad men roaming free', adding 'I'd rather play here with all the madmen for I'm quite content they're all as sane as me.' The mental hospital in which it appears he is now confined is thus revealed as a place of sanctuary; the power of those who wish to punish his deviant behaviour is effectively dissolved as Bowie's protagonist is transformed from pariah to subject of belonging. The final chorus and ending passage are positively euphoric in effect as bright, chromatic, string-like synth runs are combined with additional cymbal crashes, handclaps and multilayered vocal gestures. The sense of transcendency from the threatened confines of the mental hospital is cleverly conveyed through imaginative production effects (such as the prominent panning of the synthesizer and vocals from hard right to hard left and back again); the anticipation of the F♯m and G chords followed by the use of sustained harmony notes in the vocal 'Ahs' (providing an effective release every two bars); the gradual build in textural density as up to seven vocal parts are added to the mix; and the incessant repetition of the four-bar harmonic progression (in which there is no suggestion of closure). Thus, through his use of falsetto vocal gestures and the apparent lushness of the timbral mix, Bowie ostensibly becomes all that the album cover suggests – a sybarite who, as the song simply fades to suggest its actual continuation, basks in a perpetual state of elation.[30]

To avoid any misunderstanding of this reversal, the brief instrumental passage which follows the first chorus leads into a spoken interlude in which Bowie asks: 'Where can the horizon lie when a nation hides its organic minds in a cellar dark and grim? They must be very dim.' Here the well-known literary figure of the mad woman in the attic is replaced by the arguably more disturbing allusion to the overcrowded private madhouses of the early nineteenth century, where surprise inspections revealed patients forced to inhabit cellars:

> At Langworthy's House, Box, where there were forty patients and nine servants, Wakefield [the inspector] was not permitted to see the men, ostensibly because

---

[29]   The unpredictable nature of the song is, in fact, enhanced through the more unusual role of the kit – the excessive filling used within the chorus sections might well be expected given the often indulgent technical displays typical of the progressive rock genre; however, one would equally expect the kit to capitalize on its more traditional role of framing sectional divisions. Instead, in 'All the Madmen' there are relatively few instances where a kit fill is used to build or disperse energy levels from one section to another; indeed the chorus itself arrives with a simple repetition of the previous bar.

[30]   Sybarite meaning a luxurious, effeminate person. The original album cover for *The Man Who Sold the World* shows Bowie reclining on a chaise longue, with long, slightly curled hair, wearing what he referred to as his 'man's dress' (a gold and blue coloured gown). According to Lynch, 'Bowie told one writer that it was a take-off of a Gabriel Rossetti painting "slightly askew".' Lynch, p. 46.

it was not a day when they were allowed up. He did see two women, however, nearly naked on straw in a cellar and four others entirely naked in a completely dark room.[31]

Example 1.2    'All the Madmen' chorus 1 (vocal, bass, kit and chords)

The claim that society itself is foolish ('dim') for locking away people with functioning ('organic') minds is thus stressed in a way that draws upon common fears of wretched treatment and imprisonment. It is a device similar to that used by Szasz when he compares the function of institutional psychiatry to that of the Inquisition and witch-hunting, and appears to share his assertion that 'involuntary mental hospitalization is not only the paradigm psychiatric procedure, but that, for societies that are or aspire to be politically free, it is also the gravest moral wrong and the greatest legal embarrassment since the days of the witch-hunts and the practice of slavery'.[32]

The protagonist's desire to 'play' with the 'madmen' is also interesting and, along with the use of a child's voice in the middle section and recorder sounds in the verses (an instrument traditionally taught in primary schools, which Buckley argues gives the song a 'child-like intensity'),[33] demonstrates Bowie's exploration of the long-established idea concerning madness and its association with childishness. It is worth noting that lyrical references to play and childish subjects are present in Bowie's previous material: see for example 'There Is a Happy Land' ('where only children play') and 'Uncle Arthur' (who 'likes his mommy', 'still reads comics' and 'follows Batman'), both from his self-titled 1967 album.[34] As such, given the opportunity and the possibility that such a connection could convey a desirable

---

[31]    Minutes of Evidence (1815) Select Committee (S.C.), p. 21. Quoted in William L. Parry-Jones, *The Trade in Lunacy* (London, 1972), p. 250.

[32]    Thomas Szasz, *The Age of Madness* (London, 1975), p. xviii.

[33]    David Buckley, *The Complete Guide to the Music of David Bowie* (London, 1996), p. 8.

[34]    David Bowie, *David Bowie* (Deram, 1967).

image – the sensitive artist, the innocent madman unafraid to acknowledge the child within – Bowie's linking of such themes is not unusual and, again, appears analogous to Laing's lament regarding the loss of personal experience:

> As adults, we have forgotten most of our childhood, not only its contents but its flavour; as men of the world, we hardly know of the existence of the inner world […] Our capacity to think, except in the service of what we are dangerously deluded in supposing is our self-interest, and in conformity with common sense, is pitifully limited […] an intensive discipline of un-learning is necessary for *anyone* before one can begin to experience the world afresh, with innocence, truth and love.[35]

Taking into account the above observation, and returning to the central idea of the chorus sections (reversing traditional conceptions of madness and sanity), some obvious parallels may be drawn between Bowie's character and Alan Bates's role in the 1966 film *King of Hearts*.[36] The film is described by Fleming as 'an enduring classic among a limited number of what might be called *cult films*' and is significant in its possible influence on a youth audience in that it appealed 'primarily to college-aged adults […] enjoyed sell-out status throughout the late sixties and early seventies and then continued to get star billing on campus film series lists'.[37] Set in France during the First World War, the abhorrent self-interest of the generals and futility of the military action provide persuasive evidence from which to condemn similar acts of insanity within modern western society. While the film's concept of reversal takes longer to establish than in Bowie's song, its questioning of perceived notions of sanity and madness is equally powerful as Bates's character undergoes a form of moral conversion, casting aside his weapon and position in the front line for a life of innocent and 'true' pleasures in the mental asylum.

The portrayal of the 'mad' men and women who occupy the asylum is in stark opposition to the generals and supposed 'sane' who are engaged in battle. The 'mad' are presented as care-free individuals ('I live for the moment, that's what counts'), who entertain themselves with simple play (dressing up and acting out the roles of the evacuated townspeople). They display awareness of the hidden workings of dominant systems/institutions ('All life is spectacle, Westminster, the Military Academy … The Vatican … ceremonies, masks') and, most importantly, understand that they are different from the 'sane', actively selecting their own seclusion (returning to the asylum once the threat to the town is over, closing and locking the gates themselves).

---

[35]    Laing, *The Politics of Experience*, pp. 22–3.

[36]    A similar morality tale features in *The Madwoman of Chaillot* (1969), starring Katharine Hepburn and directed by Bryan Forbes, Warner.

[37]    Fleming and Manvell, *Images of Madness*, p. 164.

The 'sane' are, by way of contrast, presented in a negative light, with little regard for the beauty and preciousness of life. Consecutive scenes – such as the 'mad' releasing the circus animals of the town from their cages while a 'sane' German soldier shoots down a carrier pigeon to read its attached message – reveal the patent dissimilarity in behaviour between the 'mad' and the 'sane'. In a final twist on an eighteenth-century cliché of the wild madman – which Scull explains was 'emblematic of chaos and terror, of the dark, bestial possibilities that lurked within the human frame'[38] – the 'mad' try to persuade Bates's character not to return to the battlefield, warning 'the countryside is full of wild beasts, can't you hear them?', 'They'll kill you', 'There's a barrier between their world and ours. It's too dangerous; they're so wicked out there.'

Despite saving the town and witnessing troops from both sides exterminate one another, Bates's character is ordered back to the front line, whereupon he chooses instead to begin a new life – a comparatively sane life – in the mental asylum. Appearing naked, holding only a birdcage, he understands exactly the form of behaviour that will result in incarceration; and, as Fleming notes in his plot summary: 'The new king, the King of Hearts, or emotion, has finally arrived, and he has brought nothing of the old order but himself, reborn. In this childlike state he represents a rejuvenation [...] a new beginning.'[39]

In short, one can postulate that both texts seek to challenge dominant assumptions of madness and sanity in an almost identical manner – contrasting the sad and isolated state of the 'normal' world with the playfulness and community of the asylum. Bowie's keen interest in film points to the possibility of a direct conceptual influence, although this has never been acknowledged. Accepting the parallels as mere coincidence is, nevertheless, intriguing in that it illustrates the shared sympathy with which much popular literature, film and music treated the subject of madness at this time.

Before discussing characterization in more detail, I would like to return to Winick's quotation concerning the 1960s and 1970s literary portrayal of the mad as heroic and intelligent. While the bold acceptance of incarceration ('I'd rather stay here') negates the authority of those who may view the asylum as a form of deserved chastisement, thus demonstrating a form of defiance, it is within the bridge sections of 'All the Madmen' that a sense of mock bravado concerning psychiatric treatments reveals a clearer element of courageousness. Here, satire, defined by Alison Ross as 'the use of ridicule, irony, sarcasm etc to expose folly or vice'[40] informs our reading of Bowie's character in terms of his inhabiting a 'sick role' and trivializing possible psychiatric treatments.

The first part of the bridge is used to reinforce the notion of role playing. Although Bowie's protagonist avoids any direct identification of other characters in the song,

---

[38]     Andrew Scull, *Social Order/Mental Disorder: Anglo-American Psychiatry in Historical Perspective* (London, 1989), p. 59.

[39]     Fleming and Manvell, *Images of Madness*, p. 166.

[40]     Alison Ross, *The Language of Humour* (London, 1998), p. 115.

it seems clear by the various actions he describes that his allusions to 'them' and 'they' refer to the psychiatrists who treat him. Initially, he draws on stereotypical 'mad' behaviour, referring to delusions of flying and loss of self-regulation: 'So I tell them that, I can fly, I will scream, I will break my arm, I will do me harm.' In fact, it is fair to say that without due consideration of the music itself the use of such stereotypical references might be regarded as a somewhat facile means of establishing the character's state of mind, thereby reinforcing rather than challenging dominant assumptions of 'mad' behaviour. As such, this point serves to stress the futility of analysing lyrics in isolation, for when one considers the vocal's intimidatory announcement of the various actions he will take, along with the equally belligerent musical setting, an altogether more complex and plausible motive emerges.

The production of the vocal informs the sectional transition and subsequent change of tone, having moved from the excessive reverberation in verse one, through a sudden loss of reverberation in verse two, to a clearly double-tracked vocal for the start of the bridge. Musically, uncertainty abounds with the harmonic and melodic material referencing both E major and E Phrygian. The triplet rhythm of the ascending G♯ A B vocal motif moves in opposition to the straight quaver rhythms of the hi-hats, and with its uncomfortable repetition over the change in harmony to a D minor chord serves to support the assertive challenge of the vocal statement. As an addition to this final repeat of the motif, the melodic line twists accordingly upwards to a C before coming to rest on A above an F major chord. This shift in harmony to the minor 2nd once again implies Phrygian undertones and provides a disturbing metaphor for the 'mad' man's seemingly incongruous behaviour. The final statement – 'I will do me harm' – is interesting in that Bowie's character objectifies himself as 'me' rather than subjectifying himself as 'myself'. In this instance he draws the line between 'I' and 'me' being the same person, thus (along with the aforementioned double tracking) implying a possible split personality.[41] The musical gesture has playful undertones in its use of a lower chromatic auxiliary note (G♯) and rhythmic syncopation, while the unconventional phrase length (three bars followed by a 2/4 bar break) is also significant in subverting the listener's expectations of regularity and continuity (see Example 1.3).

The fact that the bridge is marked by the entry of distorted electric guitar, bass guitar and full drum kit supports the growing assertiveness of the vocal melody. The ascending octave swoops in the bass and use of high-register fills in the 2/4 bars suggest a lack of grounding (a fitting metaphor for the lyric reference to flying),[42] while the ascending electric guitar fret slide of a minor 7th over the D minor chord adds to the overall edginess. The subsequent repetition of material allows Bowie to introduce further references to stereotypical 'mad' behaviour,

---

[41]  The same method of inferring split personality was used more recently in the title of the Jim Carrey film *Me, Myself and Irene* (2000) directed by Bobby Farrelly and Peter Farrelly, TCF/Conundrum.

[42]  This lack of grounding to evidence flying has been used since Richard Wagner's famous 'Ride of the Valkyries' in Act III of *Die Walküre* (1856).

intensifying the effect through a move to the present tense while at the same time posing a direct question to the listener concerning his condition: 'Here I stand, foot in hand, talking to my wall, I'm not quite right at all, am I?'[43] The way in which the question is delivered is crucial to my interpretation: with an upward pitch inflection, one would detect genuine uncertainty; however, this is effectively denied as Bowie delivers the words 'am I?' as a spoken monotone – more a statement than an enquiry. Moreover, the sense that this is the 'real' Bowie talking, and that there is therefore a degree of sincerity behind the statement, is achieved through a sudden cut in the double tracking and a momentary return to single voice without reverberation. While playful, one could argue that the first part of the bridge thus carries a certain amount of menace in its unrelenting repetition and awkward melodic–harmonic relations.

Example 1.3   'All the Madmen' bridge part 1 (vocal, bass, kit and chords)

⁴³    Bowie's use of intertextuality is evident here in that he inserts a reworking of the lyrics 'Here I stand with head in hand, turn my face to the wall' from the Beatles' 'You've Got to Hide Your Love Away' (John Lennon and Paul McCartney, 1965).

Understanding the protagonist's relationship with whom he refers to as 'they' (the psychiatrists) requires the listener to understand the basic premise outlined by Szasz: that 'The sick role in psychiatry is typically other-defined.'[44] Bowie's recourse to threatening stereotypical behaviour ('I will scream, I will break my arm, I will do me harm') indicates that it is a role his character is prepared to 'play' – not as an admission of mental illness but as proof of an act he is able to control.[45]

The question of whether or not he's 'quite right at all' fits with the widely held opinion that madness is a condition which reveals itself through unreasonable behaviour and, as such, is diametrically opposed to reason and sanity. Behaviour that fails to comply with what the majority of society regard as 'right' and 'reasonable' is condemned through the use of a large number of popular, stigmatizing expressions: 'out of one's mind', 'not right in the head', 'not all there'. Far from constituting harmless name-calling, such references to insanity have an important function in that they may be attached to certain actions and used as a benchmark from which to maintain and uphold popular beliefs and morals. As Thomas Scheff elucidates in his work *Being Mentally Ill*:

> Why are these stereotypes resistant to change? One possible explanation is that they are functional for the current social order and tend to be integrated into the psychological make-up of all members of the society. [...] Judging from the frequency with which references to mental disorder appear in the mass media and in colloquial speech, the concept of mental disorder serves as a fundamental contrast conception in our society, functioning to preserve the current mores.[46]

Defined most concisely by Gilman: 'The other is the antithesis of the self and is thus that which defines the group.'[47] The way in which concepts of insanity serve to maintain our perception of self is consequently relevant to our understanding of the more challenging aspects of Bowie's character. As previously outlined, the song was written at a time when there was widespread interest in the examination of self and, as such, Bowie's questioning encourages the listener to consider their own notions of sanity/insanity – Am I right in the head? What is it to be right in the head?

Once the sense of role playing is established, the second half of the bridge is used to mock possible forms of psychiatric treatment. Initially, we are reminded of

---

[44]    Szasz, *The Myth of Mental Illness*, p. 194.

[45]    Given this particular reading of the text, it is ironic that the publicity text on the songbook jacket for his 1967 self-titled album actually compared him to a gifted psychiatrist: 'He [Bowie] has the eye of a newspaperman who knows his way around, the insight of a gifted psychiatrist, the heart of a loving child', quoted in Lynch, p. 27.

[46]    Thomas Scheff, *Being Mentally Ill: A Sociological Theory* (London, 1966), pp. 78–9.

[47]    Sander Gilman, *Difference and Pathology: Stereotypes of Sexuality, Race and Madness* (Ithaca and London, 1985), p. 129.

the similarities in experience for the mental patient and the prison inmate in terms of their enforced confinement, and yet the sentiments expressed unexpectedly prepare for the ensuing chorus as Bowie pleads: 'Don't set me free, I'm as heavy as can be'. The humour here is accentuated through the accompanying bass line, which swoops from the root down to the 5th of the chord and back up again as if struggling to maintain its footing. The following bar culminates in an extreme high-register melodic fill moving in metaphorical opposition to the lyric 'heavy as can be', a gesture that is given further prominence as the vocal melody also extends to its highest pitch so far.

Lyrical puns emphasized through the use of end rhyme suggest a trivialization of what would ordinarily be regarded as a grave and unpleasant situation. 'Just my Librium[48] and me, and my EST[49] makes three' could, for example, be interpreted as a mischievous allusion to the three elements within Freud's division of the psyche or, indeed, the Oedipus complex.[50] With the later repeat of this section, we find further evidence of humour being utilized as an ironic weapon as the protagonist laments 'my libido's split on me, gimme some good 'ole lobotomy'.[51]

---

[48]     Librium, or chlordiazepoxide, is a drug used to treat anxiety. The potential for becoming addicted to Librium is high, and psychological and physical withdrawal symptoms may occur if a person suddenly stops taking it. The most common side effects are drowsiness, sedation, dizziness and weakness.

[49]     EST is an abbreviation for electric (or electro)shock treatment, also called electroconvulsive therapy (ECT). It was devised by Ugo Cerletti and Lucio Bini, and first administered in 1938. While controversial, it continues to be used as a treatment for severe depression. A more thorough discussion of EST appears in Chapter 2.

[50]     The significance of the number three to these particular aspects of Freudian theory is apparent from Ussher's brief overview: 'Freud conceived of the psyche as being divided into three components, the id, ego and super-ego, which competed for energy within a closed system.' Jane Ussher, *Women's Madness: Misogyny or Mental Illness* (Hemel Hempstead, 1991), p. 125. The Oedipus complex equally centred on the relationship of three – mother, father and child: 'The Oedipus complex is the stage where the child sexually desires the parent of the opposite sex and through fear of punishment from the parent of the same sex, transfers desire, and identifies with the parent of the same sex', ibid., p. 110.

[51]     Lobotomy, like EST, was introduced in the 1930s and widely administered up until the early 1950s, when reservations concerning its effectiveness and the introduction of drug therapy resulted in it becoming almost obsolete. It is interesting that Bowie refers to the operation some 20 years after its decline, although, due to the extreme nature of the procedure and its much-publicized detrimental effects (illustrated in, for example, Kesey's *One Flew Over the Cuckoo's Nest*), it is not surprising that it should remain so prominent within the public conception of mental illness and its treatment. The following quote provides a brief description of the procedure and what it was expected to cure: 'In its more primitive form it involved the removal or destruction of nerve fibres in the frontal lobe of the brain in an operation known as the "standard leucotomy" [...] As with every new technique, psychosurgery was initially hailed as a wonder treatment and was used for a wide variety of problems: "schizophrenia", alcoholism, learning disabilities, depression, anxiety, phobias, personality disorders, for shell-shocked war veterans and even for problem

The use of slang is significant, 'good 'ole' being a term one would expect to precede something favourable, although in this instance it reveals a mock bravado similar to that exhibited by anti-hero Randle Patrick McMurphy in *One Flew Over the Cuckoo's Nest* when faced with electroshock therapy. Prior to his treatment McMurphy quips 'Don't holler, Chief [...] I'll go first. My skull's too thick for them to hurt me [...] Anointest my head with conductant. Do I get a crown of thorns?' Afterwards he ridicules its effects, claiming 'they checked my plugs and cleared my points, and I got a glow on like a Model T spark coil. Ever use one of those coils arouns Halloween time? Zam! Good clean fun.'[52] By actively requesting such extreme and controversial methods of treatment, and refusing to perform expected (submissive) patient roles, the characters are able to pose a greater challenge to the psychiatric establishment. A further observation in support of this reading concerns the words 'don't', 'heavy', 'Librium', 'helpless' and 'libido', which are all emphasized through the use of accented non-harmony notes descending to harmony tones (major 6th–5th) and appear to give the vocal melody an exaggerated, whining quality. The converse happens with the words 'EST' and 'good 'ole lobotomy', which are accented by falling from the tonic to hover uncertainly on the minor 7th; and, while the melodic phrasing during this passage becomes more regular, lower chromatic auxiliary notes continue to evoke an unpredictable, directionless quality that seems to subvert any impression of sincerity.[53]

Rather than openly criticize controversial treatments such as EST and lobotomy, their very existence is thus put forward as a matter of ridicule – a darkly humorous challenge equivalent to 'give me all you've got and then some more'. This avoidance of overt criticism is, in fact, the approach taken by Szasz, whose views on the subject may be observed in the following quote:

> Although, in my opinion, the contention that lobotomy, ECT, and the major antipsychotic drugs cause brain damage is valid – indeed, it seems to me self-evident – pushing this opinion on the public is dangerously misleading and clearly counter-productive. The reason for this is that the claim that a particular psychiatric treatment, say ECT, is bad implies, first, that it is a bona fide treatment, and hence that there is a condition justifiably regarded as mental illness [...] second, that although this particular treatment may be bad, some other treatment might not be.[54]

---

children.' Lucy Johnstone, *Users and Abusers of Psychiatry: A Critical Look at Psychiatric Practice* (London, 2000), p. 154.

[52]   Kesey, pp. 222, 229.

[53]   The lower chromatic notes, being b and c♯ respectively, also perform an important harmonic function in anticipating the move to the A major chorus passage.

[54]   Szasz, *Insanity*, pp. 125–6.

Despite his reluctance to criticize 'treatments' in detail lest it enforce the idea that such a thing as mental illness actually exists, Szasz has frequently referred to treatments as 'tortures'.[55] The final reference to lobotomy in 'All the Madmen' is similarly more acerbic in tone, as the final verse recounts the act of psychosurgery to the accompaniment of distorted guitar chops (likened to chops because of their cutting timbre and the manner in which they slice through the structural beat, anticipating beats 1 and 3 with semiquaver pick-ups) before moving into a fervent 'galloping' double time section. Bowie's vocal delivery develops accordingly for this final verse – becoming more hard and nasal in tone, replacing the legato feel of previous verses with one more detached and almost mechanical in effect. Once the offending piece of brain has been 'taken away', the lyric content suggests that the psychiatrists are free to impose their version of reality upon the 'patient': 'Day after day, they take some brain away, then turn my face around, to the far side of town, and tell me that it's real, then ask me how I feel.' Romantic portrayals of the 'mad' as tortured, creative souls have often been criticized; and yet, given radical views in which psychiatry is castigated as an institution designed to 'protect and uplift the group (the family, the state), by persecuting and degrading the individual (as insane or ill)'[56] it is not surprising that accusations of psychiatrists performing covert forms of social conditioning should find a voice within more provocative songs such as this.

In understanding Bowie's creation of character, Feder's observations regarding literary constructs of madness are useful in that they highlight the important differences between genuine experience and fictional compositions of madness:

> Although the mad characters or personae of literature may be modelled on actual persons or the authors themselves, it is also true that literary constructs of the extreme possibilities of mental experience differ in important respects from actual manifestations of madness. The very distortions of the powerful visionaries or isolated victims of the literature of madness are designed to portray the mind constructing and exposing its own symbolic framework out of fragments that all readers recognise as familiar.[57]

Hence, in the same way that Bates's character recognized the kind of behaviour that would consummate his incarceration, Bowie constructs a particular example of illness related to what he knows and a general currency of beliefs about the mentally ill. As one of the key artists to place an emphasis on theatricality in rock, Bowie's interest in acting and the impact this would have on his development of

---

[55]     See, for example: 'The mental patient, we say, *may be* dangerous: he may harm himself or someone else. But we, society, *are* dangerous: we rob him of his good name and of his liberty, and subject him to tortures called "treatments".' Szasz, *The Manufacture of Madness*, p. 308.

[56]     Ibid., p. 25.

[57]     Lillian Feder, *Madness in Literature* (Princeton and Guildford, 1980), p. xiii.

a distinctive, personal style was hinted at in a 1966 press release: 'I want to act […] I'd like to do character parts. I think it takes a lot to become somebody else; it takes some doing.'[58]

Having provided several examples of the ways in which the music encodes themes of alienation, uncertainty, instability, playfulness and ascendancy, Bowie's vocal deserves a little further investigation, for it provides an interesting insight into the methods employed to establish his notion of characterization. Singing in what appears to be an exaggerated East London accent, his vocal timbre is relatively thin and the impression is that he has not yet mastered the true expressive potential of his vocal range as witnessed in later albums (perhaps most notably *Diamond Dogs*).[59] Bowie thus concentrates on achieving a number of different vocal timbres based on performance (singing with chest voice, singing in falsetto, speaking) and production (use of excessive plate reverberation, use of double tracking, use of single unaffected voice, use of panning, use of fast tape delay and so on).

Microphone placement is also used to modify vocal timbre; for example, the use of close microphone placement without reverberation in the spoken interlude contrasts sharply with the more distant placement used in the choruses. In the spoken interlude, Bowie's vocal has also been double tracked and panned hard left and right so that the discrepancies in timing of certain words are clearly audible and the metaphor for split personality becomes clear. In fact, Bowie's interest in exploring split or multiple personalities to provide unexpected twists in his soliloquies was not new. In two previous songs, both from the *Space Oddity* album (1969),[60] he alludes first to a confusion of self-identity in 'The Wild Eyed Boy From Freecloud', singing: 'Oh, it's the madness in his eyes, as he breaks the night to cry, it's really me, really you and really me'; and second to a sense of distancing from the self in 'Janine', claiming 'I've got things inside my head even I can't face, ah Janine you'd like to crash my walls, but if you take an axe to me you'll kill another man not me at all.'

It is clear from my previous analysis that the vocal melodic construction is equally crucial to the effective delivery of the song's meaning. And yet this, in turn, relies on the support of a number of subsidiary gestures – the most noteworthy being found within the kit and bass parts – to illustrate further aspects of the protagonist's persona. Both instruments exhibit a degree of high spiritedness that, on occasion, appears inappropriate for the subject matter and general expressive tone of the vocal. For example, the kit entry in the second verse is subtle in the sense that it is limited to the bell of the ride cymbal; however, the intricate rhythmic pattern it provides (including demisemiquavers and triplet demisemiquavers) implies a shift to double time that seems oddly excessive when set against the melancholic statements of the vocal line. Moreover, both the bass and kit provide what, at times, could be considered an excessive amount of mid-bar 'fills', with

[58]  *Melody Maker* (26 February 1966), quoted in Lynch, p. 23.

[59]  David Bowie, *Diamond Dogs* (RCA, 1974).

[60]  David Bowie, 'Space Oddity'/'Wild Eyed Boy From Freecloud' (Philips, 1969).

the bass regularly occupying a noticeably high pitch register (accompanying the lyric references to 'play' and 'madmen' with flirtatious, ascending pitch swoops) and the kit descending from snare to low tom with a series of complex semi and demisemiquaver embellishments. The accompanying gestures of the recorder sounds during verses two and three are also unexpectedly lavish, with their use of non-harmony tones, chromatic runs and parallel perfect 5th intervals seeming to compete with the comparative simplicity of the vocal line. As such, I would argue that it is exactly this sense of immoderation that establishes the more flamboyant, manic aspects of Bowie's character; mania referring to an irrational excess of energy which, in the seventeenth century, was believed not only to be linked more to men than women but also to manifest itself in, among other things, excess talk, odd language and self-violence.[61]

With regard to Bowie's personal motive for exploring concepts of madness, his family history is of apparent interest to several writers keen to mention his half-brother Terry Burns's commitment to Cane Hill Mental Hospital.[62] While I believe that limiting one's reading of 'All the Madmen' to a simple description of Burns's commitment fails to observe the song's potential depth and degree of complexity, there are, nevertheless, two important points to be made regarding this matter. First, that Bowie's knowledge of particular psychiatric issues such as the lyric references to the treatments Librium and EST was, conceivably, informed by his experience of Burns's illness. Second, that certain interview statements reveal the way in which Bowie viewed his musical explorations of the subject as a form of exorcism, suggesting his ability to nullify both his fear and the risk of a similar fate by invoking and expelling the 'illness' in fictional mode: 'One reason I've never been in analysis is that I've always been afraid of what I'd find out. My brother is in a psychiatric hospital and madness has always run in our family. I have a terrible fear it's genetic.'[63] Explaining the lyric of 'Oh! You Pretty Things' to one reporter, he points to the therapeutic effects of his music: 'I hadn't been to an analyst … my parents went, my brothers and sisters and my aunts and uncles and cousins, they did that, they ended up in a much worse state, so I stayed

---

[61]     : See Joan Busfield, *Men, Women and Madness: Understanding Gender and Mental Disorder* (Basingstoke, 1996), pp. 120–21 where she outlines Michael MacDonald's observations on mania, referring to the following works: M. MacDonald, *Mystical Bedlam: Madness, Anxiety and Healing in Seventeenth-Century England* (Cambridge, 1981) pp. 121–32 and M. MacDonald, 'Women and Madness in Tudor and Stuart England', *Social Research*, 55 (1986): 257–81.

[62]     See, for example, Buckley, *The Complete Guide to the Music of David Bowie*, who claims that the lyrics for 'All the Madmen' are 'a comment on Terry's own stay at the Cane Hill mental asylum'.

[63]     From an interview with Rex Reed, quoted in Lynch, p. 5. For further information concerning Bowie's family history of mental illness see Christopher Sandford, *Bowie: Loving the Alien* (New York, 1998), pp. 14–15, and Tremlett, *David Bowie Living on the Brink*, pp. 7, 8, 17.

away. I thought I'd write my problems out.'[64] Finally, looking back over his early
career in 1993, Bowie admitted 'It scared me that my own [mind] was in question.
I often wondered at the time how near the line I was going ... how far I should
push myself.' He went on to explain how 'Ziggy and the other characters [...] had
been alternative egos', according to Sandford, 'a form of madness through which
he had meant to save his sanity'.[65] Again, certain parallels may be drawn here
with eighteenth-century interpretations of madness, most specifically that of the
melancholic poet[66] invoking inspiration from an unforgiving muse: the condition
itself, thereby perpetuating a continuing cycle of expulsion and desire.

Of course, a more cynical view asserts the possibility that Bowie's inclusion
of such themes was simply a means of attaining a certain shock value, not too
dissimilar to his sexually suggestive comments concerning, among other things,
a sexual affair with Raquel Welch's husband.[67] Tactics involving a deliberate
heightening of the media's interest in Bowie's ambiguous sexuality were also to
be found on the UK album cover (depicting Bowie reclining on a chaise longue,
wearing what he termed his 'man dress') – the resulting feminization proving
too controversial for his American record company, who insisted on a cartoon
cowboy illustration instead. Even reviewers, intending to exploit the disturbing
references to madness by linking it to brilliance of intellect, seemed to miss the
point somewhat, as the following statement reveals:

> What happens to a flower-child, when all of the world around him is going
> slightly crazy and power struggles are taking over everything, including his
> music, is that he harnesses his genius, conforms to the insanity, outpowers the
> loudest group around, and does it all just a little bit better than anybody else.[68]

Perhaps more sympathetic and relevant to this particular analysis is Cagle's
suggestion that 'Bowie and other glitter rockers *implied* that one could "try
on lifestyles" within the framework of rock'n'roll and not always "take on the
consequences".'[69] His comment on Bowie's fans 'revelling in the process of
identifying with the sexual other, whether this other was or was not intrinsic to
their own sexual orientation(s)' is certainly relevant in that the madman character

---

64    Sandford, p. 15.

65    Ibid.

66    Examples being William Cowper (1731–1800) and George (Lord) Byron (1788–
1824).

67    In an interview with John Mendelsohn, Bowie said: 'Tell your readers to make
their minds up about me when I start getting adverse publicity; when I'm found in bed with
Raquel Welch's husband.' *Rolling Stone* (1 April 1971), p. 18.

68    Chris Van Ness, *LA Free Press*, quoted in George Tremlett, *The David Bowie Story*
(New York, 1975), p. 105.

69    Van M. Cagle, *Reconstructing Pop/Subculture: Art, Rock and Andy Warhol*
(California, 1995), pp. 11–12.

may have offered a further potential source for Other identification. Moreover, in terms of dramatic potential, the madman role permits the exploration and communication of a range of contrasting emotions (from the melancholic statements of the song's opening to the humorous taunts of the bridge sections and eventual elation of the final chorus), offering the ultimate challenge to any self-confessed actor. Yet, while the appeal of such a role is clear, it is important to note that Bowie resists any vacant utilization of stereotypes that have come to represent 'mad' behaviour, and instead, through clever use of reversal techniques, humour[70] and role play, offers a critique of psychiatry that actively encourages listeners to question their own definitions of madness and sanity at the same time as espousing the potential appeal of difference. It is for such reasons that 'All the Madmen' may be identified as a text which, while shrewdly avoiding the often marginalizing identity of 'protest song',[71] manages to challenge the authority and legitimacy of the psychiatric establishment in ways that listeners are still able to derive pleasure from.

---

[70]     Here one is reminded of the following Walter Benjamin quotation: 'There is no better start for thinking than laughter.' Walter Benjamin, 'The Author as Producer', in Peter Demetz (ed.), *Reflections: Essays, Aphorisms, Autobiographical Writings* (New York, 1978), p. 235.

[71]     John Street's comparison of Tom Robinson's 'Glad to be Gay' (1976) and Rod Stewart's 'The Killing of Georgie' (1976) is useful here in that he concludes: '"Glad to be Gay" was an important political gesture, but it was not a good popular song [...] Its sneer, its fatalism, its exclusiveness and its use of categories undermine its ability to communicate', (whereas) '"Georgie" conveys a sense of injustice, avoids fatalism, and offers a glimmer of hope. It achieves all this by focusing on an individual; the group (the category) is there only by implication [...] Stewart engages the listener's attention, tells them a story and elicits their sympathy. He can do this because he is not dealing in categories.' John Street, *Rebel Rock: The Politics of Popular Music* (New York, 1986), pp. 161–2. I am suggesting that Bowie's song works in a similar way to 'The Killing of Georgie' because the methods used to question the psychiatric establishment (humour, reversal, role play) are, in and of themselves, entertaining and engender engagement and empathy from a wide audience.

# Chapter 2

# 'Kill Your Sons': Lou Reed's Verification of Psychiatry's Covert Social Function

Reportedly written during Reed's Velvet Underground period (1965–1970), 'Kill Your Sons' was finally recorded in March 1974, and appears as the fifth track on his solo album *Sally Can't Dance*.[1] The song draws on Reed's personal experience of electroshock therapy (EST), detailing the treatments he received and revealing his antipathy toward the psychiatric establishment that administered them. While there are numerous literary and film portrayals of a similar subject matter, 'Kill Your Sons' is perhaps the most detailed musical example of its kind and is seemingly unique within popular music discourse.

It is interesting that Reed neglects to reveal within the song lyrics the diagnosis he was given, but the reason behind his visits to Creedmore State Hospital in 1959, where at age 17 he underwent 24 electroshock treatments, has been thoroughly documented by many biographers. Victor Bockris writes: 'That spring, Lou's conservative parents [...] sent their difficult son to a psychiatrist, requesting that they cure Lou of his homosexual feelings and alarming mood swings',[2] while Peter Doggett acknowledges that: 'In a poorer family, Reed might have had his homosexuality beaten out of him; that would no doubt have aroused sexual difficulties of its own. In Freeport, Long Island, they called in the professionals.'[3]

In 1952 the American Psychiatric Association's *Diagnostic and Statistical Manual* (APA-DSM) provided its first official listing of mental disorders, and included homosexuality within the category of sociopathic personality disturbances. This classification is significant, for it made clear that the sufferer of such a disorder, although the victim of abstruse pathology, would typically be unaware of any stress or anxiety resulting from such. Thus, any homosexual

---

[1]     Lou Reed, *Sally Can't Dance* (RCA, 1974). For evidence of Reed writing 'Kill Your Sons' in the 1960s, see Peter Doggett, *Lou Reed: Growing up in Public* (London, 1991), where it is claimed: 'Reed actually wrote it a decade earlier. John Cale remembers it being around when they formed The Velvet Underground, though never for public consumption', p. 19.

[2]     Victor Bockris, *Lou Reed the Biography* (London, 1994), p. 2.

[3]     Doggett, p. 18. Reed is also quoted here to have said: 'They put the thing down your throat so you don't swallow your tongue, and they put electrodes on your head. That's what was recommended in Rockland County then to discourage homosexual feelings. The effect is that you lose your memory and become a vegetable. I wrote "Kill Your Sons" on *Sally Can't Dance* about that.'

who claimed no distress or mental hardship could be ignored, for it was their behaviour as opposed to their subjective opinion of it that placed beyond dispute their inherent disease.[4] DSM-I's blatant acknowledgement of the importance of social context in defining mental illness affirmed that a person diagnosed with sociopathic personality disturbance was 'ill primarily in terms of society and of conformity with the prevailing cultural milieu'.[5]

Many psychiatrists helped to establish and reinforce the belief that homosexuality was a form of mental illness[6] – from the likes of Sandor Rado, who in the 1940s espoused the view that it was simply a phobic reaction to the opposite sex; through Edmund Bergler, who labelled homosexuals 'injustice collectors';[7] to Irving Bieber, whose conceited opinion regarding heterosexuality being the 'biologic norm'[8] led to claims in the 1960s that 'every homosexual is a latent heterosexual'.[9] Common treatment involved electroshock aversion therapy which, according to sociologists David Pilgrim and Anne Rogers, prioritized men and 'was at its most exaggerated in the late 1960s and early 1970s'.[10] This crude form of 'therapy' often involved nothing more refined than showing male recipients pictures of naked men and administering an electric shock whenever arousal occurred.[11] Of course, pictures were not always used, but many accounts from those forced to undergo electroshock therapy describe the overriding sense of punishment experienced: the feeling that undesirable behaviour should be remedied lest the prescription of shocks continue. Janet Frame's *Faces In The Water* is one such example; an autobiographical account of her experience while in a mental hospital, she describes shock treatment as 'the new and fashionable

---

[4]   Ronald Bayer, *Homosexuality and American Psychiatry* (Princeton, NJ, 1987), pp. 39–40.

[5]   American Psychiatric Association, *Diagnostic and Statistical Manual, Mental Disorders* (Washington, DC, 1952), p. 34. Quoted in Bayer, p. 40.

[6]   For an in-depth discussion of psychiatry and western society's historical treatment of homosexuality, see Bayer, pp. 15–40.

[7]   Edmund Bergler, *Homosexuality: Disease or Way of Life?* (New York: Hill & Wang, 1956), p. 9. Quoted in Bayer, p. 78.

[8]   Irving Bieber et al., *Homosexuality: A Psychoanalytic Study of Male Homosexuals* (New York: Basic Books, 1962), p. 319. Quoted in Bayer, p. 30.

[9]   Bieber et al., p. 220. Quoted in Bayer, p. 30.

[10]   David Pilgrim and Anne Rogers, *A Sociology of Mental Health and Illness* (Buckingham and Philadelphia, 1999), p. 59.

[11]   For a more detailed account of this procedure, see David Cooper, *The Death of the Family* (London, 1971), p. 114. Here Cooper also writes that: 'It has been estimated that around seventy percent of homosexual men "convert" after their experience. Not one word is mentioned about the attitude of the investigator to his own homosexuality, to the reaction any person has to pain induced by electric shock, or, above all, to the quality of the nude photographs. All that seems to matter is that in the end one submits. The criterion of successful psychiatric treatment is once again seen to be the submission to the dominant values of society.'

means of quieting people and making them realize that orders are to be obeyed and floors are to be polished without anyone protesting and faces are to be made to be fixed into smiles and weeping is a crime'.[12]

Fictional literary accounts based on true experience appear to share similar objectives to that of Reed's song, casting aspersion on psychiatrists' methods and revealing the covert intention behind such therapy. Sylvia Plath's character Esther describes her equally chilling experience of electroshock in the following passage:

There was a brief silence, like an indrawn breath.

Then something bent down and took hold of me and shook me like the end of the world. Whee-ee-ee-ee-ee, it shrilled, through an air crackling with blue light, and with each flash a great jolt drubbed me till I thought my bones would break and the sap fly out of me like a split plant.

I wondered what terrible thing it was that I had done.[13]

By the late 1960s, the time of Reed's writing 'Kill Your Sons', there had been a number of significant developments concerning psychiatry's attitude towards and treatment of homosexuality. Research undertaken by Alfred Kinsey in the 1940s and Evelyn Hooker in the 1950s provided the necessary impetus to enable the emergence of a homophile movement, of which important groups were the Mattachine Society and, later, the Daughters of Bilitis.[14] It is true that the Mattachine Society, whose aim was to secure homosexuals full acceptance into society, initially supported the psychiatric establishment, for the psychiatrists could explain how a homosexual's sexual orientation was a form of mental abnormality and not a wilful act of moral solecism (better to be termed ill than criminal). Unsurprisingly, however, the movement's patience ceased once it was acknowledged that the work of psychiatrists such as Bergler and Bieber could equally be used by bigots to promote continued prejudice, and under the leadership of Frank Kameny and the influence of the Civil Rights Movement of the 1960s a more militant phase of opposition began. As Ronald Bayer explains: 'In a climate increasingly affected by the rise of nationalist movements abroad, the Black struggle at home, and a new

---

[12] Janet Frame, *Faces in the Water* (New York, 1961), extracts of which provided in Thomas Szasz, *The Age of Madness* (London, 1975), p. 203.

[13] Sylvia Plath, *The Bell Jar* [1963] (London, 1996), p. 138.

[14] The Mattachine Society was a homosexual rights group founded in 1950 with a largely male membership. The Daughters of Bilitis was an organization designed initially to defend lesbian rights. According to Bayer, its publication, the *Ladder*, 'was to emerge during the mid-1960s as the most important forum of homosexual opinion in the United States'. Bayer, p. 81.

wave of feminism, "psychiatric cure" became the equivalent of white supremacy [...] a "final solution" to the problem of homosexuality.'[15]

Despite homosexuality's categorization as sociopathic personality disturbance being revoked in the second *Diagnostic and Statistical Manual* (1968), it was not until 1973 that it was officially removed from the list of sexual deviations labelled non-psychotic mental disorders. A number of factors contributed to the eventual swiftness in which the psychiatric establishment was forced to change its position, and much of the Gay Liberation movement's rhetoric was influenced by Szasz's relentless criticism that had reached a formidable zenith in his 1971 book *The Manufacture of Madness*. In this publication, he insisted:

> It is nothing less than obscene to talk about the homosexual as a sick person whom we are trying to help so long as, by treating him as a defective thing, we demonstrate through our actions that what we want him to be is a useful, rather an annoying, *object for us*; and that what we will not tolerate is his wanting to be an authentic *person for himself.*[16]

Disruptions of the American Psychiatric Association's conventions; the Stonewall riots (June 1969) and gay pride demonstrations that followed; and the eventual, formally recognized gay presence at the APA's Dallas convention[17] helped to ensure that, while prejudice continued, claims of mental illness could no longer be used as its justification.

Clearly, the recording of Reed's 'Kill Your Sons' one year later cannot be viewed alongside Kameny's assertion that 'psychiatry is the enemy incarnate'[18] as a concomitant act of gay defiance. The song's homosexual connections are not, after all, made clear; and its impact would arguably have been greater, not least in implying a shared empathy with the movement's struggle, had he recorded it on its initial conception sometime in the 1960s. Nevertheless, I suggest that 'Kill Your Sons', at a time when many autobiographical attacks on psychiatry's methods were being published, was able to raise important questions that went beyond those of immediate concern to the Gay Liberation movement. More specifically, the various themes explored within the song – the role of his parents, the after-effects of the treatments he received, his evident scepticism of so-called mental normality – provide the listener with a further insight into what Szasz would term the covert social function of psychiatry.[19]

---

[15]     Ibid., p. 85.

[16]     Thomas Szasz, *The Manufacture of Madness* [1970] (London, 1973), p. 287.

[17]     See Bayer, pp. 97, 105 and 107 for details of these events. Following the Stonewall riots, the adoption of the word 'gay' signifies a difference in the reception of what it means to be homosexual.

[18]     *The Advocate* (26 May 1971), p. 3. Quoted in Bayer, p. 105.

[19]     Thomas Szasz has tirelessly claimed that psychiatry serves to silence and dispose of society's scapegoats.

It is worth first considering the song's auditory impact, for the tempo appears deliberately slower than that typically employed to breathe life into a rhythmic arrangement so intent on crotchet beat emphasis. The incessant use of crash cymbal, coupled with the guitar's two bar progression of crotchet power chords, produces a brashness of timbre normally associated with faster tempos where the sounds have little chance to register as separate hits. In this case, however, the tempo of 80 beats per minute (bpm) contributes to a feeling of intense sluggishness that provides an evocative backdrop for Reed's delivery of the verbal text. The first verse is essential in setting the scene for the rest of the song, informing the listener of the prescription of electric shock and the ensuing memory loss:

> All your two-bit psychiatrists
> Are giving you electric shock […]
> But every time you tried to read a book
> You couldn't get to page seventeen
> 'Cause you forgot where you were
> So you couldn't even read

While the vocal delivery itself is arguably the dominant signifier for the disabling effects of memory loss – as Doggett details in his biography: 'like the victim of a lobotomy, Reed droned out the lyrics beneath a distant buzz of guitars: this is what you've reduced me to, he seemed to say, as he catalogued the mental vacuity caused by his treatment'[20] – it appears that the staid yet timbrally jarring musical setting likewise contributes to the dolorous, belligerent character of the song.

Doggett's observation concerning Reed droning out the lyrics is a valid one, particularly as a number of critics have attempted to summarize his delivery in terms of a monotonal voice. At the same time, however, it is a rather simplified account of what is actually a distinctive and intriguing vocal style. Once the precise nature of Reed's phrasing is examined there is actually far more to conclude regarding the possible ways in which melodic contour, pitch inflection, vocal timbre and rhythmic construction inform the listener's reading of the musical text.

The amorphous quality of the phrasing, slightly flat pitching and interminable repetition of notes result in a somewhat insipid delivery, perfect for illustrating the sentiment of the lyric content. Granted, such characteristics are indicative of Reed's usual vocal style; but in 'Kill Your Sons' they are noticeably exaggerated in a manner seemingly illustrative of the adverse effects of electroshock.[21] Each change

---

[20]   Doggett, p. 94.

[21]   See other songs from *Sally Can't Dance*, for example 'Ennui' and the title track, which demonstrate greater adherence to the structural beat and largely consonant phrase endings.

in pitch is typically followed by between two and six restatements of the same note, resulting in what Cagle refers to as Reed's 'anti-melodic vocals'[22] (see Example 2.1).

Example 2.1 'Kill Your Sons' verse 1 (vocal)

In terms of producing a sense of monotony, this device is most effective at points when the pitch repeats in an unrelenting fashion against notes of the embellished bass line. During the first verse, the best example of this occurs with the lines 'giving you electric shock' and 'couldn't get to page seventeen', where the vocal's repetition of the note 'c' finally culminates on the word 'shock', below which the bass sounds semiquaver B♭s. The resulting interval clash of a major 2nd causes a momentary point of awkwardness, implying that the vocal has outstayed its welcome; that the phrase has been handled in a clumsy manner. As such, the lack of conventional resolution at the ends of many vocal phrases could be perceived as a metaphor for the loss of mental functioning caused by the shock treatment.[23]

The rhythmic articulation of the verses adds a further dimension to this particular reading of the text, since the vocal progresses from an apparently free, syncopated opening of phrase to a more confined conclusion where repeated semiquavers emphasize the structural beat and the monotonal pitch is, as a result, highlighted (see Example 2.1). Given that the lyrics 'giving you electric shock', 'instead of mental hospitals', 'couldn't get to page seventeen', and 'couldn't even read' are all end points of phrase, the listener is thus encouraged to consider the restrictive, dehumanizing elements of not only the subsequent memory loss but also the prescription and delivery of the treatment itself. The grinding repetition of the guitar's two-bar power chord progression (G/D, D/A, F/C, C/G) compounds

Example 2.2 'Kill Your Sons' intro and verse (bass)

---

[22]     Van M. Cagle, *Reconstructing Pop/Subculture: Art, Rock and Andy Warhol* (Thousand Oaks, CA, 1995), p. 222.

[23]     Peter Breggin briefly details the adverse effects of electroshock to be 'loss of everyday memory, as well as associated effects such as losing one's train of thought, incoherent speech or slowness of affect'. Breggin, *Toxic Psychiatry*, p. 247.

the effect, leaving the responsibility for directing any sense of forward motion to the bass, which utilizes ascending chromatic embellishments that aid linkage between bars (see Example 2.2). Despite this, the apparent concentration on bass frequencies simply adds to the ponderous feel of the verses.

The criticism of psychiatrists and details of memory loss that occur during verse one are addressed directly to the listener, placing the singer in the role of observer and messenger – a position that is strengthened in the chorus as Reed asks: 'Don't you know they're gonna kill your sons?' While psychiatrists are part of a medical profession that is intended to heal people, their portrayal within literature and film has often contravened this belief. *When the Clouds Roll By* (1919) was one of the first films to explore the plot of doctor–patient reversal, where the psychiatrist is eventually revealed to be an escaped patient from the New York Insane Asylum. The notion of such a scam going unnoticed would prove a popular source of irony and humour, and, while suggestive of incompetence, was arguably less harmful than more veritable subjects. As Fleming notes in his account of filmic representations of psychiatrists, *Mr Deeds Goes To Town* (1936) is one such example where the David and Goliath theme is played out between Deeds, the simple, modest protagonist, and the conceited psychiatrist who challenges his sanity: 'It is this very plausibility that could have left the audience feeling that all psychiatrists, like the one in the film, were self-serving egocentrics who felt that they understood reality while in fact they had never really lived it.'[24] While more positive images of psychiatrists appeared in films such as *The Three Faces of Eve* (1957) and *Pressure Point* (1962), by the time of the release of 'Kill Your Sons' the desire for shock and drama had resulted in an abundance of negative representations as witnessed in works such as *Peeping Tom* (1962) and *Coogan's Bluff* (1968).[25] As such, Reed's derogatory reference to 'two-bit psychiatrists' would be understood as a part of that tradition and demonstrates an affinity with Szasz, who laments the fact that the public are 'eager to be led – and deceived – by psychiatrists posturing as medical scientists'.[26]

During the 1960s and 1970s there was growing public awareness of what electric shock treatment – more commonly referred to as electroshock (EST) or electroconvulsive (ECT) – was, if not always a clear idea of its efficacy and indeed validity. Most literary accounts, as mentioned previously, advocated suspicion regarding its intended usage, and this was mirrored by anti-psychiatrists such as David Cooper, who wrote:

> It is no sheer chance that Cerletti discovered electro-convulsive 'treatment' in the abattoirs of Rome, where pigs were killed by electrocution. Those pigs who did not die showed noticeable changes in their modes of behaviour; and

[24]   Michael Fleming and Roger Manvell, *Images of Madness: The Portrayal of Insanity in the Feature Film* (London, 1985), p. 174.

[25]   Ibid., p. 177.

[26]   Szasz, *The Manufacture of Madness*, p. 234.

then of course he started giving electroshocks to mental patients to change their behaviour, just as Hitler killed 60,000 mental patients 'experimentally' as well as to 'improve the race'.[27]

Electroshock was first administered in 1938 and is a means of producing unconsciousness and a convulsion by passing an electric current through the brain. Peter Breggin's account of the treatment serves to illustrate its supposedly curative process:

> The shock induces an electrical storm that obliterates the normal electrical patterns of the brain, driving the recording needle on the EEG up and down in violent, jagged swings. This period of extreme bursts of electrical energy often is followed by a briefer period of absolutely no electrical activity, called the isoelectric phase. The brain waves become temporarily flat, exactly as in brain death, and it may be that cell death takes place during this time. [...] Typically the treatment is given three times a week for a total of at least six to ten sessions. After several sessions of shock, the patient awakens in a few (sometimes many) minutes in a state of apathy and docility.[28]

Examining literary portrayals of electroshock therapy from the period reveals the most common after-effect described to be that of memory loss. Janet Frame's depiction is typical: 'At first I cannot find my way, I cannot find myself where I left myself, someone has removed all trace of me. I am crying.'[29] In Charles Willeford's short story *The Machine in Ward Eleven*, the main character, Blake, likewise describes a fellow patient prior to their discharge from hospital following a series of electroshocks:

> after a few treatments he'd developed a frowning, perplexed expression. He was unable to recall entering the hospital, or any of the events that had led up to his admission. I had talked to him several times before his release, and except for his memory block, which worried him very little, he was a rational, perfectly normal – nothing – that was it nothing! He was neither excited nor depressed. He was stonily indifferent to his past and future, and had believed Dr Fellerman when he was told that his memory would return, all in good time[30]

When threatened with the same treatment himself, Blake attacks his psychiatrist and subjects him to a fatal dose of electric current, admitting: 'The body convulsions

---

27    Cooper, *The Death of the Family*, p. 86.

28    Breggin, pp. 241–2.

29    Frame, *Faces in the Water*, extracts of which provided in Szasz, *The Age of Madness*, p. 212.

30    Charles Willeford, *The Machine in Ward Eleven* (New York, 1963). Found in Szasz, *The Age of Madness*, pp. 347–8.

were terrible to see, and I turned my head away. I couldn't bear the sight of this long skinny body buckling and jerking beneath the steady flow of electricity.'[31] By comparison, Reed's depiction is surprisingly mild, and yet the sentiment remains the same: his reference to memory loss is intended to facilitate a sense of doubt within the listener concerning the validity of electroshock therapy. With regard to Breggin's work, where precise details of the after-effects are provided, it appears that such questioning is perfectly logical:

> To the extent that it works at all, shock has its impact by disabling the brain. It does so by causing an organic brain syndrome, with memory loss, confusion, and disorientation, and by producing lobotomy effects. For a few days or weeks the patient may be euphoric or high as a result of the brain damage, and this may be experienced as 'feeling better'. In the long run the patient becomes more apathetic and 'makes fewer complaints'.[32]

Neurologist John Friedberg put it even more bluntly in his contribution to the *American Journal of Psychiatry* in 1977, writing: 'Assuming free and fully informed consent, it is well to reaffirm the individual's right to pursue happiness through brain damage if he or she so chooses. But we might well ask ourselves whether we, as doctors sworn to the Hippocratic Oath, should be offering it.'[33]

The fact that Reed avoids recounting the horrors of his treatment in the first person is significant, since reminding listeners that it is *their* psychiatrists who are giving *them* electric shock serves to generate feelings of both vulnerability and culpability. The use of heavy 'telephone voice' equalization (where the frequency band occupied by the vocal is limited to between 500Hz and 3,000Hz) lends a metallic edge to Reed's vocal timbre in the chorus. The effect enhances the mode of expression; the message that the psychiatrists are 'gonna kill your sons' appears to be delivered from a telephone receiver, where, as the other senses are redundant, the act of listening is more concentrated. The vocal is also processed through an analogue tape delay to achieve two audible repeats of the word 'gonna' following the lead-in phrase 'don't you know they're gonna'. The use of this device has a subtle yet noticeable impact: the fact that the vocal temporarily ceases its flow, leaving only the diminishing echoes, ensures that its eventual furtherance ('kill your sons') receives due attention. Upon subsequent repeats of this phrase, the word 'kill' is emphasized through its placement on the first beat of the bar, its crotchet duration and, most importantly, the indolent fashion in which Reed delivers it – with a descending pitch inflection, like a half-spoken sneer.

---

[31]   Ibid., p. 354.

[32]   Breggin, *Toxic Psychiatry*, p. 245.

[33]   John M. Friedberg, 'Shock Treatment, Brain Damage and Memory Loss: A Neurological Perspective', *American Journal of Psychiatry*, 134 (1977): 1010–14. Quoted in Lucy Johnstone, *Users and Abusers of Psychiatry: A Critical Look at Psychiatric Practice* (London, 2000), p. 192.

The threat of such horrific action is accompanied by an increase in momentum, as the bass's alternating octave quavers provide a relatively 'bouncy' and seemingly incongruous accompaniment. The functional harmonic progression (I–V–IV–I in F major) serves to strengthen the sense of direction, breaking away from the verse's stagnant cycle of repetition to become a metaphor for the predicted act. The concluding phrase 'kill your sons until they run, run, run, run, run, run, run, run away' makes no literal sense, although does perhaps warn of a potential breakdown in parent–child relations while appealing to a teenage sensibility: the secret desire to punish one's carers and promote self-identity through leaving home. The vocal's descending crotchet F Dorian melody, doubled in the guitar and bass (where it becomes embellished with triplet semiquaver turns), appears to symbolize the growing distance that emerges as a result of the running. Only on the very last repetition of the word 'run' does the melody unexpectedly lurch upwards, accompanied by a dissonant guitar string bend, in an attempt to regain its starting pitch for the subsequent verse.

Addressing the chorus to a parent or future parent anticipates the content of the second verse. The bitter snapshot of his mother's and sister's marital relations shifts the lyric subject away from the intensity of personal reflection towards the wider issue of what constitutes normal, sane behaviour.

Reed's mother confides in him that she 'doesn't know what to do about dad' since he 'took an axe and broke the table'. Reed's sardonic response: 'aren't you glad you're married?' – which he delivers in an impassive, monotonal slur – is given added poignancy as he goes on to describe his sister's wedlock resulting in a husband who is big and fat and 'doesn't even have a brain'. The implication is that the son, in this case Reed's protagonist, is pleasantly free of such problems since he has resisted the pressures of social conformity by disregarding the institution of marriage. The suggestion that his sister's husband is an automaton, taking the train (presumably to work) but lacking a brain, demonstrates a certain affinity between Reed's thinking and David Cooper's critique of society's institutions and his description of what he termed 'the well-conditioned, endlessly obedient citizen', writing:

> This is a state of being in which one is so estranged from every aspect of one's experience, from every spontaneous impulse to action, from every bit of awareness of one's body for oneself [...] from all carefully refused possibilities of awakening change, that one might truly and without metaphorical sleight-of-hand regard this normal person as being out of his mind.[34]

The evident criticism of the subject's family, while lacking real enmity, nevertheless implies that it would be totally unreasonable, given their own inadequacies, for such parents to judge their son's state of mind; and is perhaps why at this point

---

[34]     Cooper, *The Death of the Family*, p. 13.

in the song the listener is able to reflect more clearly upon the bitter irony of the chorus lyric.

By all accounts, Reed was a rebellious teenager: 'slithering around the house like a snake on speed [...] he alternately slashed screeching guitar chords on his electric guitar, practised an effeminate way of walking [...] drew his sister aside in conspiratorial conferences that excluded his parents, and threatened to throw the mother of all moodies if everyone didn't pay complete attention to him immediately.'[35] But his parent's decision to question such behaviour and subsequently accept the psychiatrist's diagnosis enables Reed to comment with some authority on the covert way in which family and psychiatric institutions might conspire to control threatening behaviour. Again, there is a certain affinity here with Cooper's belief that it is the family unit that invents the notion of disease, formulating a list of symptoms which medical science, via the discipline of psychiatry, can then apply a classification to and treat. With specific reference to schizophrenia, Cooper argues that it is typically a family's inability to deal with difficulties surrounding adolescence that leads to accusations of illness:

> symptoms are virtually whatever makes the family unbearably anxious about the tentatively independent behaviour of its offspring. These behavioural signs usually involve issues such as aggression, sexuality, and generally any form of autonomous self-assertion. These may be the customary expression of the needs of an adolescent person, but, in certain families, even these are quite unacceptable and must, if necessary by some desperate means, be invalidated. A most respectable and readily available form of invalidation is to call such behaviour 'ill'.[36]

Leonard Frank – who was institutionalized by his parents in 1962 and, in the same year that 'Kill Your Sons' was released, co-founded the Network Against Psychiatric Assault – provides a similarly scathing account of how one might be singled out for 'treatment':

> If you're earning a living – if you're playing the game – almost anything goes; if you're not, almost nothing does. People dropping out without sanctions would set a bad example from the standpoint of the stick-it-outs. If the dropouts aren't punished, similarly inclined people might be encouraged to follow their example, and soon the game might have to be called for lack of players – or at least the rules of the game might have to be changed, and that's something people generally don't like, especially if they happen to be in the winning side at the time.[37]

---

[35]    Bockris, p. 2.

[36]    Cooper, *Psychiatry and Anti-Psychiatry*, pp. 24–5.

[37]    Leonard Frank 'From Victim to Revolutionary: An Interview with Leonard Frank', in Seth Farber, *Madness, Heresy, and the Rumor of Angels: The Revolt Against the Mental Health System* (Chicago, 1993), p. 190.

Of all the anti-psychiatrists, Cooper was the most vehement in his critique of family relations, arguing that psychiatry is 'after educational institutions, the third rung of family defence against autonomy on the part of its members'.[38] Within his works *Psychiatry and Anti-Psychiatry* (1967) and *The Death of the Family* (1971), he proposed that breakdown in family relations was not only a probable cause for an individual member to exhibit behaviour likely to be categorized as mental illness, but also that a family's inability to coerce its members to function in a mutually beneficial fashion was often remedied by either the threat or actual assignment of psychiatric treatment.[39] It is possible that Lou Reed's experience would have offered Cooper the perfect case in point, for it was his refusal, albeit subconsciously perhaps, to conform to what was deemed acceptable, normal behaviour that resulted in his own course of 'treatment'.

Underpinning all of Cooper's protestations is his criticism of a society in which the right to assert one's self-centred interests is quashed by institutions designed to encourage capitulation and obedience for the greater good of all:

> the family specializes in the formation of roles for its members rather than laying down the conditions for the free assumption of identity [...] characteristically in a family a child is indoctrinated with the desired desire to become a certain sort of son of daughter (then husband, wife, father, mother) [...] Instead of the feared possibility of acting from the chosen and self-invented centre of oneself, being self-centred in a good sense, one is taught to submit.[40]

Unsurprisingly, Cooper viewed the classification of homosexuality as a mental illness as a specific example of the way in which society attempted to curtail sexual emancipation:

> sexuality is the most feared object of the psychiatric service which needs its madmen and is terrified of losing its unreasonable *raison d'être*. So the outpatient clinics multiply, as do the variety of tranquillizer drugs, as do the literal or metaphorical electronic eyes that, in the interest of some remote and

---

   38   Cooper, *The Death of the Family*, p. 11.

   39   Lucy Johnstone documents one particular case where a young person experiences problems growing up and finds the hospital simply reinforcing child-like behaviour: 'she had to go to bed and get up at specified times, ask permission to have a bath, stay in her nightgown, and comply with various other ward regulations. In a tragic repetition of the situation in her family, her rebellion against these rules, against taking her drugs and against the very fact of her containment, was seen not as healthy assertiveness or understandable protest but as further evidence of her illness. The more she struggled, the more entangled she became.' Johnstone, p. 74.

   40   Cooper, *The Death of the Family*, p. 25.

crazy family ideal, destructively control every ecstatic possibility of experience and any tentative move to sexual liberation.[41]

Reed's clever mocking of the idyllic family façade – where there is a mother, a father and a happily married sister (whose loving husband dutifully goes off to work each morning) – may also be related to R.D. Laing's contemptuous accusation regarding the hidden purpose of the family unit, whereupon he wrote:

> The family's function is to repress Eros: to induce a false consciousness of security: to deny death by avoiding life [...] to create, in short, one-dimensional man: to promote respect, conformity, obedience: to con children out of play: to induce a fear of failure: to promote a respect for work: to promote a respect for 'respectability'.[42]

The appeal of such subject matter to Reed's established audience is obvious, in that he becomes the ultimate martyr for all adolescents struggling to assert their own sense of individuality and indignation at what society expects of them. Moreover, the medium within which Reed chooses to confront his past proves that he is no *passive* victim – the powerful and rebellious connotations of hard rock demonstrating his successful ascendancy to one of the ultimate platforms for the communication of self-identity and self-promotion.

By introducing the family element to his critique, Reed aligns himself with what is often termed 'social judgement theory' (the belief that someone is diagnosed mentally ill on the basis of a social judgement as opposed to tangible medical evidence) without the necessity of tackling the much more intricate and, at the time, taboo subject of homosexuality. Such a theory provides a means of criticizing the psychiatric establishment by highlighting the way in which any person exhibiting behaviour that differs from, or challenges, cultural norms is prone to a definition of mental illness.[43] Lucy Johnstone details some of the evidence utilized in the defence of social judgement theory, the clearest being 'perhaps the most spectacular instant cure achieved by modern psychiatry, when homosexuality was dropped as a category of mental illness from the Diagnostic and Statistical Manual III in 1973 and millions of people thus "recovered" overnight'.[44]

---

[41] Ibid., p. 119.

[42] Ronald D. Laing, *The Politics of Experience* [1967] (Harmondsworth, 1978), p. 26. Note the reference is to Herbert Marcuse's work *One-Dimensional Man: Studies in the Ideology of Advanced Industrial Society* (1964).

[43] Thomas Szasz has arguably been the most prolific expounder of such a theory, claiming in 1963 that 'mental health [...] has come to mean conformity to the demands of society. According to the common sense definition, mental health is the ability to play the game of social living, and to play it well. Conversely, mental illness is the refusal to play, or the inability to play it well.' Szasz, *Law, Liberty and Psychiatry* [1963] (London, 1974), p. 205.

[44] Johnstone, p. 221.

By exposing the hypocrisy of the protagonist's own family members (an axe-wielding father, a brain-dead brother-in-law), there is also the possibility of challenging definitions of sanity and madness through a process of reversal, the premise being that what, on the surface, may appear sane is actually mad and vice versa. Writers such as Laing and Cooper effectively utilized this method to suggest that sanity amounts to little more than an 'absence of experience'. To illustrate such claims, Cooper documents the life story of a typical conformist, highlighting the conventional, static and forgettable nature of their existence. He warns that this is the destiny for the majority designated mentally healthy, and suggests that emancipation may be possible but that by pursuing more genuine and less stereotypical prospects 'one runs the risk of being thought mad and one is then in danger of psychiatric treatment'.[45] Like Reed, Cooper includes examples designed to initiate a questioning of what constitutes 'mad' behaviour, the most powerful of these being his reference to the vast amount of irrational and violent behaviour undertaken by, or in the name of, the sane majority compared to the very small instances of violence committed by those considered mentally ill.[46]

It is interesting to note that within 'Kill Your Sons' any sense of personal recollection is left until the third verse where references to drugs such as Thorazine, alongside the mention of clinics such as Creedmore and Paine Whitney, imbue the narrative with an essential sense of authenticity that is perhaps compromised up to this point through the lack of first person narrative. Reed's vocal melody and delivery continues in the same manner as previous verses, although the reference to Paine Whitney being 'even better' appears purposely immature in effect, with clumsily stressed syllables and an upward slur on the word 'better' suggestive of the defiant tone of an adolescent.

Reed's reference to all the drugs 'we took' and how much fun it was appears akin to someone reminiscing about schoolboy shenanigans, in that the intention and potentially negative effects of their prescription remains inconsequential. This blasé approach does, however, have implications for possible interpretations of his experience, in that the potential for the treatment to represent some form of chastisement is effectively nullified. Any serious warning is left to the last line where, reflective of the possible chronology of his treatment (Thorazine being a major tranquillizer usually given following treatment with lesser-strength drugs), he alerts listeners to the unpleasant after-effects of Thorazine injections, claiming 'you choke like a son of a gun'.

---

[45]     Cooper, *Psychiatry and Anti-Psychiatry*, p. 17. For Cooper's documenting of the conformist's life, see ibid, pp. 15–17.

[46]     See, for example, the following quotation: '"They" [psychiatric inmates] hurt or kill one or two other people, if that. "We" normal people murder not only them but countless millions of people across the world. The behavioural patterning of "them" and "us" is identical. The extent of destruction in "our" case, involving all the rationalizations of imperialism over the whole world scene, is incomparable with "theirs" – it is just so much bigger and so much less in the light of day.' Cooper, *The Death of the Family*, p. 138.

The allusion to specific drugs allows a widening in the song's critique of psychiatry, for it corroborates previous suggestions that the treatment administered results in undesirable side-effects. Doggett's description of Reed's vocal delivery being synonymous with the compromised functioning of a lobotomized patient is especially pertinent here, although it should be clarified that the suggestion is one of chemical as opposed to surgical lobotomy. According to Peter Breggin, the year 1954 represented 'a landmark in psychiatry, when the neuroleptic drug Thorazine began to flood the state hospitals throughout the nation'.[47] Of specific reference to Reed's experience, Breggin laments that: 'too often they are administered to children with behaviour problems, even children who are living at home and going to school'.[48] The evidence he provides of the first report detailing the effects of the drug is also of relevance to my interpretation of Reed's deliberately compromised melodic construction and vocal delivery: 'Sitting or lying, the patient is motionless lying in his bed, often pale and with eyelids lowered. He remains silent most of the time. If he is questioned, he answers slowly and deliberately in a monotonous and indifferent voice.'[49] Rather than simply drawing on the public's arguably more prevalent fears of psychosurgery, Reed's account thus offers the possibility of raising awareness regarding the damaging effects of its chemical equivalent, as Breggin explains:

> Most psychosurgery cuts the nerve connections to and from the frontal lobes and limbic system; chemical lobotomy largely interdicts the nerve connections to the same regions. Either way, coming or going, it's a lobotomy effect [...] Chemical lobotomy can have no specifically beneficial effect on any particular human problem or human being. It puts a chemical clamp on the higher brain of anyone.[50]

As opposed to simply showing off his knowledge of drugs, one can therefore argue that Reed's critique is of greater contemporary relevance than many similar songs of its time which instead utilized more stereotypical (and arguably outdated) signifiers of psychiatric practice. Involuntary hospitalization and surgical lobotomy, to give two such examples, were no longer customary forms of psychiatric treatment following the advent of the neuroleptic drugs, and yet the potential dangers of this new medication were nonetheless frightening.

---

[47]     Breggin, *Toxic Psychiatry*, p. 3. To provide some indication of its prevalence, Breggin explains that: 'The first neuroleptic was chlorpromazine, whose trade mark is Thorazine. In a 1964 publication entitled "Ten Years' Experience with Thorazine", the manufacturer, Smith, Kline and French, estimated that fifty million patients had been prescribed chlorpromazine in the first decade of its use (1954 to 1964).' Ibid, p. 63.

[48]     Ibid., p. 62.

[49]     Delay and Deniker, *Congres des Medecins Alienistes et Neurologistes de France*. Quoted in Breggin, *Toxic Psychiatry*, p. 67.

[50]     Breggin, *Toxic Psychiatry*, pp. 69–70.

The allusion to Reed's personal experience of psychiatric diagnosis and treatment within 'Kill Your Sons' provides an interesting example of what psychologists Alexandra Adame and Gail Hornstein term 'psychiatric oppression' narratives[51] – these being subjective accounts that reference some form of psychiatric mistreatment with the possible intention of voicing objection to such action, increasing public knowledge and confronting the psychiatric establishment. Their observation regarding the variety of ways in which a writer can structure his or her narrative of illness is relevant here, for it is fair to say that the accusations of abuse and consequential sense of protest within 'Kill Your Sons' could be much more blatant if so desired. However, the way in which a narrative is constructed and tempered is inevitably informed by the chosen medium and genre, and for Reed there was a need to sustain his construction of the non-conformist, rebellious, self-assured, degenerate hard rocker that fans had come to believe in. Too much preaching and direct protesting would be anomalous with the air of defiant indifference typical of Reed's earlier works, and so a fine line is traversed in which the ill effects of ECT treatment are detailed while at the same time access to freely prescribed drugs is celebrated.

The entire narrative rests on a backdrop of bitter irony in which the very people advocating psychiatric treatment (the protagonist's family members) are the ones most in need of assistance. In this way, Reed constructs an image in which he stands outside ordinary experience as both observer and social outcast. He secures empathy from listeners by detailing the negative effects of his shock treatment, but resists the victim role by mocking the psychiatric establishment for its attempt to cure him of his extraordinary character.

---

[51]     Alexandra Adame and Gail Hornstein, 'Representing Madness: How Are Subjective Experiences of Emotional Distress Presented in First-Person Accounts?' *The Humanist Psychologist*, 34/2 (2006): 135–58. Adame and Hornstein define 'psychiatric oppression' as 'the feeling of being in some way abused, mistreated, coerced, or denied human rights by mental health professionals; by a diagnosis or label of mental illness; by a hospital or institution; or by treatments such as medication, electroconvulsive therapy (ECT), hydrotherapy, or restraint', pp. 146–7.

# Chapter 3

# Reversing Us and Them: Anti-Psychiatry and Pink Floyd's *The Dark Side of the Moon*

> The mind of man has been poisoned by concepts. Do not ask him to be content, ask him only to be calm, to believe that he has found his place. But only the madman is really calm.
>
> (Antonin Artaud, 1925)

An appreciation of the way in which perceptions of madness have changed throughout history is crucial when examining the relationship between a musical text and contemporary medical, social and cultural beliefs surrounding mental illness. While it is likely that contemporary beliefs will manifest themselves in entirely observable ways (for example, with reference to specific treatments that may or may not be considered beneficial) there are often additional themes contributing to the depiction offered that are drawn from much earlier historical periods – notions that have, for whatever reason, remained prominent within the public conception of mental illness despite evident developments in psychiatric opinion. One such example, relevant to Pink Floyd's 1973 album *The Dark Side of the Moon*,[1] is the notion that those labelled madmen are, in fact, enlightened individuals capable of perceiving the true reality of human existence and experience. It is an assumption that first became popular in fictionalized mode within the farces of the Middle Ages wherein the character of the fool or madman would appear 'center stage as the guardian of truth'.[2] Although its portrayal was initially intended for comedic value, the enduring fascination of the mystery of madness has ensured it is a theme that has continually reappeared (as I explore in detail in Chapter 5).

The opinion that madness could possibly constitute a heightened state of awareness certainly became more prevalent during the late 1960s and early 1970s when, for once, the stark opposition between reason and unreason was used not to ostracize the madman but to draw attention to the sickness within a society seemingly bent on its own destruction. Those who mourned the 'insanity' of society itself frequently enforced their claims by following this reversal to its natural conclusion: if behaviour generally believed to be 'normal' could be proven insane, then surely conventionally labelled 'mad' behaviour could conceivably be sane. It was a reversal of conceptions that held favour within the work of R.D.

---

[1]   Pink Floyd, *The Dark Side of the Moon* (Harvest Records, 1973).

[2]   Michel Foucault, *Madness and Civilization: A History of Insanity in the Age of Reason*, trans. R. Howard (London, 1997), p. 14 (originally published in French in 1961 as *Histoire de la Folie*; first published in Great Britain in 1967 by Tavistock Publications).

Laing and, as this chapter seeks to reveal, provides the very foundation upon which *The Dark Side of the Moon* communicates its critique of contemporary society and promise of a more meaningful existence.

Initially, the album appears to focus on the fatuous, routine and temporal nature of life as both 'Breathe' and 'Time' illustrate the various ways in which normal man is blinded by a false existence. The effective communication of this message relies on the way in which the listeners' expectations are continually yet subtly denied. 'Breathe', for example, begins with a variety of timbral and melodic gestures that appear to connote sublime predictability and comfort. The slide guitar is suitably unhurried in its smooth transition between notes (aided by the use of slow attack), its pure tone contributing to the bell-like arpeggiated motif of the Hammond organ and mellowness of the bass timbre to offer a warm, textural ambience. In slight contrast to this the slightly distorted accompanying guitar plays descending, picked arpeggios that lead effortlessly onto the beat, where the tones are left to ring and pulsate; the kit adds to this shimmering quality with the use of ride cymbal quavers and occasional soft cymbal crashes. The first vocal statements of section A are perfectly suited to such accompanying gestures, responding in an agreeably lazy fashion through the delayed entry of phrases and use of appoggiaturas over the A major chords to suggest sighs of contentment on the words 'air', 'care' and 'me'. The alternating i–IV progression in E Dorian imposes no fixed sense of direction, and with the major 6th degree offering an attractive brightening to what would otherwise be a natural minor, the harmony maintains an appealing sense of stasis and security.

Once the B section is underway it would appear, however, that such contentment is misplaced. The use of a descending bass and kit fill results in a perceived decrease in energy level at the pivot junction between sections, preparing for the depressing revelation that the price to pay for such contentment is a life without meaning or distinction: 'And all you touch and all you see is all your life will ever be'. While brief in duration, the four bars of section B are given prominence through the sudden lack of fluency in the kit part as it appears to pause on its first crotchet following the activity of the preceding fill and proceeds to use toms to punctuate at the half bar rather than relax back into a continual pattern. Its crotchet beat emphasis in the final bar, while evoking a slowing of time, helps to emphasize the contrasting increase in harmonic rhythm as the chords push downwards to the inescapable repetition of section A. The chord progression of section B is also significant, allowing a descending line – symbolic of the dissipation of section A's deceptive invulnerability – to be traced from the first two bass notes through to guitar and Hammond organ:

| Section B chords: | Cmaj7 | Bm | F | G | D7#9 | D#dim7 |
|---|---|---|---|---|---|---|
| Descending movement: | C | B | A | G | F | E♭ (D#) |
| | | | | | | |
| | Bass … | | Guitar and organ … | | | |

The vocal motif equally descends to emphasize harmony notes (C, B, A) across the first three bars and, while more continuous than the melodic statements of section A, the line's unrelenting repetition and certainty of stress on beat 1 works to suggest an unstoppable/inescapable truth (Example 3.1).

Example 3.1 'Breathe' section B (lead vocal and upper harmony vocal)

As the song progresses, the repeat of section A begins to evoke a distinct element of misfortune as subtly disruptive gestures such as the organ glissando and melodic syncopation with repetition (derived from the phrasing of section B) convey a dawning awareness of the need to awake from the opening reverie, alongside a realization of the futility of work itself. The final prophetic statement of section B indicates the inescapability of man's mortality: it is possible to maintain an unconscious approach to life's progression in which case 'all you touch and all you see is all your life will ever be', but try to 'catch up' and commit yourself to the drudgery of work and you face only 'an early grave'.

Such criticism of 'normal' man's existence – in which he is perceived to be restrained, even trapped, by western society's necessity for conformity and an illusory world of contentment – formed a key premise for R.D. Laing,[3] who argued that coercion was the source of this pitiful state: 'What we call "normal" is a product of repression [...] The "normally" alienated person, by reason of the fact that he acts more or less like everyone else, is taken to be sane.'[4] David Cooper, the psychiatrist who first employed the term 'anti-psychiatry', was even more vehement in his appeals for a reawakening of man's true potential, insisting, like Laing, that 'the well-conditioned, endlessly obedient citizen' could 'without metaphorical sleight-of-hand' be regarded as being 'out of his mind', asking in dramatic conclusion: 'How do we turn around the signs at the entrance of the psychiatric prison so that we can see ourselves as the violently disturbed inmates of a rather larger bin?'[5]

---

[3]   See my previous references to Laing's theory of man's estranged state in Chapter 1.

[4]   Ronald D. Laing, *The Politics of Experience* [1967] (Harmondsworth, 1978), pp. 23–4.

[5]   David Cooper, *The Death of the Family* (London, 1971), pp. 13, 138.

Given Pink Floyd's allegiance to the British counter-cultural movement and the evident appeal of Laing's theory to the Bohemian fringe, who Roszak claimed were 'grounded in an intensive examination of the self' and 'the buried wealth of personal consciousness',[6] it is perfectly plausible that such thinking could influence the nature of critique favoured within *The Dark Side of the Moon*. Furthermore, an identification with such radical opinion could convey a desirable image for the band – to be regarded as 'normal' and 'one-dimensional' is, after all, the very worst indictment one can level at an artist as 'normalcy can be destructive to the imagination, to creativity, to the intellect, to the soul. The only way we grow as people is through confronting our dark side, because if all you want is the quiet and safety, you're giving up reality.'[7]

The opening of 'Time' quite literally demands the aforementioned desire for wakefulness as the cacophony of bells, chimes and alarms enters in unpredictable discord, lasting for what seems an interminable duration of 30 seconds. Like 'Breathe' the song is divided into repeated A and B sections, although here the A sections are more direct in their criticism of life's rituals: 'And you run and you run to catch up with the sun, but it's sinking, and racing around to come up behind you again'; while the B sections lament wasted opportunities: 'And then one day you find ten years have got behind you, no one told you when to run, you missed the starting gun.' David Gilmour's strained throat voice produces a more assertive vocal delivery, and his occasional use of melisma (for example on the words 'day' and 'way') suggests an attempt to break free from the confines of the phrase, thereby enhancing the suggested frustration of the lyric content. The strength of the vocal is also conveyed through its reliance on the root notes of the chords on accented beats; yet its confined nature, utilizing a repeated alternation with the seventh degree, draws attention to the tedious dissipation of time (see Example 3.2). While the

Example 3.2   'Time' section A (vocal, bass and kit)

---

[6]     Theodore Roszak, *The Making of a Counter Culture: Reflections on the Technocratic Society and Its Youthful Opposition* (London, 1970), p. 62.

[7]     John Carpenter (director of *Halloween*, 1978) quoted in *Clive Barker's A–Z of Horror* (1997), mini UK TV documentary hosted by Clive Barker, directed by Ursula Macfarlane, Production Companies: Arts and Entertainment Video, BBC. Distributor: BBC.

rhythm section's activity (bass and kit working in rhythmic unison) creates the impression that time is passing, the repetition of melodic motif and repeated F♯ Aeolian chord progression suggest that life itself remains uniform/unchanged.

The B sections of 'Time' are reminiscent of the comfort witnessed in the A sections of 'Breathe'. The change in drum pattern and shift to a more sustained bass line establish a half-time feel that, alongside Richard Wright's softer vocal timbre and calming choir gestures, creates a relative tranquillity. The simple alternation of tones within the melody continues through the change in harmony to provide an unassuming, lazy feel over the brightness of the major seventh chords (VI–III in F♯ Aeolian). Once again, however, it appears that the listener has been lulled into a false sense of security, for there follows a subtle break in the expected continuity of phrase that draws attention to the twist in the lyric content: the result of such laziness being that ten years have passed without notice. The harmonic descent from Dmaj7 to C♯m then Bm appears to illustrate this depressing shift before rising up to deliver the final revelation: 'You've missed the starting gun!'

'Time' then is significant in the way in which it embellishes the aforementioned theme of a false existence, but it also forms a crucial part of the album's conceptualization of time itself. From the very beginning, the heartbeat and diverse ticks of three clocks in 'Speak to Me' encourage the listener to ponder their own mortality and the transient nature of time. 'On the Run' offers a more subtle expression of time, the repeating synthi-A riff representing a sense of eternity/timelessness while auxiliary sounds punctuate and move around the spatial dimension, occasionally descending in pitch to represent the Doppler effect and underpin the spoken vocal statement; 'live for today, gone tomorrow, that's me'. Whereas the activity of clocks at the opening of 'Time' pre-empts the returning concept of the dangers associated with a life of 'lying in the sunshine', the spaciousness achieved in the remainder of the introduction (through excessive reverb on the roto-toms, wide gap in frequency range between bass and xylophone, and apparent freedom of the pitched motives) encourages further reflection upon time's all-encompassing nature. The following vocal sections (as outlined above) capture both feelings of frustration and regret at the inability to halt temporal movement and recapture missed opportunities.

In this instance, one is reminded of the character Billy Pilgrim in Kurt Vonnegut's *Slaughterhouse-Five*, who becomes 'unstuck in time': 'The second hand on my watch would twitch once and a year would pass.'[8] This recognition is, however, a source of awakening for Pilgrim as Patrick Shaw explains: he is then able to comprehend the 'negligibility of death, and the true nature of time'.[9] This was also a view held by Laing, who claimed that: 'We are socially conditioned to

---

[8] Kurt Vonnegut, *Slaughterhouse-Five: or, The Children's Crusade, a Duty Dance with Death* (New York, 1969), p. 20.

[9] Patrick Shaw, 'The Excremental Festival: Vonnegut's Slaughterhouse-Five', *Scholia Satyrica*, 2/3 (1976): p. 5. Quoted in Barbara Tepa Lupack, *Insanity as Redemption in Contemporary American Fiction* (Gainesville, FL, 1995), p. 110.

regard total immersion in outer space and time as normal and healthy. Immersion in inner space and time tends to be regarded as anti-social withdrawal, a deviancy [...] in some sense discreditable.'[10] In the inner world he claimed that 'Mundane time becomes merely anecdotal, only the eternal matters'[11] and that one way to access this was through an impulsive curative process involving some of the people whom society labels schizophrenic. Thus, madness was conceived by Laing as a possible pilgrimage to rediscover inner space and time, destroy the false self and be reborn through the re-establishment of a new ego:

> Instead of the mental hospital, a sort of re-servicing factory for human breakdowns, we need a place where people who have travelled further and, consequently, may be more lost than psychiatrists and other sane people, can find their way *further* into inner space and time, and back again [...] This process may be one that all of us need, in one form or another. This process could have a central function in a truly sane society.[12]

While the first half of *The Dark Side of the Moon* makes no reference to this view of an enlightened form of madness, the numerous references to time that expose the folly of being either too blasé or, conversely, too absorbed in its external passing – and the evident encouragement to ponder its inner, eternal existence – appear to support Laing's premise.

Moving on from 'Breathe' and 'Time' the album offers more specific examples of society's sickness, as the negative themes of commodity fetishism and war are explored within the tracks 'Money' and 'Us and Them'. Initially, 'Money' reminds listeners of their restricted existence within modern capitalist society: the opening irregular 7/4 loop of sound effects (each paper tear, dropping money bag, opening of cash register and so forth representing a single crotchet beat) determines the metre of the ensuing bass riff and vocal sections, acting as a metaphor for man's perfunctory existence. The deviation from regular metre is significant, for it evokes a sense of unnatural progression, enhancing the mechanistic nature of the sound effects and their unrelenting repetition. Once the bass riff and kit enter, the beat grouping of the metre (3+3+1) is also consequential as the final crotchet appears as a turnaround device. The effect is produced by the way in which the bass reaches its tonic goal on beat 6 and then utilizes beat 7 to flip up to the third before returning to the tonic once more for beat 1 of the following bar; the intervallic shape of the riff and cymbal crashes on both beat 7 and beat 1 offer the impression that the loop's repetition is being mechanically activated.

While the first half of verse one appears to condone a reasonable amount of financial striving (getting a 'new job' with 'more pay' so that you're 'okay'), subsequent passages reveal the attendant pressures and levels of deception

---

[10]     Laing, *The Politics of Experience*, p. 103.
[11]     Ibid., 109.
[12]     Ibid., pp. 105–7 (emphasis original).

as people become divorced from the functioning reality of life. Desire for the procurement of material wealth as opposed to the more substantive attainment of emotional wealth is evident in the pronouncements 'Grab that cash with both hands' and 'I'm all right, Jack, keep your hands off my stack', the accompanying guitar and organ gestures serving to highlight the vocal's authoritative nature through alternating crotchet stabs. The manipulation of bass riff, coupled with the vocal's refusal to conform to regular phrase patterning (beginning on beat 7 as opposed to the anticipated beat 1), further enhances the comfortless sentiments of such self-serving beliefs.

A number of musical devices help to illustrate the greedy accretion of material goods, the unstoppable force of the capitalist ideal. One such example occurs in the final two lines of verses one and two where, while listing the various possessions that money can buy, the vocal, doubled by guitar and bass, appears to run away with itself, providing a continuous stream of ascending and descending pitches with no breaks in delivery (see Example 3.3). The metre becomes ambiguous at this point, adding to the sense of unbridled movement by moving to two bars of 4/4 and a bar of 6/4. Moreover, the brief departure from Bm to F♯m then Em suggests that the only means of establishing a sense of individual direction (signified by the break with the bass riff) is through pursuing the ambition of furthering one's economic status within society. As such it is merely an illusory freedom, the individual imagining that they possess a life defined by the style of the commodities purchased: 'I'm in the hi-fidelity first class travelling set and I think I need a Lear jet.'

Example 3.3 'Money' final two lines of verse 1 (vocal, bass and kit)

The critique of capitalism offered in 'Money' is, as Sheila Whiteley observes, 'all-inclusive. None of us is free from this social disease, the sentiments are universal.'[13] Being the most acerbic critic of capitalism among those termed 'anti-psychiatrists', Cooper repeatedly called for a revolution that would involve 'both an external, mass-social, and internal, personal and private, divorce from all the

---

[13]    Sheila Whiteley, *The Space Between the Notes: Rock and the Counter-Culture* (London, 1992), p. 111.

mechanizations of capitalist-imperializing society'.[14] The belief that an obsession with material wealth would overshadow, even negate, the pursuit and experience of life's true pleasures was equally shared by Laing, who asked: 'What is to be done? We who are still half alive, living in the often fibrillating heartland of a senescent capitalism – can we do no more than reflect the decay around and within us?'[15] Again, there appears to be a similarity between such thinking and the sentiments exhibited in 'Money', as further evidenced by Roger Waters's admission in the *Washington Post* of 28 April 1993: 'I'm obsessed with truth and how the futile scramble for material things obscures our possible path to understanding ourselves, each other and the universe.'[16]

'Us and Them' continues the aforementioned critique by drawing on the 'anti-war philosophy of the counter-culture' and 'fears of manipulation'.[17] Given the social climate of the time, such choice of subject matter is hardly remarkable; and yet the make-up of the critique deserves further mention, bearing, as it does, remarkable similarities in its exploration of human nature to Laing's chapter of the same name.[18] The title, 'Us and Them', is used in both texts as a means of questioning the possible methods and reasons by which humans label (Them) and hence disconnect from each other to generate and secure a sense of identity (Us). Laing articulates this idea by claiming: 'The invention of Them creates Us, and We may require to invent Them to re-invent Ourselves',[19] this being similar to anti-psychiatrist Thomas Szasz's opinion that: 'Social man fears the Other and tries to destroy him; but [...] paradoxically, he needs the Other and, if need be, creates him, so that, by invalidating him as evil, he may confirm himself as good.'[20]

In the song 'Us and Them' a sense of opposing identities is established through both use of lyrics (us/them, me/you) and harmonic language: 'us' and 'me' being accompanied by the tonic major (D major), while 'them' and 'you' work in dialectical opposition, moving to the relative minor chord vi (B minor). The use of echo results in six audible statements of each word and serves to signify the collective identity of the group, while panning – most noticeable on the word 'them' – to left, centre, then right suggests the imagined threat of the encircling Other. The sincerity of the following absolving statements – 'And after all, we're only ordinary men' and 'God only knows it's not what we would choose to do' – is undermined by the ensuing progression to tonic harmonic minor (Dm, maj7), an unexpected and uncertain chord (due to its minor 3rd and major 7th construction), which is finally resolved by a deceptively soothing plagal cadence (G–D).

---

14      Cooper, *The Death of the Family*, p. 139.

15      Laing, *The Politics of Experience*, p. 11.

16      Roger Waters, quoted in *The Washington Post*, 28 April 1993.

17      Whiteley, p. 114.

18      The fourth chapter of Laing's 1967 book *The Politics of Experience* is likewise entitled 'Us and Them'.

19      Laing, *The Politics of Experience*, p. 76.

20      Thomas Szasz, *The Manufacture of Madness* [1970 (London, 1973), p. 319.

Such statements are akin to the song's introductory spoken vocals in which the participants attempt to justify their use of violence – 'I was in the right/I certainly was in the right', followed by the admission and repetition of 'I don't know, I was really drunk at the time' – and once again bear a striking similarity to the opinions expressed by Laing in his chapter of the same name wherein he bemoans man's apathetic existence and lack of personal responsibility:

> At this moment in history, we are all caught in the hell of frenetic passivity […] Everyone will be carrying out orders. Where do they come from? Always from elsewhere. […] They are created only by each one of us repudiating his own identity […] each person claims his own inessentiality: 'I just carried out my orders. If I had not done so, someone else would have.' […] Yet although I can make no difference, I cannot act differently. No single other person is any more necessary to me than I claim to be to Them. But just as he is 'one of Them' to me, so I am 'one of Them' to him. In this collection of reciprocal indifference, of reciprocal inessentiality and solitude, there appears to exist no freedom.[21]

The dramatic crotchet descent of distorted guitar, bass and piano, accompanied by a semiquaver drum fill, marks the arrival of the B section wherein the texture immediately swells, to signify the sense of combined endeavour suggestive of the forward movement of troops. As the lyric content becomes descriptive of military action, various musical gestures serve to evoke the impending sense of doom, the bass and piano pushing down with pounding crotchets towards the principal point of tension on the word 'died' where the use of sevenths and ninths in the backing vocals eventually resolve to chord tones of the following C chord. The kit punctuates the texture with dynamic cymbal crashes on beats 3 and 4 adding further emphasis to the lyrics 'forward', 'cried', 'rear', 'front', 'rank' and 'died', while a triplet semiquaver snare fill, suggestive of gunfire, follows the lyric 'the general sat', serving to highlight his inert posture. The fruitlessness of the struggle is confirmed not only by the lyric content – 'forward he cried from the rear and the front rank died' – but equally by the insinuated modulation to G major that fails to achieve due recognition. The section begins ominously enough in B Aeolian and progresses to chord VII (A major) before falling to chord VI (Gmaj7) which, when followed by the unexpected C major chord, may be understood as a pivot (functioning as both chord VI in B Aeolian and chord I in G major). However, despite the I–IV movement of the Gmaj7 to C, the root of B appears only momentarily undermined, and with the repetition of the entire phrase alongside the lyrics 'The General sat and the lines on the map moved from side to side', the emptiness of the gesture, both physically and metaphorically, becomes clear.

In Laing's text he too chooses the brutality of war to illustrate the senselessness of human division and asinine fear of imaginary enemies, writing:

---

21    Laing, *The Politics of Experience*, pp. 65, 66, 70, 71.

> In the name of our freedom and our brotherhood we are prepared to blow up the
> other half of mankind, and to be blown up in turn [...] it is on the basis of such
> primitive social phantasies of who and what are I and you, he and she, We and
> Them, that the world is linked or separated, that we die, kill, devour, tear and
> are torn apart.[22]

The sense of futile struggle is summed up in the following statement: 'As war
continues, both sides come more and more to resemble each other [...] We are
Them to Them as They are Them to Us'[23] – a view that is echoed in the second
verse of 'Us and Them' with the lines: 'Black and blue, and who knows which is
which and who is who/Up and down/And in the end it's only round and round'.

Returning to my opening premise concerning the possible reversal of
conceptions of madness and sanity and how this may be the very axis on which
*The Dark Side of the Moon* articulates its critique of contemporary society, it is
now necessary to identify the ways in which the final two songs establish the
possibility of a more meaningful, enlightened existence. 'Brain Damage' appears,
at first, to conform to stereotypical representations of madness, reliant upon the
belief that madness is a condition which reveals itself through unreasonable
behaviour and, as such, is diametrically opposed to reason and sanity. The musical
text communicates the Otherness of madness through a number of compositional
devices, each constituting a form of opposition to conventional, functional and
logical musical processing. Derek Scott's examination of demonic signifiers is
useful here, reminding us that: 'In music, terms that form binary oppositions are
rarely of equal status. One term is usually the negative rather than the opposite
of another, its identity is, as it were, that of the other term with a minus sign.
Dissonance is a lack of consonance, yet consonance is not a lack of dissonance.'[24]
As such, it is possible to identify chains of signifiers (for example, non-functional
harmonic progressions, rhythmic phrases that challenge the structural beat,
undirected melodic constructions and so forth) that are dependent on the listeners'
understanding of utilitarian musical devices in order that their illogical character
may be read as representative of the irrational identity of madness.

Initially, the verse of 'Brain Damage' utilizes a non-functional progression (D–
G7) that repeats without evident purpose/direction and incorporates descending
chromatic tones (F♯–F). As outlined above, the lack of 'rational' progression
is significant; but so too is the use of chromaticism for, unlike the dialectical
opposition located in 'Us and Them', the lunatic is effectively positioned as
neither major nor minor. Consequently, by drawing on the frequently diagnosed

---

[22]  Ibid., p. 79.

[23]  Ibid., p. 83.

[24]  Derek Scott, *From the Erotic to the Demonic: On Critical Musicology* (Oxford,
2003), p. 129.

behaviour of the psychotic, the lunatic is portrayed as lacking a binary opposite, and thus existing as neither 'us or them' but rather as both 'us and them'.[25]

Seemingly devoid of emotion, the vocal delivery is soft and relaxed, utilizing chest tone within a comfortable, yet noticeably limited range. The rhythmic construction, being heavily syncopated, evokes a further sense of disconnection, the effect being that of an observer commenting on events from a distance. The reference to 'lunatics' in the first two lines harks back to the mid-nineteenth century, when in 1845 the Lunatics Act was introduced in an attempt to alleviate the poor, unregulated conditions of private madhouses. Considered an acceptable term for the insane then, by the 1970s it would be recognized as a stigmatizing vulgarism: a term utilized to conjure up negative images of insanity that may be attached to certain actions and put forward as a benchmark from which to maintain and uphold popular beliefs.

Two further stereotypes underpin the remainder of verse one, the first alluding to the long-established idea concerning madness and its connection with childishness ('Remembering games and daisy chains and laughs'), while the second promotes the necessity of policing the insane ('Got to keep the loonies on the path'). The simplicity of the accompanying gestures, particularly the lilting guitar arpeggiation and naïve bass fills, appears to support the childish sentiments – although the bass's refusal to acknowledge the eventual chord change to E (continuing instead to sound octave Ds), along with the tritone interval of the vocal harmony, results in an unexpected dissonance that suggests a sense of foreboding despite the

Example 3.4  'Brain Damage' verse 1 (vocal, guitar and bass)

---

[25]    For further theoretical discussion of this matter, see Gilles Deleuze and Felix Guattari, *Anti-Oedipus*, trans. R. Hurley, M. Seem and H.R. Lane (London, 1984).

innocence of the lyric 'daisy chains and laughs' (see Example 3.4). Harmonically, the brief departure from the uncertainty of the alternating D–G7 to the functional movement of D, E7, A7, D (I, V of V, V, I) serves to reinforce the statement 'Got to keep the loonies on the path', implying both the reasonableness of such action and, through the use of a perfect cadence, the legitimacy of the path itself.

Intensifying the ominous undertones, the beginning of verse two builds upon our conventional fear of madness: the lead guitar's eerie 4–3 appoggiatura that echoed the vocal's F♯–F movement a tritone higher in verse one now becomes a direct repetition of the vocal pitches, resulting in a dissonant clash between the major (F♯) and minor 7ths (F) of the accompanying G7 chord. This disturbed response to the enclosing madness, 'the lunatics are in the hall', is further stressed through subtle variation in the vocal's rhythmic phrasing, whereupon the revelation that they are in 'my hall' is emphasized through a slight, yet noticeable delay in the delivery of the word 'hall' until beat 1 of the following bar. It is just after this point, where a keen sense of anticipation has been created, that the listeners' expectations are denied and the notion of reversal – and through this a reinterpretation of the song's opening – is revealed.

Initially, the verbal text alone is responsible for the sudden turn of events, the final two lines – 'The paper holds their folded faces to the floor and every day the paper boy brings more' – revealing that 'the real madmen are not the ones you label mad, but the politicians on the front pages of the morning papers'.[26] The statement dissolves the supposed threat of the imaginary 'loonies' and exposes the more likely danger of those who hold the power of life and death, summarizing, as it were, Laing's cautionary tale:

> A little girl of seventeen in a mental hospital told me she was terrified because the Atom Bomb was inside her. That is a delusion. The statesmen of the world who boast and threaten that they have Doomsday weapons are far more dangerous, and far more estranged from 'reality' than many of the people on whom the label 'psychotic' is affixed.[27]

Following this revelation, the chorus serves to normalize such fears by engendering an emotional high that supports the positive sentiments of the lyric content. The preceding bar allows the listener a brief pause for reflection while enhancing the build in energy levels through the addition of organ with rotary speaker effect, giving rise to a whirling crescendo. The harmonic pivot into the chorus is equally assertive, the D7 chord moving with evident purpose onto G (V–I).

The major chord progression of the chorus (G, A, C, G) connotes strength and, through its Lydian inflection (the A chord introducing the augmented 4th of G

---

26     Whiteley p. 116.
27     Laing, *The Divided Self*, pp. 11–12.

Lydian), a sense of striving.[28] Instead of appearing directionless, the descending chromaticism discernible within the vocal harmonies appears purposeful, progressing D–C♯–C–B while being complemented by ascending, contrary motion bass movement to resolve on a plagal cadence. The vocal is rhythmically more secure and continuous than in preceding sections, resulting in an expressive increase in momentum. Moreover, it employs greater use of chord tones, thereby enhancing the harmony's assured advance from the insecure verse statements. The smooth consonant movements and lush texture of the vocal choir help to soothe feelings of anxiety resulting from the knowledge of society's ills: 'And if the dam breaks open many years too soon,/And if your head explodes with dark forebodings too'. There is also a suggestion of intertextual meanings: the lyric 'And if there is no room upon the hill' being reminiscent of the Beatles' 'Fool on the Hill' (1967), which is similarly implicative of the fool's heightened powers of perception. The final statement of the chorus is one of welcoming reassurance, the unison vocal phrase 'I'll see you on the dark side of the moon' evoking feelings of combined endeavour and collective strength.[29]

The first chorus of 'Brain Damage' thus marks a critical moment in the album's reception; to rouse oneself from society's illusory sphere of contentment and comprehend its numerous afflictions may result in accusations of deviancy and mental abasement, yet the resulting awareness of truth and appreciation of potential experience will provide a form of sanctuary and solace. While previous songs question the sanity of society's actions, 'Brain Damage' shifts the focus toward an exploration of madness itself, encouraging listeners to ponder its definition and the methods by which it is 'treated'. Most importantly, the final lines of verse two and the ensuing chorus suggest an identification with what has been termed the conspiratorial model of madness: 'Mental health [...] has come to mean conformity to the demands of society. According to the common sense definition, mental health is the ability to play the game of social living, and to play it well. Conversely, mental illness is the refusal to play, or the inability to

---

[28]     Deryck Cooke's interpretation regarding the function of the augmented 4th is useful here: 'the sharp fourth [...] acts as an accessory and more powerful major seventh on the dominant, its semitonal tension towards the dominant being alone capable of performing the "heroic" task of lifting us into the key of the dominant. [...] Functioning in this way, the sharp fourth expresses the same violent longing (upward semitonal tension in a major context) as the major seventh, but not in a context of finality; rather in a context of pushing outwards and upwards, aspiring towards something higher.' Deryck Cooke, *The Language of Music* (Oxford, 1959), p. 81. Apart from 'Climb Every Mountain', this move is also evident in the theme tune for the fantasy film *E.T.: The Extra-Terrestrial* (1982) used when E.T. takes the children for a ride in the air on their bikes.

[29]     The syncopation of the phrase is also significant in that the word 'moon' anticipates beat 1 of the concluding G chord, intensifying the aforementioned sense of harmonic striving.

play it well.'[30] As indicated in previous chapters, no critic has been more vocal and persistent in their attack on the medical model of psychiatry than Thomas Szasz, and the relevance of his beliefs to *Dark Side of the Moon* becomes clear when one considers the musical and lyrical text of the third verse of 'Brain Damage', where references to psychiatry's employment of physical 'treatment' and restraint imply covert forms of social conditioning.

The transitionary chord progression at the end of the first chorus serves to dispel the previous dynamism, utilizing minor chords iii and vi in G major followed by a firm V–I cadence in D to signal a return to the joyless sentiments of the verse. While the harmonic and intervallic construction is similar, the rhythmic delivery is subtly manipulated in verse three to suggest a sense of confusion regarding the latest revelation: that 'the lunatic is in my head'. Both statements of the phrase involve a slight delay in the enunciation of the word 'head', whereas the uniform phrasing and literal repetition of the following lines – 'You raise the blade, you make the change' – lack the rhythmic variety witnessed in previous verses and illustrate the clinical sterility of psychosurgery. The implied hesitancy in acknowledging the presence of the lunatic and the skilful way in which the listener is inculpated in the action of lobotomy – '*you* raise the blade, *you* make the change, *you* rearrange me till I'm sane' (my emphasis) – serve to generate feelings of culpability and uncertainty concerning the acts of diagnosis and enforced therapy. The laughter (first heard in the opening 'Speak To Me') that interjects the first two vocal phrases – due to its inappropriateness of expression – may be read as either a stereotypical signifier of lunacy[31] or a mocking riposte to the protagonist's admission of 'illness'. Either way, its inclusion effectively contrasts the sombre, sustained organ accompaniment (which now lacks rotary speaker effect to allow a more fitting metaphor for the suggested death of the self), encouraging further empathy on the part of the listener.

Suspicion surrounding the possible means by which the state might manage deviant behaviour, rather than act in the individual's best interest, was at a peak in the early 1970s: 'complaints of abuses, as well as a growing suspicion of government's big-brother role and the social pressures for conformity, now make it necessary to explore the history and workings of the therapeutic state, which is steadily acquiring the tools for control and, indeed, the modification of man'.[32] As

---

[30]     Thomas Szasz, *Law, Liberty and Psychiatry* [1963] (London, 1974), p. 205. This requires listeners to understand Szasz's basic premise that 'The sick role in psychiatry is typically other-defined.' Thomas Szasz, *The Myth of Mental Illness: Foundations of a Theory of Personal Conduct* [1961] (London, 1972), p. 194.

[31]     Laughter lacking in apparent cause, and hence irrational, has often been used to suggest a protagonist's unstable mind. A more recent example can be heard on The Dead Weather song 'I'm Mad' (2010) wherein Alison Mosshart ends each vocal phrase with a marked 'ha ha': 'I'm mad, ha ha. A hundred ways, ha ha.'

[32]     Nicholas N. Kittrie, *The Right to Be Different: Deviance and Enforced Therapy* (London, 1971), p. 4.

such, Waters's use of the term 'rearrange' as opposed to 'cure' suggests a particular identification with contemporary critics who questioned the validity of extreme physical treatments. The fact that prefrontal lobotomy had resulted in changed personalities was common knowledge, as Kittrie explains: 'Research disclosed that the operation destroyed the capacity to form abstract thought and robbed the individual of ambition, conscience, and planning abilities. The lobotomized person could react quickly to stimuli but was unable to reflect before reacting on the wisdom or effects of his response.'[33] Understandably, Laing was keen to denounce any intervention that dealt with behaviour to the exclusion of experience: 'Any technique concerned with the other without the self [...] and most of all, with an object-to-be-changed rather than a person-to-be-accepted, simply perpetuates the disease it purports to cure.'[34]

Further evidence of the possible influence of anti-psychiatry is apparent within the repetition of the verse's B section, which enables a continuance of imputations regarding the management of mental illness, this time drawing on fears of involuntary incarceration: 'You lock the door and throw away the key, there's someone in my head but it's not me.' Since the late 1950s, Szasz had continually demonstrated his fervent opposition to such treatment, writing in 1970: 'For some time now I have maintained that commitment – that is the detention of persons in mental institutions against their will – is a form of imprisonment.'[35] Equally pertinent was Laing's renunciation of established psychiatric institutions in favour of the Kingsley Hall therapeutic community, which in 1965 posed a particularly visible attack on conventional medical intervention.

In response to the distressing content of the third verse, the final chorus brings a resurgence of comforting emotion that is heightened by the choir's improvised embellishments. The possible reference to former band member Syd Barrett has been well documented,[36] but it is the reassurance concerning the importance of individual expression and conviction that is most evident. The voices are not perfectly balanced, allowing scope for individual assertion, while the cracked/strained delivery supports the previously discussed harmonic vigour suggestive of sustained endeavour: 'And if the cloud bursts thunder in your ear, you shout and no one seems to hear'. Conceptually, the notion of striving may have two possible

---

[33]    Ibid., p. 306.

[34]    Laing, *The Politics of Experience*, p. 45.

[35]    Thomas S. Szasz, *Ideology and Insanity: Essays on the Psychiatric Dehumanization of Man* [1970] (London, 1973), p. 113.

[36]    'Although Syd was the trigger for the song, providing inspiration for the line "And if the band you're in starts playing different tunes [...]" Waters later gave the song a broader perspective.' Cliff Jones, *Another Brick in the Wall: The Stories Behind Every Pink Floyd Song* (reprinted edn London, 1999), p. 101. 'The final chorus draws heavily on Syd Barrett's breakdown [...] Here there is a subtle change in rhythmic emphasis from the last chorus as if to underline Syd's lack of co-ordination – "and if the band you're in starts playing different tunes".' Whiteley, p. 116.

motives, the first focusing on the necessity for maintaining faith in one's own beliefs irrespective of conventional opinion, hence drawing upon Szasz's view of the so-called 'mentally ill' as 'society's official and principal scapegoats';[37] the second relating to Laing's conceptualization of mental illness as a possible journey to potential enlightenment, a journey that was likely to be both arduous and frightening: 'in our present world, that is both so terrified and so unconscious of the other world, it is not surprising that when "reality," the fabric of this world, bursts, and a person enters the other world, he is completely lost and terrified'.[38]

The final instrumental passage of 'Brain Damage' appears to demonstrate an identification with Laing's belief that madness may well constitute a form of personal redemption: a rebirth that would embrace an appreciation of innocent, true pleasures long since lost to 'grown-up' sensibilities. The bass lead-in – moving in stepwise ascending motion (A–B–C♯–D) from the A7 chord to the D chord (and repeated upon the two subsequent statements of this chord progression) – is reminiscent of early country music, serving to connote simplicity, honesty and genuine values. In addition, a sense of playful nostalgia is introduced through the synthesizer's smooth articulation and rhythmically unhurried parallel chromatics in sixths (typical of the sentimental Tin Pan Alley ballads that country music absorbed). Despite utilizing the uncertain chord progression of previous verses, the sense of foreboding is effectively banished as the bass complies with the eventual shift in harmony to the E chord and the prominent tritone intervals no longer appear (Example 3.5).

Example 3.5 'Brain Damage' final instrumental passage (synth, guitar and bass)

---

[37]   Szasz, *The Manufacture of Madness*, p. 271.

[38]   Laing, *The Politics of Experience*, p. 103.

The spoken vocal segments seem facile in both content and delivery, and the new laughter lacks the mocking, oppressive undertones characteristic of the old. In lamenting the loss of personal experience Laing stressed that: 'As adults we have forgotten most of our childhood, not only its contents but its flavour [...] an intensive discipline of un-learning is necessary for *anyone* before one can begin to experience the world afresh, with innocence, truth and love.'[39] It is thus possible to view the final section of 'Brain Damage' as a momentary indulgence, an opportunity to evoke an imaginary utopia – a glimpse of the untainted existence that may await those journeying to the 'dark side of the moon'.

As mentioned previously, the belief that madness could constitute a heightened state of awareness was not unique to the period in question; and yet, evidence points to a definite escalation of such ideas prior to the album's conception: 'Madness is a tentative vision of a new and truer world to be achieved through de-structuring – a de-structuring that must become final – of the old, conditioned world', wrote anti-psychiatrist David Cooper.[40] Unsurprisingly, such beliefs occasionally adopted a pseudo-religious quality, elevating the notion of increased insight into a form of mystical, divine power: see, for example, Laing's description of the 'madman' as 'the hierophant of the sacred. An exile from the scene of being as we know it, [...] a stranger, signalling to us from the void [...] a void which may be peopled by presences that we do not even dream of.'[41] As such, it is perhaps not coincidental that the transition into 'Eclipse' encapsulates an impassioned feeling of spiritual ascendancy. The metre change to 6/8 (while maintaining the same quaver pulse) results in an increased occurrence of accents that produces a more driven feel. There is a noticeable dynamic growth aided by the return of full rotary effect on organ and half-bar kit fills which capitalize on the use of toms and cymbals. Despite essentially descending in stepwise motion (D–C–B♭–A), the bass activity is equally vivid in terms of its presence and role in strengthening the anticipated sense of arrival/accession. Its use of an ascending octave slide below the final A7 chord serves to emphasize the eventual cadential movement into D major, a progression that represents the end of the suggested journey towards the dominant of G (initiated by the use of the augmented fourth – leading note of D major – during the choruses of 'Brain Damage').

In many respects, 'Eclipse' encapsulates the overriding message of the album, its list of potential experiences marking a final, climactic appeal to its listeners. In drawing our attention to the collective significance of every thought and every action, the enormity of individual responsibility becomes clear, and once more we are reminded of the choice that must be made between a life of sublime ignorance or pained awareness. The musical text imparts the strength necessary to align oneself with the latter, utilizing a lead vocal melody based on the root or 5th of each chord and a strong functional progression D–B♭maj7–A–A7 (I–ii–V–V7

39   Ibid., pp. 22–3.
40   Cooper, *The Death of the Family*, p. 85.
41   Laing, *The Politics of Experience*, pp. 109–10.

with tritone substitution of chord ii to allow smooth semitone movement onto the A chord). The amount of literal phrase repetition and gradual accretion of vocal layers secure a palpable build in tension that appears to reach its zenith on the final statement: 'and everything under the sun is in tune, but the sun is eclipsed by the moon'. This final phrase, due to the density of texture, slight *rallentando* and varied harmonic construction, appears stronger in terms of reiterating a sense of arrival than attaining mere closure. The dominant chord is omitted in favour of a B♭maj7–D progression that, while not cadential, offers a slight moment of uncertainty before the F and B♭ move inwards in semitones to form a welcome point of condensation upon the F♯ and A of the D chord.

Despite the apparently strong, even celebratory, connotations of the musical gestures within 'Eclipse', the use of the word 'but' has led many writers to suggest a more pessimistic reading of the album's closing statement. The final spoken vocal is often referenced as a means of affirming this conclusion, although it has the possibility to be viewed, alongside many of the earlier examples, as a defensive posture. And yet, there is a further conceivable interpretation, one that appears to fit more comfortably within the established tradition of esoteric meanings witnessed throughout the album's progression. That the immense power of the sun may be eclipsed by the infinitely smaller body of the moon may well be viewed as a metaphor, propagating the value of personal endeavour. The notion of mystical power is, once again, implicit and may be linked to Laing's remark that: 'The light that illumines the madman is an unearthly light. It is not always a distorted refraction of his mundane life situation. He may be irradiated by light from other worlds.'[42] Moreover, once the sun is eclipsed by the moon, the 'dark side' is actually resplendent with brightness – a phenomenon that prompts an interpretation more in keeping with the exhilarated character of the musical text. Thus, the album acknowledges the ultimate sadness resulting from an awareness of society's ills, while simultaneously revealing the possible reward of self-realization: gaining access to our inner consciousness – reaching, as it were, the metaphorical dark side of the moon.

---

[42]     Ibid., p. 114.

## Chapter 4

# 'The Ballad of Dwight Fry': Madness as Social Deviancy, and the Condemnation of Involuntary Confinement

I envy you your other world; you've chosen your own home. But I have to live here in this terrible prison, in a world my torturers have forced upon me, in a world I hate [...] I'd prefer death a thousand times. But I can't die. That is the decree for all of us madmen who suffer without being guilty. We're tortured as if we were the worst criminals. (Walpurg)[1]

In his 1923 play *The Madman and the Nun*, Stanislaw Witkiewicz critiques the enforced confinement of the 'mad' in a similar manner to that later witnessed in Alice Cooper's epic song 'The Ballad of Dwight Fry'.[2] While Witkiewicz's protagonist, Alexander Walpurg, finds himself imprisoned against his will in an insane asylum with suicide proving the only means of liberation, the subject of Alice Cooper's tale is likewise confined in an intensive care ward and left to repeatedly plead for his unlikely release. The captive state of both characters is amplified through the use of straitjackets, Walpurg protesting: 'I'm suffocating. My arms are pulling loose from their sockets',[3] while Fry laments: 'sleeping don't come very easy in a straight white vest'. With reference to the Alice Cooper stage show, it is also possible to identify commonalities in the eventual demise and resurrection of both characters: Walpurg hanging himself, only to return from the dead to witness the self-inflicted downfall of his captors; Fry falling victim to the electric chair before re-emerging for a triumphant encore.

While there is no evidence to suggest a direct influence from Witkiewicz on the thematic content of 'The Ballad of Dwight Fry', similarities in approach may be, at least partially, attributed to the interest Cooper had in the Theatre of Cruelty,[4]

---

[1]   Stanislaw I. Witkiewicz, *The Madman and the Nun/Wariat i zakonnica* (1923), in *The Madman and the Nun and the Crazy Locomotive: Three Plays by Stanislaw Ignacy Witkiewicz*, edited, translated and with an introduction by Daniel C. Gerould and C.S. Durer [1966] (New York, 1989), p. 14.

[2]   Alice Cooper, *Love it to Death* (Straight Records, Warner Brothers, 1971).

[3]   Witkiewicz, p. 14.

[4]   I refer here to Antonin Artaud's theoretical essays (also commonly referred to as manifestos): 'The Theatre of Cruelty' and 'Theatre and Cruelty', in Antonin Artaud, *The Theatre and its Double*, Collected Works, vol. 4, trans. Victor Corti (London, 1974), in which he criticizes contemporary theatre experience as passive voyeurism. Artaud's

and the suggestion that Witkiewicz was a forebear of such techniques. Jan Kott directed *The Madman and the Nun* at San Francisco State College in 1967, and with reference to Witkiewicz's work argues:

> If we consider the Theatre of the Absurd, the Theatre of Cruelty, and the Theatre of Happenings as the most significant theatrical phenomena of the fifties and sixties, it no longer seems difficult to draw their historical genealogy [...] In both Artaud's and Witkiewicz's plays, even before the body of a character who has died has time to cool down, he stands up and walks.[5]

The live spectacle of an Alice Cooper show relied on confronting audiences with extreme, but not impossible, events that were cleverly designed to shock and challenge conventional boundaries between artist and audience. Van Cagle identifies this as being a particular trait of the early 1970s Detroit music scene: 'In Detroit, the performance schemata was analogous in principle to Artaud's "theater of cruelty" in that the technique was to "incite a kind of virtual revolt" by absolving the boundaries between audiences and performers.'[6] During the *Love It to Death* tour, such activity would involve Alice partaking in mock acts of violence towards fellow band members; once the desired levels of musical and dramatic tension were attained, he would shower the audience with feathers, receiving both gratitude and applause.[7]

The bizarre theatrical appeal of Alice Cooper is widely acknowledged, and yet his innovative use of characterization is often undervalued. Too often his shock-horror antics have provoked reviews offering a somewhat banal description of conceptual ideas/events: 'Then someone brings something on the stage, but it's covered with a sheet. Alice walks over to it, and pulls the sheets off. It's an electric chair with a doll in it. Alice, who by this time has a pitch fork in his hands, takes the doll and begins to stab it.'[8] In fact, many early reviewers failed to understand

---

theatre instead promoted participation through the experience and confrontation of fear, the intention being that the audience would undergo a significant metaphysical encounter and emerge cleansed.

[5]     Witkiewicz, pp. xii–xiii.

[6]     Van M. Cagle, *Reconstructing Pop/Subculture: Art, Rock and Andy Warhol* (Thousand Oaks, CA, 1995), p. 96. According to Cagle, Alice Cooper and Iggy Pop embodied the basis of the 1967–70 Detroit scene, which, in a similar fashion to the Velvet Underground's incorporation of the Factory influence, adopted a form of performance comparable to Artaud's 'Theatre of Cruelty'. As evidence for this, Cagle cites Iggy Pop's stage diving antics and Cooper's predilection for prowling the corners of the stage and catapulting objects (parts of dolls, feathers and so on) into the audience.

[7]     For full details of such stage antics, see Elaine Gross's article 'Where Are the Chickens?' *Rolling Stone* (15 October 1970).

[8]     Trevor Dollier, 'Swing the Sword, Paint your Face, and Electrify the Stage, it's Alice Cooper Time', *Rock On* (13 August 1971), sourced from the Alice Cooper eChive at http://www.alicecooperechive.com (retrieved 2 August 2005).

the distinction between artist and persona, condemning the band for their blasé approach to such macabre themes.[9] Any yet, it was precisely the provocatively insensitive and, in many instances, comic approach of Alice Cooper that enabled an effective critique of contemporary American society. Ironically, had the band attempted a realistic depiction of madness, murder and electrocution they would almost certainly have been derided for manufacturing gratuitous violence for consumption. Notable exceptions include Lester Bangs's 1972 review of the album *Killer* in which he claimed Cooper had 'brought the Hollywood manipulation of fantasies and attitude to brilliant new levels of cheerful cynicism. Some regard it as contemptuous, nihilistic exploitation [...] but I think he's one of the most upfront stars we've ever known.'[10] Indeed, Cooper's ability to capitalize on the nonsensicality of certain facets of American society encouraged his audience to discover not only their own relative levels of autonomy but also the extent to which irrational fear may be revealed and overcome through caricature and dramatic performance.

'The Ballad of Dwight Fry' is widely heralded as the most influential track from Alice Cooper's 1971 album *Love It to Death*. Cooper himself has acknowledged its importance, proclaiming it to be 'the definitive Alice song'.[11] While the two preceding albums had involved the establishment of Alice Cooper's performance ethos, it was *Love It to Death* that presented the first opportunity for the band's distinctive hard rock to be released on a major label. The theme of incarceration provided a powerful means by which Alice could exploit a wide range of musical and dramatic gestures. It was a theme he would return to for his 1978 album *From the Inside*,[12] rumoured to have been inspired by people he met while receiving treatment for alcoholism at a New York psychiatric hospital.

Rather than simply expound a common fear of psychiatric imprisonment, Cooper's musical narrative critiques such treatment by highlighting its cruel and damaging effects. In this way, the band aligns itself with the revolutionary work of Erving Goffman and his condemnation of 'total institutions' first outlined in his 1961 work *Asylums: Essays on the Social Situation of Mental Patients and Other Inmates*.[13] While sociologists such as Edwin Lemert[14] and the better-known

---

[9]     Cagle blames such ignorance on certain rock critics' resistance to 1970s thematic developments: 'rock commentators who were still embedded in 1960s countercultural themes and philosophies found that they couldn't bear the idea that this "comic book madman" with "no values" was emerging as an idol to 15- and 16-year-olds'. Cagle, p. 121.

[10]     Lester Bangs, 'Killer', *Rolling Stone* (6 January 1972).

[11]     The Record Buyer Interview: 'You've Read About the Man – Now Let's Meet Him', *Record Buyer* (July 2000).

[12]     Alice Cooper, *From the Inside* (Warner, 1978). Note that all songs were co-written with lyricist Bernie Taupin.

[13]     Erving Goffman, *Asylums: Essays on the Social Situation of Mental Patients and Other Inmates* [1961] (London, 1991).

[14]     See Edwin M. Lemert, *Social Pathology* (New York, 1951).

Thomas Scheff[15] began developing their accounts of 'labelling theory', it was Goffman who first evaluated the process and experience of commitment and its impact on the individual designated as mentally ill. Akin to contemporary ideas challenging the medical model of psychiatry (Szasz's *The Myth of Mental Illness* being published in the same year), Goffman's *Asylums* proposed that behaviour exhibited by hospital 'inmates' considered to be both symptom and evidence of their pathology was, in fact, an understandable reaction to their treatment and the passive role/career they were encouraged to adopt. The 'passage from civilian to patient status'[16] resulted in the self being 'systematically, if often unintentionally, mortified',[17] while the provision, and subsequent strengthening of diagnosis, had no apparent medical justification:

> I want to stress that perception of losing one's mind is based on culturally derived and socially engrained stereotypes [...] Similarly, the anxiety consequent upon this perception of oneself, and the strategies devised to reduce this anxiety, are not a product of abnormal psychology, but would be exhibited by any person socialized into our culture who came to conceive of himself as someone losing his mind.[18]

Evidence to support a reading of 'The Ballad of Dwight Fry' – based on the challenging theories of Goffman, Szasz, Cooper, Scheff and the early works of Laing – will be presented in this chapter via an exploration of its family setting; the narrative exposition of events concerning the protagonist's experience of hospitalization; and the suggested effects of involuntary incarceration. Additional themes that interweave the musical text (the infantilization of the mad; the suggested solidarity of hospital 'inmates'; and mental illness as social deviancy) will be examined in an attempt to understand the attraction and efficacy of Alice Cooper's use of characterization.

In preparation for the first person narrative that constitutes the majority of the song, the introductory material serves to establish the protagonist's familial circumstances. A female voice, childlike in tone and delivery, asks: 'Mommy, where's Daddy? He's been gone for so long. Do you think he'll ever come home?' The questions, while failing to solicit a literal response, are underpinned by musical gestures that encourage an empathetic view from the listener. At the same time, they suggest an uneasiness concerning the possible reasons for 'daddy's' absence. The first four bars offer delicate counterpoint between metallophone and piano; the harmony progressing effortlessly via a chromatic bass movement from

---

[15]    Thomas J. Scheff, *Being Mentally Ill: A Sociological Theory* (London, 1966).

[16]    Erving Goffman, 'The Moral Career of the Mental Patient' [1959], in Thomas Szasz, *The Age of Madness* (London, 1975), p. 254. Goffman's chapter is an abridged version of 'The Moral Career of the Mental Patient', *Psychiatry*, 22/2 (May 1959): 123–42.

[17]    Goffman, *Asylums*, p. 24.

[18]    Ibid., pp. 123–4.

A major to D major (A–A/G♯–A/G–D). The ballad feel is established through the flowing quaver accompaniment; a triplet crotchet articulation in the left hand of bar two; and repetition of a simple melodic motif over changing harmony. The overall feeling is one of almost maudlin purity – not something an audience of early 1970s heavy rock would anticipate experiencing within an album of this nature. As such, its duration is understandably short-lived, as the introduction of child's voice initiates an unexpected move to a B♭ major chord. This use of tritone substitution for the chord of E, resulting in chromatic movement back to A major, is further emphasized through an accented appoggiatura in the metallophone melody. Its effect, while not interrupting the music's sense of fluency (which is actually enhanced through a metre change to 6/8), is to imbue the text with a subtle sense of apprehension (see Example 4.1). Furthermore, the subsequent repetition of ascending, non-functional chords (F–G–Asus2) resists closure, encouraging the listener to ponder 'daddy's' unexplained and ostensibly unending absence.

Example 4.1  'The Ballad of Dwight Fry' introduction (metallophone)

Given that rock artists conventionally convey a pre-marriage identity, the selection of a presumably post-marriage, or at least paternal, identity for Alice Cooper's protagonist is unusual. Indeed, this approach is more typical of country music, where themes of lovin' and cheatin' are paramount; however, neither of these features within the story of Dwight Fry. One possible interpretation involves an understanding of the family's role in identifying mad behaviour and initiating treatment for such. To imply parental conspiracy, involving the protagonist's mother/father being responsible for his commitment, would be detrimental to Alice Cooper's rebellious image (implying that he remains under their control). As such, the suggestion of fatherhood is more appropriate in that it presupposes a greater degree of autonomy while at the same time establishing a context for his commitment fitting contemporary theories of family conspiracy.

In their 1964 work *Sanity, Madness and the Family*,[19] Laing and Esterson suggested that the behaviour of certain patients deemed schizophrenic was actually understandable in terms of their individual family contexts: their diagnosis could either be a result of family conspiracy or, perhaps less controversially, a result of their relatives driving them frantic. While not challenging the medical model

---

[19]     Ronald D. Laing and Aaron Esterson, *Sanity, Madness and the Family* (Harmondsworth, 1964).

as such – for the possibility of accurately identified schizophrenia remained a definite option – the work encouraged the consideration of an individual's family relationships within the process of both diagnosis and treatment. This 'conspiratorial theory of schizophrenia'[20] was subsequently adopted and furthered with evident zeal (and a fair degree of wit) by David Cooper, who wrote:

> It is, however, still almost revolutionary to suggest that the problem lies not in the so-called 'ill person' but in the interacting network of persons, particularly his family, from which the admitted patient, by a piece of conceptual sleight of hand, has already been abstracted. Madness, that is to say, is not 'in' a person, but in a system of relationships in which the labelled 'patient' participates: schizophrenia, if it means anything, is a more or less characteristic mode of disturbed group behaviour.[21]

Cooper believed that removing the so-called 'patient' from their family context resulted in the creation and classification of fake problems – 'all genuine problems having vanished unnoticed through the hospital gates (along with the departing relatives)'.[22]

The fear of false commitment to a mental institution by one's family has existed within public consciousness since the days of the private asylums. Henry Russell's Victorian ballad 'The Maniac' (1846)[23] exploits this very subject matter, and with good reason, as Szasz demonstrates: 'Psychiatry began with the relatives of troublesome persons seeking relief from the suffering the (mis)behaviour of their kin caused them. Unlike the regular doctor, the early psychiatrist, called mad-doctor, treated persons who did not want to be his patients, and whose ailments manifested themselves by exciting the resentment of their relatives.'[24] With the rapid proliferation of state mental asylums during the eighteenth and nineteenth centuries, it became evident that the state's desire to assist families with their problematic relatives had a less altruistic purpose: 'a person who spurns our core values – that life, liberty, and property are goods worth preserving – endangers not only himself and his relatives but, symbolically, society and the social fabric itself'.[25]

---

[20]     The term 'conspiratorial theory' is identified by Miriam Siegler, Humphrey Osmond and Harriet Mann, 'Laing's Models of Madness', in Robert Boyers and Robert Orrill (eds), *Laing and Anti-Psychiatry* (Harmondsworth, 1972).

[21]     David Cooper, *Psychiatry and Anti-Psychiatry* [1967] (London, 2001), pp. 28–9.

[22]     Ibid., p. 29.

[23]     'The Maniac' is sung in the persona of someone falsely committed by their relatives.

[24]     Thomas Szasz, *Cruel Compassion: Psychiatric Control of Society's Unwanted* (New York, 1994), p. 103.

[25]     Ibid., p. 106.

By establishing the family context in the opening passage, Alice Cooper (the band) offer the possibility of a more in-depth, and empathetic, interpretation of the protagonist's circumstances – one that is analogous with the aforementioned emerging and, in the case of Cooper and Szasz, established anti-psychiatric theories. Later songs, such as 'Inmates (We're All Crazy)', return to this theme with tongue-in-cheek lyrics ('Lizzy Borden took an axe and gave her mother forty whacks') that resonate with contemporary autobiographical accounts of family conspiracy, the most notorious of these being Frances Farmer's *Will There Really Be a Morning?*:

> 'I'm just about at the end of my rope with you,' she warned. 'I've just about had all I can take. I've put up with you for years and what do I get for it? Nothing! Absolutely nothing! But you're my daughter and you're going to do exactly as I say, or back you go. Do you understand me? Back you go! And this time … for keeps.'[26]

The shift to first person narrative – whereupon the 'ballad' of the protagonist commences – is heralded by an ascending sequence of major chords (F, G, A, B, C, D) and change in instrumentation. As the piano and metallophone texture dissipates, the introduction of acoustic guitar, followed by bass and then kit, advocates a move away from the dreamlike scenario of the opening to a more 'genuine' articulation of experience: that of the committed madman. The harmonic and melodic content serves to animate certain aspects of the lyric, while the vocal delivery is responsible for conveying the notion of role play. With E being established as the central pitch axis (receiving accentual stress at the start of the harmonic sequence E–G–D–C), the progression from E major to E natural minor and descending D–C movement evoke a distinctly melancholic feel.

The accompaniment remains relatively simple in construction, its subdued character and lack of evident word-painting allowing full focus to be placed on the vocal. Initially, the delivery appears to lack conviction, ascending to the minor 3rd in anticipation of the Aeolian feel before falling back to the minor 7th and remaining confined between it and the minor 6th for its consequent phrase. This, coupled with the soft, half-sung/half-spoken tone and unexpected pitch bends, serves to underpin Fry's uncertain recollection of events: 'I was gone for fourteen days, I could'a been gone for more. Held up in an intensive care-ward, lyin' on the floor.' An inability to recollect the correct passage of time is a widely understood side-effect of involuntary confinement, and one which Jan Knott chose to portray in his production of *The Madman and the Nun*, with slide projections used 'to penetrate into Walpurg's mind […] clocks running backward and at different

---

[26]  Frances Farmer, *Will There Really Be a Morning? An Autobiography by Frances Farmer* [1972] (Glasgow, 1983), p. 17. This passage involves Farmer's mother threatening to send her back to a state asylum for the insane.

speeds created the sense of deranged time within the confines of the cell, cut off from all contact with normal life'.[27]

The melodic contour appears unnecessarily uncomfortable at points, but this is crucial to the establishment of Fry's character. The articulation of 'care-ward' is an obvious example, where attention is drawn to both its existence and the protagonist's potential feelings towards it by a descending fall from the minor 3rd and unwieldy rise from minor 6th to minor 7th (see Example 4.2). The ungainly use of pitch, lack of first beat emphasis, laboured rhythmic phrasing and disturbing tone all convey an apparent sense of abnormality that is likely to be interpreted as justification for the protagonist's confinement. However, this impression is quickly thwarted as the shift up an octave and employment of throat voice for the ensuing, more conventional, phrase 'I was gone for all those days' reveals Fry's ability to merely 'play' the role of the madman. As such, the protagonist is not necessarily perceived as being, in reality, mad. Rather, he demonstrates the ability to slip in and out of a madman 'role' in a conscious, predetermined manner.

Example 4.2 'The Ballad of Dwight Fry' verse 1 (vocal and chords)

Further evidence to support this reading of the text comes from the abundant, and evidently considered, manipulation of vocal tone throughout the song wherein three main modes of delivery are exploited: soft, half-sung/half-spoken voice; clear tone chest voice; and shouted, strained throat voice. With reference to the continuation of verse one, for example, the soft, half-spoken tone returns to reinforce the use of slurred, non-harmony tones (9th to the 7th) that re-establish a sense of abnormality for the unexpected: 'But I was not all alone'. The statement that follows then introduces clear tone, mid-range chest voice to instil the lyric 'I made friends with a lot of people' with a feeling of integrity, before the use of restricted throat voice snarls the concluding phrase: 'in the danger zone'. One possible interpretation is to perceive such manipulation as evidence of the protagonist's mental instability, but this denies a deeper understanding of the way in which the vocal delivery enlivens the lyric text. Instead, one could argue that the return to clear tone, chest voice encourages the listener to question their own insecurities concerning the kinds of people Fry may have met during his

---

[27]     Witkiewicz, p. 4.

commitment, while the snarled condemnation of the ward being a 'danger zone' identifies the true threat of the psychiatric establishment itself.

The suggested solidarity of mental patients ('I made friends with a lot of people') has proved a popular theme within literature and film, and commonly incorporates the suspicion that the lunatics will eventually depose those in authority. Goffman views such unity as a reasonable response to treatment received within the institution, describing how:

> A sense of common injustice and a sense of bitterness against the outside world tend to develop [...] Sometimes special solidarities extend throughout a physically closed region such as a ward or cottage, whose inhabitants perceive they are being administered as a single unit, and hence have a lively sense of common fate.[28]

For such an idea to gain popular recognition, the belief that the mental hospital could conceivably do the patient more harm than good, must receive equal emphasis. By referring to Fry's place of confinement as a 'danger zone', Alice Cooper link the aforementioned ideas and draw on earlier critiques of mental institutions that emerged during the period 1950–70. Goffman, for example, makes it quite clear why an 'inmate' may have cause to question their personal safety, making explicit reference to certain forms of treatment: 'Beatings, shock therapy, or, in mental hospitals, surgery – whatever the intent of staff in providing these services for some inmates – may lead many inmates to feel that they are in an environment that does not guarantee their physical integrity.'[29] David Cooper expanded this theory by applying the proposed threat to the patient's mental integrity, referring to the 'mutilation' of 'personal reality' occurring as a consequence of the necessity to conform to staff preconceptions. As a result: 'The violence that commences in his family is perpetuated in the conventional psychiatric ward.'[30]

The first half of verse two is used to provide justification for Fry's apparent scepticism concerning the curative potential of the ward. His voice traverses the pitches with apparent uncertainty, ascending between non-harmony tones (major 6th–minor 7th) before cracking hoarsely on the word 'weight' to suggest the unnecessary fatigue he's endured: 'I think I lost some weight there, and I'm sure I need some rest, sleepin' don't come very easy in a straight white vest'. Attention is drawn to the use of physical restraint through the use of end rhyme (rest/vest) and prolonged note duration, ending with noticeable accents on the final consonants. The fact that straitjackets are also commonly used within prisons strengthens his

---

[28]    Goffman, *Asylums*, pp. 58–9.

[29]    Ibid., p. 30.

[30]    Cooper, *Psychiatry and Anti-Psychiatry*, p. 28. Cooper clarifies his definition of violence earlier in the book: 'To comprehend my present usage of the term "violence", we shall have to understand it as the corrosive action of the freedom of a person on the freedom of another. It is not direct physical assaultiveness, although this may issue from it' (p. 18).

critique of the mental hospital by implying that both deal first and foremost with controlling unwanted behaviour.

Fictional accounts of the brutal employment of straitjackets have assisted its prominent place within public consciousness as an instrument of imprisonment and torture; *Star Rover* by American writer Jack London[31] is one such example:

> The jacket is spread on the floor. The man who is to be punished, or who is to be tortured for confession, is told to lie face-downward on the flat canvas. If he refuses he is manhandled [...] On occasion, when the guards are cruel and vindictive, or when the command has come down from above, in order to ensure the severity of the lacing the guards press with their feet into the man's back as they draw the lacing tight.[32]

Even comic books have utilized striking imagery of their heroes in frenzied yet futile attempts to break free from straitjackets as a means of enhancing anticipated levels of peril. *The Incredible Hulk* and *Animal Man*[33] have both contained front cover examples of such; but perhaps the most interesting scene is found within the lesser-known *Law Breakers Always Lose!* Here, in an amusing reversal of the Victorian novel (whereupon it was typically the 'mad' wife being locked away in the attic), a femme fatale attempts to have her husband committed to a sanatorium, while the hero, who has infiltrated the hospital, vows to 'bust wide open this phoney sanatorium racket!'[34]

The first interlude section of the song embellishes the aforementioned theme of physical confinement through a number of musical gestures that evoke feelings of confusion, frustration, anger and entrapment. A return to the song's sparse opening texture, prepared by a noticeable ascending bass swoop, suggests a move to somewhere less stable than the preceding chorus. The reintroduction of metallophone and piano reminds listeners of the negative associations of the song's opening, while the incessant repetition of undulating melodic figures over the same four-bar verse harmonic progression serves to illustrate the protagonist's state of captivity. Use of tritone and minor 2nd intervals in the piano (bar 2: C♯ over G; bar 3: A and G♯ over D; bar 4 F♯ over C) provides subtle dissonances that contradict the purity of the timbral associations, while the high pitch range of both

---

[31]     Jack London, *The Star Rover* (New York, 1915). The protagonist, tormented by prison guards, discovers a means to endure the pain of the 'jacket' by exploring his inner space.

[32]     London, *The Star Rover*, contained in chapter 7. Available online at http://london.sonoma.edu/Writings/StarRover/chapter7.html.

[33]     Information regarding *The Incredible Hulk* (Marvel, February 1995) and *Animal Man* #60 (DC/Vertigo, June 1993) was sourced 5 June 2007 from http://sj.blacksteel.com/media/books.cgi.

[34]     *Law Breakers Always Lose* #4 (Marvel Comic Group, #1 Spring 1948–#10 October 1949). Sourced 5 June 2007 from http://sj.blacksteel.com/media/images/lawbreakers.jpg.C

parts ensures they remain audible once the full instrumental texture is reinstated in bar 5. In the previous bar, the electric guitar signals the imminent return of bass and kit with a descending slide that augments the melancholic atmosphere, cutting through the delicate texture as if mimicking a dog howling for its master's return.

The apparent denied possibility of either melodic or harmonic closure results in a growing tension that perfectly complements the repeated and increasingly frantic vocal appeals: 'I wanna get out of here'. The vocal passage begins in a tentative manner as the phrase starts mid-bar with an irregular grouping in simple time (triplet quavers against the accompanying straight quaver rhythms) before utilizing a triplet quaver rest on beat 1 of the following bar to convey a sense of hesitancy. The disjunctive feel between vocal and accompaniment becomes increasingly prominent as the four-bar backing repeats unremittingly while the vocal's rhythmic and hoarse timbral character intensifies. Beginning with a normal, albeit hesitant, spoken delivery, the vocal quickly progresses through to high-pitched shouting and finally screaming, with each phrase involving a faster rhythmic delivery of the same statement. The second phrase, for example, maintains the faltering feel of the first, repeating the word 'I' on the offbeat of beats 1 and 2 of the bar before cramming the words 'I wanna get outta' into three triplet and two straight semiquaver rhythms.[35]

While the vocal passage appears to be largely improvised, it nevertheless remains rhythmatized throughout, and this is relevant to the way in which the protagonist's mental state may be interpreted. A lack of structured time could serve as a metaphor for a lack of rationality/reason, in which case the use of restraint might be read as justifiable and the critique of such would be undermined. Instead, by maintaining an adherence to structured time, and behaving in a manner that Goffman points out to be a perfectly comprehensible response to such treatment,[36] a more sympathetic reaction to the protagonist's plight is assured. The notion that Fry's frustration and anger is perfectly explicable is reinforced by the accompaniment's unremitting character and the fact that the tempo of such increases slightly in what could be viewed as a mocking rejoinder to Fry's increased protestations. Empathy from the

---

[35]  Many fan websites offer information concerning the recording of this vocal passage. Rumour has it that it took place while Vincent Furnier was confined below a heap of folding chairs in an attempt to mimic the physical restraint of a straitjacket. During his live concerts, Furnier would be taken offstage by a 'nurse' before re-emerging in a straitjacket to deliver this section of the song.

[36]  According to Goffman, once a person enters the mental hospital they may behave in a way which refuses to concede what they have 'become in the eyes of others', for example, by being 'out of contact' or 'manic'. Goffman, *Asylums*, p. 136. Most importantly, such signs of hostility can then be used by the establishment as further evidence of their rightly diagnosed illness: 'In short, mental hospitalization out-manoeuvres the patient, tending to rob him of the common expressions through which people hold off the embrace of organizations – insolence, silence, *sotto voce* remarks, uncooperativeness, malicious destruction of interior decorations, and so forth; these signs of disaffiliation are now read as signs of their maker's proper affiliation.' Ibid., p. 269.

listener is additionally encouraged by the way in which the final frenzied vocal statements, despite reaching a dynamic high and continuing into the ensuing chorus, are overtaken in the mix to suggest both his captor's indifference and Fry's resulting abandonment. The implied tragedy of his surpassed screams is akin to Cooper's description of psychiatry's unheard violence: 'If one speaks of violence in psychiatry, the violence that stares out screaming, proclaiming itself as such so loudly that it is rarely heard, is the subtle, torturous violence that other people, the "sane ones", perpetrate against the labelled madmen.'[37]

Aside from fictional accounts concerning the employment of straitjackets, contemporary autobiographies of formerly committed patients offered a shocking insight into their potential misuse. Frances Farmer's description of such treatment explains exactly how one's understandable resistance could be misconstrued as evidence of their mental illness:

> I began to scream and tried to run, but they [two uniformed men] grabbed me. I fought like a cornered animal but was easily overpowered and wrestled to the floor. They straddled me, and I felt the rough canvas of the straitjacket wrap around me and buckle into place. My arms were nearly stretched from their sockets as I was locked into it [...] And so it was, on May 22, 1945, at 3.25 in the afternoon, that I was delivered bound and gagged to the state asylum like a dog gone mad.[38]

Goffman referred to the transition from civilian to mental patient as being perceived as an act of betrayal, with various factors strengthening the 'inmate's' sense of abandonment: 'I am suggesting that the pre-patient starts out with at least a portion of the rights, liberties, and satisfactions of the civilian and ends up on a psychiatric ward stripped of almost everything.'[39] This stripping was, Goffman argued, the beginning step in the establishment of an 'inmate's' moral career as a mental patient.[40] It is a view that receives evident support when one considers the chorus passages of 'The Ballad of Dwight Fry', whereupon the concluding evidence that Fry is driven insane by his commitment becomes arguably the most plausible interpretation of both lyric and musical texts.

The chorus harmony – being an E Mixolydian minor VI–VII–I progression (parent key: A ascending melodic minor) – is relatively predictable in its ascent to chord I, and less ambiguous than the non-functional verse sections. The fact that the resting chord I is major rather than minor moves it away from the

---

[37]     Cooper, *Psychiatry and Anti-Psychiatry*, p. 14.

[38]     Farmer, pp. 32, 34. According to Andrew Roberts, in 1978 Frances Farmer's autobiography 'generated a lot of unwelcome publicity' for the Western State Hospital, where she had been a patient. Andrew Roberts, *American History Timeline*, http://www.mdx.ac.uk/www/study/America.htm (retrieved 19 July 2005).

[39]     Goffman, *Asylums*, pp. 257–8.

[40]     Ibid., pp. 252–3.

Aeolian modal inflection of the verse, and gives a brighter feel that supports the potential revelation of the chorus message. The harmonic rhythm lends further emphasis to chord I as, unlike the previous VI and VII chords which are of minim duration, it is held for a full semibreve. Similarly, the melodic content is also more straightforward than the verse sections, centring on the harmony notes of the accompanying chords – with the exception of chord I, where the minor 3rd (G natural) conveys a bluesy feel before resolving to the central pitch axis of E. The vocal remains consistently within a comfortable and strong chest tone, and is supported in bars one and five by a harmony vocal in 3rds. The aforementioned gestures ensure that the chorus itself is distinguished as the most important section in terms of formal hierarchy, but they also impact on one's reading of the lyric text. There is a noticeable shift to the present tense as Fry implores the listener to witness his mental breakdown: 'See my lonely life unfold, I see it every day. See my only mind explode, since I've gone away.' The strength of the musical gestures imparts a sense of confidence and sincerity that assists in the communication of the song's principal message: that rather than offering rest and cure, involuntary confinement and 'treatment' in a psychiatric ward actually has a detrimental effect on a person's mental well-being.

Each chorus repeats the reference to the protagonist's mind exploding. The second is more explicit in linking the event to a state of mental illness: 'See my lonely mind explode when I've gone insane', while the third – 'See my only mind explode, blow up in my face' – suggests that, being the only mind he possesses, its detonation is irreparable. The tragedy of such is represented by a metaphorical iconic signifier: a sound effect of an actual explosion which is almost comical in effect, highlighting as it does the difference between metaphor and reality. The same symbol for the mind's disintegration is found in Frances Farmer's autobiography as she describes her attempts to assess her own mental state: 'I was alone, and I was confused, but was I insane? Was this uncommon reality in which I lived insanity? Had my mind exploded beyond reality or repair, or was I, instead, the result of some dreadful caricature?'[41]

Other writers have also identified Fry as a casualty of his captivity: for example, Cagle notes that, in his live performance of the song, Cooper 'described the frustrations of a man who had been locked away in a mental institution. As the song's tempo increased, Cooper revealed "his" condition as an insane "victim" who had lapsed into a paranoiac state.'[42] Contemporary critics equally recognized Alice Cooper's condemnation of involuntary incarceration: John Mendelsohn's review of the album for *Rolling Stone* summarized the song's narrative as 'the story of a man who's gone temporarily insane and finds himself going gradually more insane as a result of being confined in a mental institution'.[43] It is also significant that further parallels may be drawn in this respect between 'The Ballad of Dwight Fry'

---

[41] Farmer, p. 31.

[42] Cagle, p. 123.

[43] John Mendelsohn, 'Love It to Death', *Rolling Stone* (15 April 1971).

and Stanislaw Witkiewicz's play *The Madman and the Nun* wherein the principal character, Walpurg, delivers a similar accusation concerning the injurious mental effects of the lunatic asylum:

> But no one gets well here. You can see that for yourself. As a matter of fact I'm in full possession of my senses [...] Whoever comes here is finished. Because their type of cure only pushes you further and further into madness; you can try to tell them lies, but eventually you do something stupid, you make one false step and you're locked up forever.[44]

Evidence attesting to Fry's mental breakdown may be identified following each chorus passage. The first instance occurs during the second half of verse two, where references to childlike behaviour point towards Fry's mental regression. The use of grammar appears deliberately naïve: 'should like to see that little children, she's only four years old'; and attention is drawn to the young age of the child by a repetition of the word 'old' using an ascending 6th–7th slur (A–B against the accompanying chord of C) that fails to resolve. Allusions to childish play – 'I'd give her back all of her play things, even the ones I stole' – and the impression that such toys were important enough to pilfer (the voice cracks in apparent distress for the words 'all of her play things') establish that Fry's mind has regressed to an infantile state. The rhythmic delivery of the half-spoken/half-sung phrases appears to mimic the insecurity of a child, resulting in an awkward repetition of the word 'even' that breaks with the established rhythmic patterns of previous phrase endings. The final word 'stole' is unnaturally emphasized, being drawn out over a semibreve with an audible accent on the end letter, as if its exaggerated pronunciation is part of the protagonist's juvenile effort to gain attention (Example 4.3).

Example 4.3   'The Ballad of Dwight Fry' verse 2 (vocal)

The idea that institutionalization could, if not reduce a person's mental functioning to that of a child, at least encourage them to adopt infantile behaviour by limiting their accustomed levels of autonomy may be found within a number of critiques concerning both the nature and methods of psychiatric care. Goffman,

---

[44]    Witkiewicz, p. 17.

in his analysis of the social situation of mental patients, claimed that: 'total institutions disrupt or defile precisely those actions that in civil society have the role of attesting to the actor and those in his presence that he has some command over his world – that he is a person with "adult" self-determination autonomy, and freedom of action'.[45] Similarly, Lucy Johnstone states that: 'the hospital environment, as we have seen, tends to reinforce all of a person's most childlike aspects'.[46] For Szasz, who has consistently protested against involuntary commitment, the identification and treatment of the supposed insane as if they were infants, and encouragement of this within public perception, has long had a hidden motive. In the early twentieth century, justification for the confinement of practically all persons diagnosed mentally ill came from the fact that 'Psychiatrists and the public alike viewed the insane person as an irresponsible child and/or dangerous criminal, who neither needed nor deserved liberty. Instead he needed to be protected from himself, and society needed to be protected from him.'[47] Indeed, according to Szasz, the very progression to becoming a labelled madman required that the person be stripped of all rights and 'Reframing the political status of the insane adult as similar to that of a child accomplishes this task.'[48]

The clearest verification of Fry's mental collapse follows the explosion event that serves to highlight the structural boundary between third chorus and second (instrumental) interlude. As the explosion fades, there is a noticeable drop in dynamic level, textural density and tempo that provides a keen sense of aftermath and anticipation about what will follow. The kit enters first with simple crotchet beats, the slowness of which appears amplified by the way in which the drumstick is allowed to bounce nonchalantly on the skin of the snare. In the second bar, the metallophone adds an unexpected high E (over two octaves above middle C) on the second half of beat 3 that seems to further heighten the level of suspense. From here, the texture continues to grow as reversed guitar chords bring a sense of familiarity but also dread as the same harmonic progression witnessed in previous verses and the first interlude suggests that circumstances for Fry remain unaltered. The chords begin on the second beat of each bar and swell to a sharp accent due to the reversed attack of the notes. The effect, while not groundbreaking in production terms, nevertheless suggests a sense of disorientation that supports the notion of dazed discovery.

Once the aforementioned, unnerving atmosphere is established, the bass initiates a little more continuity and drive playing, the usual verse riff to strengthen the sense of unmovable background/setting. What *has* changed, however, is Fry's mental state, and this is imaginatively portrayed through an atonal guitar solo wherein pitch bends (falling and ascending apparently randomly) provide a fitting metaphor for his supposedly warped mind. The slow rhythm of the solo

---

[45]   Goffman, *Asylums*, p. 47.

[46]   Johnstone, p. 74.

[47]   Szasz, *Cruel Compassion*, p. 169.

[48]   Ibid., p. 104.

ensures the dissonance has maximum effect; the starting pitches, all of which are non-chord tones, create an initial sense of conflict that seems heightened through excruciating portamento effects that find no sense of resolution. After the first four bars, the phrases become an unconventional five bars in length, yet the ascending pitch direction suggests an unwieldy attempt to regain some sense of identifiable direction when all else appears confused. The dislocation of the lead guitar from the surrounding arrangement is furthered by the haunting return of metallophone and piano materials from interlude one. From this point onwards the tempo begins to increase, winding up tension in preparation for the vocal's anticipated return.

The bizarre and unpredictable feel of the second interlude is maintained in the ensuing subject matter as the final verse tells of an escape attempt that appears a likely product of Fry's delusional state rather than a real occurrence. The narrative seems to adopt a quasi-comic book style; the detailed action seems clumsily scripted and highly improbable given his desperate desire for freedom: 'I grabbed my hat, and I got my coat, then I ran into the street'. The seemingly irrational desire to be properly presented could also be a way of implying that normality is simply a façade. The feel of reminiscing is strengthened by the detached, half-spoken delivery, with the words 'and I' and 'then I' being delivered in semiquaver bursts followed by quaver rests suggestive of an out-of-breath condition. Unlike previous verses, the melodic line begins as a monotone, with a noticeably hoarse timbre that conveys a sense of frantic excitement. The suggestion that this may all have been a figment of Fry's imagination is then delivered by way of a reminder of his regressive mental state (witnessed previously in verse two). While reverting to a more rounded, conventional vocal tone, the actual enunciation of words appears unnecessarily exaggerated and deliberately childlike in character as Fry describes how he was distracted by a man choking, prompting the following facile thoughts: that he obviously couldn't breathe; that such behaviour was strange; and that he was glad it wasn't him.

The reverie of this final verse is eventually broken by a sudden shift to present tense that establishes a sense of immediacy and informs listeners of Fry's ultimate fate. In a half-shouted tone, his perpetual terror of enforced confinement is once again revealed: 'but now I hear those sirens calling, and so I am not free'. The reference to a siren, like that of the straitjacket, conjures up images of policing as opposed to medical assistance, and serves to reinforce the song's criticism of the psychiatric establishment. Szasz refers to the way in which psychiatrists have been 'classified by other physicians and the public at large, as "not real doctors," or medical jailers';[49] and the belief that enforced treatment for mental illness was, and still is, used as a means of regulating behaviour deemed undesirable and potentially damaging to society at large has obviously fuelled such classifications. Andrew Scull traces the origins of this covert function back to the eighteenth century:

---

[49]     Szasz, *Ideology and Insanity*, p. 53.

Very early on in the history of the asylum, it became apparent that its primary value to the community was a handy place to which to consign the disturbing, the vaguely menacing, the unwanted, and the useless – those potentially and actually troublesome people who posed threats to social order and to the business of daily living which were not readily subject to control by the legal system.[50]

According to Szasz, the perpetuation of this function has been made possible by psychiatry's taxonomy of so-called 'mental conditions':

Social deviance, renamed 'mental illness,' became the subject matter of psychiatry; social outcasts and other incompetent, troubled, oppressed, and persecuted individuals, renamed 'neurotics' and 'psychotics,' became the 'patients' whom psychiatric 'physicians' were expected to 'treat'; and the doctors who assumed the task of verbally or physically controlling troublesome individuals, renamed 'psychiatrists,' became the scientifically accredited experts in their diagnosis and treatment of 'mental diseases.' Nearly all of this is humbug.[51]

Fry's resistance to being recaptured, and the fact that he appears to have committed no real crimes, encourages further questioning concerning the morality of involuntary confinement. In a shouted, strained, monotone delivery he repeats the words 'I didn't wanna be' in semiquaver bursts that develop to include triplet semiquavers, before proclaiming a more clearly delivered: 'Don't touch me!' The vocal remains rhythmatized while managing to convey an acute sense of drama and violent struggle. As the final chorus enters to accompany the scene, we are reminded of the detrimental effects of his treatment; the final phrase – 'see my lonely mind explode, when I've gone insane' – culminates in a two-bar descending glissando, with a noticeably increased reverb applied to the word 'insane', illustrating his further descent into madness. Attention is focused on this fall by a sudden cut in instrumental texture to strummed acoustic guitars and a sustained E chord. The sense of drama is then heightened via a continuation in harmonic stasis (a further two bars of E) alongside the re-entry of full band playing pounding, unison semiquavers that evoke feelings of intense frustration. The eventual release into a final instrumental chorus is accompanied by a resolute pedal E on lead guitar that seems especially poignant given the absence of vocal and implied reasons for such.

A criticism of enforced confinement was revisited in Alice Cooper's later work 'The Quiet Room', where a more detailed description of setting was offered while the suggested feelings of loneliness and isolation remained: 'They've got this place where they've been keeping me [...] the quiet room is sterilised and

---

50   Andrew Scull, *Social Order/Mental Disorder: Anglo-American Psychiatry in Historical Perspective* (London, 1989), p. 352.

51   Szasz, *Ideology and Insanity*, p. 67.

white, it's like a tomb [...] Its haunted atmosphere has heard so many scream [...] A mattress on the floor, no handles on the door. I really need nothing here, I'm all alone.' The attempt to secure empathy from listeners by describing such miserable conditions, and their resultant denial of freedom, further aligns the band with the work of Szasz and his belief that, within the psychiatric establishment, incarceration is typically concealed as hospitalization.[52] Moreover, unlike early (eighteenth-century) attempts to expose instances of wrongful confinement wherein the imprisonment of *accurately* defined madmen and madwomen was never in question, by playing the role of the madman, Alice Cooper, like Szasz, questions the compulsory confinement of *all* persons diagnosed mentally ill. The fact that the protagonist in 'The Quiet Room' is kept in a padded cell to avert his would-be suicide – 'They've got this place where they've been keeping me, where I can't hurt myself. I can't get my wrists to bleed' – results not only in a questioning of enforced physical restraint, but also a challenge to the denial of a person's right to take their own life.

*From the Inside* encouraged further associations to be drawn between mental institutions and prisons by using the common euphemism for prison occupation: being '*inside*' and containing the song 'Inmates (We're All Crazy)'. Goffman, who referred to all mental patients as 'inmates' of 'total institutions', clarified their understanding of such in the following way: 'The full meaning for the inmate of being "in" or "on the inside" does not exist apart from the special meaning to him of "getting out" or "getting on the outside".'[53] The notion that being a mental patient was akin to being a convict was equally promoted within personal recounts of hospital life aimed at exposing poor conditions within early twentieth-century mental hospitals. Frances Farmer's *Will There Really Be a Morning?* begins by identifying her position as a prisoner: 'For eight years I was an inmate in a state asylum for the insane'.[54] An enforced lack of freedom is, of course, the primary reason for such connections; however critics such as Goffman and Szasz have equally stressed the important similarities in social role:

> Long before I became a psychiatrist, I was impressed by the fact that in modern societies many individuals are incarcerated like prisoners in institutions – but are called *patients* [...] The social role of the mental hospital patient resembles the role of the prison inmate much more than it resembles the role of the medical patient.[55]

---

[52]     Szasz, *Cruel Compassion*, p. 113. Here Szasz also writes that since initial efforts by writers such as Daniel Defoe to uncover instances of wrongful confinement, 'Psychiatrists became more sophisticated, concealing incarceration as hospitalization and torture as treatment.'

[53]     Goffman, *Asylums*, p. 23.

[54]     Farmer, p. 11.

[55]     Thomas Szasz, *Insanity: The Idea and Its Consequences* (New York, 1987), p. 112.

By constructing a victim role for their protagonist, and stressing themes of isolation and loneliness as opposed to cure and rehabilitation, it may be argued that Alice Cooper promote similar beliefs.

'The Ballad of Dwight Fry' offers no real insight regarding the possible causes of Fry's incarceration, although the idea that punishment for deviant behaviour could be at its root is perhaps the most likely interpretation' given the band's contemporary image and outrageous stage antics.[56] The later song 'Inmates (We're All Crazy)' is far more blatant in suggesting deviancy, albeit it in an extreme form, as sufficient cause for involuntary commitment to a mental hospital. Teenage pranks take on a deliberately exaggerated appearance as the 'inmates' describe acts of arson, sabotage and gravedigging: 'It's not like we did something wrong, we just burned down the church while the choir within sang religious songs. And it's not like we thought we were right, we just played with the wheels of a passenger train that cracked on the tracks one night.' The verse sections comprise tongue-in-cheek attempts to excuse the aforementioned acts – the first ending with a humorous attack on the efficacy of psychiatrists: 'It's not like we ain't on the ball, we just talk to our shrinks, huh, they talk to their shrinks, no wonder we're up the wall.' Furthermore, an acknowledgement of the inmates' ability to impact negatively on obedient American citizens (giving rise to their ultimate punishment of incarceration) suggests an alignment with theories that expound madness as a form of social deviancy: 'We're not stupid or dumb, we're the lunatic fringe who rusted the hinge on Uncle Sam's daughters and sons […] And it's not like we don't know the score, we're the fragile elite they dragged off the street, I guess they just couldn't take us no more.'

Multiple layered vocals repeat the sing-song refrain 'We're all crazy' in a manner that suggests the potential to overwhelm and ultimately absorb listeners into the ever-growing texture, an invitation to recognize themselves as potential 'inmates'. Such a reading is supported by the fact that the album came complete with a ready-to-sign 'Certificate of Insanity' while its reverse cover pictured the ready-to-be-opened door of a psychiatric hospital. Alice Cooper thus celebrate *playing* the deviant while at the same time mocking stereotypical beliefs surrounding madness and its treatment. The refrain's nursery-rhyme melodic line and banal repetition once again serve to highlight beliefs that the diagnosed mentally ill are akin to reckless children justifiably denied their freedom for their

---

[56]     The album cover alone would have established an alternative and extrovert identity for the band, exhibiting as it does theatrical poses, make-up and clothes that would have been considered effeminate and outrageous by many at the time of its release. Other songs on the album such as 'I'm Eighteen' and Black Juju' strengthen the sense of adolescent rebellion with lyrics that propagate the desire to break free while celebrating the vitality of youth: 'I gotta get out of this place, I'll go runnin in outer space' ('I'm Eighteen'); 'Clutching and biting my soul has caught on fire, my evil is now and I'm caught up in desire, everything I'm living for is all that I am, liking it and loving it that's all in the plan' ('Black Juju').

own good. The exaggerated nature of the musical gestures and engaging use of humour result in a theatrical parody of conservative American values; the threat of incarceration is defeated by the suggestion that its occurrence simply affirms one's deviancy and hence rightful place as an Alice Cooper fan.

Given that Szasz has argued: 'Being considered or labelled mentally disordered, abnormal, crazy, mad, psychotic, sick, it matters not what variant is used – is the most profoundly discrediting classification that can be imposed on a person',[57] the above helps to explain the attraction of playing the madman role, for it allows the band to express deviant behaviour crucial to the construction of their hard rock identity. Elements of danger, volatility, excess and profanation are successfully communicated by relying on listeners' awareness of beliefs circulating about madness at the time. Indeed, Feder identifies similar possibilities for the film artist, wherein 'madness is principally a subject whose depiction probes the darkest and most hidden side of our being'.[58] The allure of madness as the ultimate site of rebellion should not be underestimated, and Alice Cooper's exaggerated characterization offers a means for fans to identify and revel in the kind of behaviour society dreads, as David Cooper identifies:

> The most prevalent fear, for the most part secret, or ill expressed or unexpressed in first-world societies, is the fear of a madness that knows no limits, a madness that shatters the pre-structured life not only of one person, the person who 'goes mad,' but beyond that a whole social region of life [...] the fantasy runs on, the world will go to pieces, we shall all go to pot, all our minds blown out, uselessly and finally.[59]

As opposed to simply confirming their fans' 'sanity' by denoting abnormal behaviour that constitutes 'madness', Alice Cooper offer an invitation to fantasize about the ultimate breach of societal norms. It is a theatrical approach whose origins may be traced back to the Victorians' predilection for asylum visits wherein one's desire to witness both the bizarre attributes of madness and its safe confinement could be satisfied.

While it seems clear that Alice Cooper exploited such beliefs to augment their own theatrical appeal, the act of dramatic performance equally served to expose the arguably damaging stereotypes in part responsible for the labelling and confinement of all 'mad' men and women. The band's innovative use of characterization has been well documented by writers such as Cagle who, while acknowledging the use of non-musical concepts by earlier bands, makes the important distinction that 'these bands did not take on theatrical roles as actors; group members did not "become" characters that they had created in their narratives. In an opposite manner, Cooper attempted to enact the roles of the characters he sang about; he

---

[57]     Szasz, *The Manufacture of Madness*, pp. 267–8.

[58]     Lillian Feder, *Madness in Literature* (Princeton and Guildford, 1980), p. 17.

[59]     Cooper, *The Death of the Family*, p. 101.

became the demented psychopath on stage.'[60] Cagle also points out that by 1972 both his fans and would-be castigators within the press were well aware of his actor status, and as such the band's potential threat to society was diminished for 'Cooper had done an excellent job of reinforcing the notion that he was a reflection of culture, not a threat to it'.[61]

In reference to the celebration of teen rebellion in songs such as 'School's Out' and 'I'm Eighteen', Cagle's observation is without doubt most relevant; however, for 'The Ballad of Dwight Fry', 'Inmates (We're All Crazy)' and 'The Quiet Room' it may be argued that the identification of role play is actually central to one's reading of the musical text as a critique of contemporary, and past, psychiatric practices and beliefs about madness. In fact, without the perceived distinction between reality and theatrical impersonation, one could speculate that, at best, the band would have received derision for exploiting the mental illness of their frontman, and at worse been without his continued contribution due to a certification of insanity. By drawing on past representations of madness within literature and film; mixing these with commonly understood notions of what constitutes 'mad' behaviour; and amplifying the end product, Alice Cooper not only expose such stereotypes for public scrutiny but also highlight the potential for society's misuse of psychiatric classification and care. If behaviour is deemed 'mad' simply because it fails to conform to the general consensus of normality, and the term 'psychiatric care' is simply a more palatable definition for the policing of society's deviants, then what better way to expose it than by acting out the part of a madman within a narrative full of overstated clichés?

Attempting to retrace the conscious intentions of Alice Cooper during the writing, recording and performance of the aforementioned songs is not the objective of this study; however, Cagle's description and assessment of the protagonist's resurrection during live shows offer further evidence to suggest that the use of characterization was a deliberate ploy to initiate questions concerning definitions of both sanity and madness. In the aftermath of Fry's electrocution 'Cooper tossed posters and dollar bills toward the audience and he watched triumphantly as they fought to grab these objects. This manifestation of "crowd psychosis" resulted in Cooper's resounding question: "Who is crazy? Them or me?"'[62] By spinning the voyeuristic lens 180 degrees, Alice Cooper demonstrate how easily one can find oneself engulfed within acts of apparent irrationality; the implication is that acts of greed and 'real' violence are far more threatening to society than the kind of behaviour exhibited by their invented protagonist. It is also worth noting that the same technique is utilized in Witkiewicz's play *The Madman and the Nun*, although here the notion of reversal is applied more literally as the matron and

---

[60] Cagle, pp. 125–6.

[61] Ibid., p. 126.

[62] Ibid., p. 122.

attendants responsible for maintaining Walpurg's confinement admit to being mad themselves and begin to beat each other.[63]

Cooper's simulated electrocution seemingly acts out what Szasz claims institutional psychiatry and modern totalitarian movements have in common in that:

> each represses certain individual and moral interests and, in general, sacrifices the 'one' for the 'many,' the 'I' for the 'we' [...] to strengthen group cohesion, each channels – by systematic propaganda accompanied by the brutal show of force – enmity towards a symbolic offender to whom the impending disintegration of the social order is attributed.[64]

In 'The Ballad of Dwight Fry' the protagonist ('I') is offered up to the audience ('We') as the 'symbolic offender'; his eventual execution and rebirth serves to unite the crowd in their own final act of madness as they applaud his antics and struggle to secure mementos of the show. While none of this is actually real, in the sense that both band and audience are acting out make-believe roles, the uncomfortable question of how closely such behaviour mirrors real life remains. It is for this reason that Alice Cooper cannot be dismissed as merely 'playing' with explicit themes such as madness, murder and electrocution for their shock value alone. Indeed, in the 'The Ballad of Dwight Fry' the band's exposure of frequently deceptive public beliefs relating to definitions of madness and its treatment reveals the considerable potential for the re-evaluation and revision of such by means of a popular idiom.

---

[63]    'In my declining years I cannot tell anymore who is mad – you or I [...] oh, my God, my God! Take pity on me. Perhaps I've already gone mad' (Sister Barbara); 'We're the madmen now. They've locked us up for good' (Alfred, the first attendant); 'He's the one – he's the worst madman. Hit him Fred! Give it to him! Harder! Till you can't lift your arm anymore!' (Paphnutius, the second attendant). Witkiewicz, p. 31.

[64]    Szasz, *The Manufacture of Madness*, p. 86.

# Chapter 5

# The Fool's Demise: Critiques of Social Exclusion Found in the Beatles' 'The Fool on the Hill' and Elton John's 'Madman Across the Water'

The fool is a multifaceted character who has inhabited our world in both real and fictional form for centuries. Regarded as 'a certain type of madfolk'[1] in medieval through to Elizabethan times, the fool was synonymous with the court jester – a real person in the employment of important, wealthy persons, whose role was not simply to provoke laughter but to offer critical opinion on a variety of matters. While their feigned stupidity provided a means of generating laughter, their conveyance of wisdom through shrewdness and wit allowed them to critique the supposedly rational schemes of everyday life. In this way, the fool is associated with the role of truth-sayer and, as Beatrice Otto observes: 'There is a plethora of proverbs and quotations testifying to the belief that a fool (and by extension a feigned fool) could be relied on to expose the folly of those purporting to be sane.'[2]

Otto's reference to a 'feigned' fool is interesting, for it points to her exploration of two related, yet distinct, fool identities: the 'natural' and the 'artificial'. The 'natural' fool was typically identified through having a reduced intellectual capacity and/or some form of physical abnormality, either or both of which served to classify them as Other. While typically pitied for being unable to comprehend and/or experience the full extent and complexities of social systems and relationships, this allowed them a certain freedom in which to speak basic truths – an ability that was often interpreted as evidence of a gift of special insight. Indeed there were some who believed in the possibility of the 'innocent' or 'natural' having divine connections: 'The fool as simpleton, the natural, was laughed at and whipped, but he was also held in awe as a potential mouthpiece for God.'[3] It is possible that R.D. Laing was influenced by such mythology when, in his 1967 work *The Politics of Experience*, he described the madman as 'the hierophant of the sacred'.[4]

---

[1] Roy Porter, *A Social History of Madness: Stories of the Insane* (London, 1996), p. 125.

[2] Beatrice K. Otto, *Fools Are Everywhere: The Court Jester Around the World* (Chicago and London, 2001), p. 103.

[3] Ibid., p. 33.

[4] Ronald D. Laing, *The Politics of Experience* [1967] (Harmondsworth, 1978), pp. 109–10.

Though reliant on the 'natural' fool identity as a basis for impersonation,[5] 'artificial' fools were generally characterized by their high level of intelligence which resulted in an ability to perceive the world in a way that was often concealed from so-called 'normal' men and women. There is not the same sense of unearthly mystery as with the 'natural', but a clear acknowledgement of their powers of perception with respect to exposing apparent 'truths'. The entertainment factor came in the form of verbal wit, with clever selection of words, word play and riddles to engage listeners and generate humour. In particular, there was a certain predilection for reversal, as Roy Porter notes: 'Jest-books, plays and paintings tell us much at one or more removes about such lords of misrule, temporarily licensed to wreak cultural havoc and spin the world upside down.'[6]

In this chapter I will explore the way in which the Beatles' fool differs in identity from that of Elton John's while demonstrating how both texts offer a critique of social exclusion and supposed 'normality' that is concomitant with much anti-psychiatric writing of the time. This will involve an examination of the difference in portrayal of character, setting (in terms of both historical and physical location), treatment and social interaction. In an attempt to explain the differences in portrayal with respect to the fools' treatment, I will draw on the work of Michel Foucault and especially his well-known work *Madness and Civilization*,[7] while the differences in terms of subject position will be related to a discussion of musical style and period.

'The Fool on the Hill' appeared on the Beatles' EP (extended play disc) *Magical Mystery Tour*[8] and was written and recorded in 1967. The song was originally composed by McCartney in March 1967 and it is *his* voice which appears on the final recording. Various writers have commented on the likely source of inspiration for the fool character: Ian MacDonald suggesting that the LSD-inspired rejuvenation of interest in western occultism meant that McCartney 'may have been thinking of The Fool in the Tarot pack',[9] while Alistair Taylor, a personal friend of McCartney, traces it to a particular real-life incident involving the sudden appearance and mysterious disappearance of a man on Primrose Hill.[10] Whatever its origin, some common conclusions have been drawn with respect

---

[5]     Otto refers to artificial fools 'donning the apparel of the natural'. Otto, p. 37.

[6]     Porter, *A Social History of Madness*, p. 125.

[7]     Michel Foucault, *Madness and Civilization: A History of Insanity in the Age of Reason*, trans. R. Howard (London, 1997). Originally published in French in 1961 as *Histoire de la Folie*; first published in Great Britain in 1967 by Tavistock Publications.

[8]     The Beatles, *Magical Mystery Tour* (Parlophone, 1967).

[9]     Ian MacDonald, *Revolution in the Head: The Beatles' Records and the Sixties* (London, 1994), p. 218.

[10]    Alistair Taylor, *Yesterday: The Beatles Remembered* (London: Pan Macmillan, 1988). Sourced from Steve Turner, *A Hard Day's Write: The Stories Behind Every Beatles Song* (London, 2006), p. 143.

to suggested interpretations of the song's meaning, these being largely based on themes of detachment and innocence.

Before examining these themes in detail, it is worth noting the significance of the chosen subject position in relation to the period in which the song was written. McCartney's decision to relay the narrative of events from a third person perspective means that he does not 'play' the part of the fool himself. Rather, he adopts the neutral position of observer – a stance that had proved effective in earlier songs such as 'Eleanor Rigby' (1966), 'Penny Lane' (1967) and 'She's Leaving Home' (1967).[11] While love songs in the first person remained standard fare in 1967, the personae inhabited were ultimately believable because they confronted situations common to most ordinary people. In contrast to this, personae that could be classed as unusual in a potentially threatening or negative way were rarely encountered. Instead, they would be described from a safe distance – one in which the singer was able to occupy the, usually attractive, position of judicious observer. This is not to suggest such songs are necessarily weak in their ability to provide some form of social critique, more that the modes of both conception and reception were not yet sufficiently developed in the late 1960s to allow for the recognition of subversive theatrical role play. Philip Auslander's observation regarding the mutable relationship between the performer's real self and their inhabited persona is relevant here: 'The ideology of sixties rock insisted that the musician's performing persona and real self be presented and perceived as identical – it had to be possible to see the musician's songs and performances as authentic manifestations of his or her individuality.'[12] With this in mind, McCartney's third person perspective is clearly understandable, for 'playing' the fool may simply have been dismissed by contemporary audiences as inauthentic or, worse still, may have risked imbuing McCartney's own star persona with the undesirable associations of madness.

The listener then never hears the voice of the fool, but perceives his character type through the singer's description (verbal and melodic) and accompanying musical gestures. The song's opening promotes feelings of simplicity and innocence while establishing the fool's constant yet detached presence. The one-

---

[11]     'Eleanor Rigby' appears on the 1966 album *Revolver* and is credited to both Lennon and McCartney. McCartney is generally acknowledged as the originator of the first verse: see MacDonald, *Revolution in the Head*, p. 162. 'Penny Lane' was released as an A-side single alongside 'Strawberry Fields Forever' in February 1967 and is credited to both Lennon and McCartney. Both writers contributed to the lyric but, according to MacDonald, it was McCartney 'who went on to set it to music'. MacDonald, p. 177. 'She's Leaving Home' appears on the 1967 album *Sgt. Pepper's Lonely Hearts Club Band* (Parlophone, 1967) and is credited to Lennon and McCartney. According to MacDonald, 'Its succinct and compassionately observed lyric is McCartney's except for Lennon's lines in the chorus.' MacDonald, p. 195.

[12]     Philip Auslander, *Performing Glam Rock: Gender and Theatricality in Popular Music* (Ann Arbor, MI, 2006), p. 66.

bar introduction, involving repeated crotchets on piano with two sustained flutes emphasizing the 3rd and 5th of a D major triad, anticipates the vocal's similar use of repeated harmony tones to underpin the words 'day after day' and 'perfectly still'. The one-bar alternation of chords I and ii (D and Em7/D) during the first four bars of the verse fails to impose a clear sense of direction despite the fluent quaver articulation. As such, these gestures impart a feeling of stasis and eternity that immediately distances the fool from everyday experience. The fool, we are told, remains 'alone on a hill' – the gradual ascent in pitch serving as a metaphor for his lofty position while the concentration on harmony tones, acoustic timbres, unaffected vocal tone, first-beat emphasis and accompanying sustained flute gesture impart feelings of ease and innocence. References to the fool's 'foolish grin' and perpetual immobility suggest an unnaturalness that is born out of their lack of apparent cause.

The second half of the first verse is marked by an increase in harmonic rhythm (to two chords per bar)[13] and use of a functional ii–V–I progression (Em, A, D) which results in a strengthening of direction to support the move away from purely describing the fool and his location to detailing the way in which he is perceived by others. The shift is prepared via a counter-melodic lead-in on flute, and the sense of progression is further enhanced by subtle developments in the instrumental arrangement (added bass notes in the piano, continuation of flute counter-melody and harmonica crescendos). The predictable nature of the ii–V–I harmonic movement lends an air of naturalness to the lyric 'but nobody wants to know him, they can see that he's just a' (fool) – the inference being that their instinctive conclusion and consequential disregard of him is precisely right – while the denial of extended closure on chord I is also significant as the minor chord vi follows to accompany the word 'fool'. Melodically, the word 'nobody' is given emphasis through its irregular triplet rhythm, and a high-pitched 6–5 appoggiatura serves to accentuate the words 'know him'. The fool's unremitting silence is conveyed through the lack of melodic resolution (notes E–F♯ over an A7 chord), the ascending pitch and unresolved 6th degree metaphorically endorsing the phrase 'he never gives an answer'. In terms of the accompanying instrumental arrangement, the addition of harmonica and its conspicuous minim crescendos contrasts with the previous evenness of tone and timbre and hints at the subsequent change of mood about to occur in the refrain.

Arriving earlier than expected, the refrain is placed in dialectical opposition to the verses through an unexpected modulation to tonic minor. The final two chords of the verse (Em7, A7) suggest a predictable cadence (ii–V–I) onto tonic major (D major) which would adhere to the conventional structure of an eight-bar

---

[13]        McCartney's skill as a songwriter is evident when one considers his attention to varying the harmonic rhythm. The song 'Yesterday', for example, utilizes a move to crotchet chord movement to enhance the poignancy of the lyric 'had to go, I don't know'. The effect of this contrast is heightened by the fact that it follows minim chord movement and the use of sustained anticipation in the melody line to underpin the question: 'why, she'.

verse. However, the move to tonic minor and lack of melodic closure – the leading phrase 'but the fool' suggesting a turn of events – instead mark the beginning of the refrain, and effectively undermine the straightforward simplicity and certainty of the previous passage. Indeed, the refrain's lyric and musical gestures work to suggest that the summation of the 'fool' offered in verse one is both misleading and inadequate: the 'fool', in fact, possesses special powers of perception – an ability to use the 'eyes in his head' to 'see the world spinning round'.

Several musical features enable the listener to interpret the refrain section as an initial point of revelation as opposed to a lament on the fool's detached existence. Initially, the move to D natural minor (Aeolian mode) and concentration on the minor 6th degree (B♭) lend a melancholy feel that is accentuated through the melodic word painting for the lyric 'sun going down' (a descending phrase using a triplet rhythm for the words 'going down' that implies both the setting of the sun and a consequential slowing in momentum). The sense of possible stagnation is also suggested through the two flutes' repeated semibreves and the relatively weak harmonic progression utilizing chords Dm, Gm 2nd inversion, B♭ 1st inversion (i, ivc, VIb). The addition of snare rattle (perhaps resulting from the use of brushes on the skin) and delicate finger cymbals adds an unusual element to the timbral mix which imparts an air of mystery. Out of this, however, comes an awakening, a move back to the tonic major that shrewdly asserts the fool's hidden depths. The ascending Aeolian chord movement from the previously mentioned B♭ 1st inversion through C7 to Dm (VIb, VII, i) produces a point of closure which is extended through the sounding of the tonic major chord in the following bar. This is the exact point of revelation, and appears as a responding affirmation to the vocal's intimation regarding the fool's unique powers: 'the eyes in his head see the world spinning round'.

The repeated ascending melodic figures lend thematic unity to the refrain and also stress the words 'but the fool', 'sees the sun', 'and the eyes' and 'see the world'. As well as drawing attention to the fool's powers of sight, the gestures push into subsequent bars, aiding momentum and building a sense of anticipation for the eventual awakening. The melody actually ends before the 'revelation' tonic major chord and achieves closure through the use of a suspended E which skips up to the note F before resolving downwards from E to D, the suddenness of the embellishment serving to underline the word 'spinning'. The brightness of the responding 'revelation' tonic major chord is actually enhanced through major 3rd to tonic crotchet movement in the first flute and bouncy, staccato, arpeggiated quavers in the second flute. This sudden activity produces an audible contrast to the previous semibreves and is thus liberatory in effect.

From the above analysis it would appear that the Beatles' fool displays the majority of characteristics necessary for him to be identified as a 'natural', a child of nature: simplicity, innocence, special powers of insight and a certain detachment from everyday experience. Both MacDonald and Terence J. O'Grady's descriptions of 'The Fool on the Hill' concur with the presence of such features: O'Grady claiming that the song 'celebrates the wisdom of innocence',[14] while MacDonald refers to 'its air of childlike unworldliness'.[15] Taking the first three characteristics (simplicity, innocence and powers of insight), it is clear that the song draws on what Porter terms 'the belief in the wisdom of fools [which was] passed down through the tradition of the Court jester'.[16] Indeed, it offers a combination of features best summed up by Cecil Collins in his work *The Vision of the Fool* (1981): 'I believe that there is in life, and in the human psyche, a certain quality, an inviolate eternal innocence, and this quality I call the Fool. It is a continuous wisdom […] It is the joy of the original Adam in men.'[17]

The proposed link between madness (be it identified in terms of the fool or the schizophrenic) and uncommon insight may be found in the work of R.D. Laing and David Cooper, both of whom stressed the need to return to a simpler and more truthful form of existence. For Cooper, madness itself is 'a tentative vision of a new and truer world',[18] while the very identification of so-called mental *disease* was regarded as evidence for the denial of intense personal reflection: 'We choose to conjure up this disease in order to evade a certain moment of our own existence – the moment of disturbance, of penetrating vision into the depths of ourselves, that we prefer to externalize into others.'[19] The notion of madness enabling a deeper understanding of the inner world was similarly expounded by Laing in his work *The Politics of Experience* – 'schizophrenics have more to teach psychiatrists about the inner world than psychiatrists their patients'[20] – and may be directly related to the lyric 'eyes in his head see the world spinning round'. The suggestion is that of internal insight and a more profound level of consciousness, one that enables a reading of the world unhindered by external disruptions. But, as Laing identified, such powers are rarely valued, for engagement with one's inner world ultimately results in disconnection from one's outer (social) relationships; and herein lies the threat of recrimination: 'Immersion in inner space and time tends to be regarded as anti-social withdrawal, a deviancy, invalid, pathological *per se*, in some sense discreditable.'[21]

---

[14]     Terence J. O'Grady, *The Beatles: A Musical Evolution* (Boston, MA, 1983), p. 144.

[15]     MacDonald, p. 218.

[16]     Porter, *A Social History of Madness*, p. 130.

[17]     Cecil Collins, *The Vision of the Fool* (Chipping Norton: Kedros, 1981). Quoted in Otto, p. 232.

[18]     David Cooper, *The Death of the Family* (London, 1971), p. 85. In the same work, Cooper examines the notion of truth in more detail, concluding that: 'Truth is an unspeakable madness. Truth is a lethal awakening', p. 141.

[19]     Cooper, from his introduction in Foucault, *Madness and Civilization*, p viii.

[20]     Laing, *The Politics of Experience*, p. 91.

[21]     Ibid., p. 103. In the same work, Laing elaborates further on the issue of detachment, describing the madman as 'An exile from the scene of being as we know it, he is an alien, a stranger', p. 110.

The detached existence of the fool is, in part, what allows him his special powers of insight. It permits critical distance to be established between him and all he observes. And yet this very characteristic leads to a potential diagnosis of mental abnormality, as Ian Inglis demonstrates when he concludes that 'The Fool on The Hill' – together with four other Beatles' songs ('I'm Only Sleeping', 'She Said She Said', 'I'm So Tired' and 'Mean Mr Mustard') – provides a representation of schizophrenia: 'The Fool on the Hill' being one of three that 'are narratives, which tell of a third party, whose behaviour is typified by the perceptual difficulties, thought disorders and emotional disturbances associated with the illness'.[22] With specific regard to the Beatles' fool, Inglis notes that he is 'characterised by his remoteness and indifference towards life',[23] and may also be considered an *idiot savant* – a term which contains similar associations to those of the 'natural' because such persons simply 'know' things, as opposed to having to learn them. Lee Warren's definition of the idiot savant is useful here:

> The word idiot usually refers to a simpleton, in contrast to the word 'savant' in French that means 'learned one.' [...] Now the irony of an idiot-savant is that this group of individuals does not acquire knowledge by learning as the average human does. They mysteriously 'know' explicit, exact, correct information. One may wonder: 'How do idiots savants know certain information or possess certain skills?' By whatever means they obtain this information, they undermine current definitions about intelligence.[24]

It is this undermining of normality that ascribes them their mystical associations while at the same time highlighting their Otherness.[25]

Inglis's interpretation of the Beatles' fool identity is especially persuasive when considered alongside contemporary writers' observations concerning artists' knowledge of schizophrenia. Jeff Nuttall, in his work *Bomb Culture* (1968), wrote that 'schizophrenia was ill-defined. At best it meant, means, someone who was isolated and therefore not adjusted to the patterns of society. The language was anyway familiar to artists.'[26] It is possible, therefore, that regardless of whether or

---

[22]   Annette Hames and Ian Inglis, 'And I Will Lose My Mind ... Images of Mental Illness in the Songs of the Beatles', *International Review of the Aesthetics and Sociology of Music (IRASM)*, 30/2 (1999): 173–88, p. 180.

[23]   Ibid.

[24]   Lee E. Warren, 'The Power Latent in Man: Idiot Savant', PLIM Report (November/December 1996), retrieved 9 December 2007 from http://www.plim.org/2idiots.html.

[25]   Steve Turner offers a similar interpretation of the Beatles' fool: 'The song was about an idiot savant, a person everyone considers to be a fool but who is actually a misunderstood visionary. Paul was thinking of gurus like Maharishi Mahesh Yogi who were often derided and an Italian hermit he once read about who emerged from a cave in the late 1940s to discover that he'd missed the entire second world war.' Turner, p. 143.

[26]   Jeff Nuttall, *Bomb Culture* [1968] (London, 1970), p. 108.

not the Beatles intended such associations, listeners may nevertheless have drawn similar conclusions, linking the aloof and mysterious qualities of the fool with the general fascination with madness, and more specifically schizophrenia, at that time.

While accepting the aforementioned, early seventies rock arguably gave rise to the 'natural' fool being surpassed by something altogether more synthetic and potentially challenging: the artificial fool capable of passing judgement on a society seeking to contain such critical insight. Elton John's *Madman Across the Water*[27] was released in November 1971 and, like other songs on the album, the title track features lyrics by Bernie Taupin and an instrumental arrangement by Paul Buckmaster. The album received mixed reviews upon its release – according to biographers Claude Bernardin and Tom Stanton the negative press was 'partly because it marked Elton's fifth release in eighteen months'[28] – but despite this, it continued to sell well 'due to interest generated by "Tiny Dancer," "Levon" and the title track'.[29] As with 'The Fool on the Hill', attempts to identify the likely source of inspiration for the lyric content have been acknowledged by various writers, the most common relating to Taupin's denial that the madman protagonist was based on Richard Nixon[30] (a highly unlikely proposition when one considers the lyrical and musical texts in any depth).

Unlike McCartney's third person perspective for 'The Fool on the Hill', in 'Madman Across the Water' Elton John *plays* the part of his protagonist, the identified 'Madman', and, in so doing, offers first-hand evidence of personal thoughts relating to his location, treatment and social relationships. Unsurprisingly then, John's vocal delivery is far more varied in tone and dynamic than McCartney's as he expresses the extreme emotions of his 'mad' protagonist (involving sudden shifts from self-pity to extreme anger) and inhabits the voices of the protagonist's relations. It is this characteristic which, despite John's bluesy vocal embellishments and evident natural musicality, adds a palpable sense of theatricality to the song; and, again, Auslander's theory concerning the difference in performance personae between 1960s counter-cultural rock and 1970s glam rock is of value here: 'By insisting that the figure performing the music was fabricated from makeup, costume, and pose, all of which were subject to change at any moment, glam rockers insisted on the constructedness of their performing identities and implicitly denied their authenticity.'[31] With this in mind, it is important to recognize that this 'constructedness' was also firmly rooted within the music itself, as evidenced by not only the varied vocal delivery but also the

---

[27]     Elton John, *Madman Across the Water* (DJM Records, 1971).

[28]     Claude Bernardin and Tom Stanton, *Rocket Man: Elton John from A–Z* (Westport, CT, 1996), p. 120.

[29]     Ibid., p. 120. In fact, Bernardin and Stanton rate this particular album as 'the quintessential Elton John piano album', p. 121.

[30]     Ibid., p. 184.

[31]     Auslander, p. 66.

complex forms of the songs involving multiple and markedly contrasting sections. While Auslander utilizes the more obvious glam figures of David Bowie and Marc Bolan to illustrate his arguments, songs such as 'Madman Across the Water' derive from the same performance and compositional ethos.

The song begins with a repeated one-bar acoustic guitar riff (doubled by piano from bar three) which lends a sense of intimacy but also trepidation as a reverse reverb effect is added to the right channel (the reverse effect produces a crescendo in dynamic onto beat two where a dotted quaver note results in a perceived stoppage in fluidity before the ensuing semiquavers of beat three). Harmonics also feature on the last semiquaver of beat three and last quaver of beat four to suggest a lack of grounding which is enhanced by means of the riff's undulating pitch contour. The four-bar introduction thus demonstrates careful attention to atmospheric detail, a feature not characteristic of other songs on the album.

The vocal melody in verse one makes expressive use of non-harmony tones and melismas, but primarily emphasizes harmony tones to impart feelings of sincerity and honesty concerning the protagonist's claims to 'see' and 'know' 'very well'. The use of an anacrusis[32] for the first two phrases suggests an eagerness to convey the lyric's message; the fact that the beginnings and ends of phrases fail to conform to the strictness of bar lines also serves to enhance the aforementioned sense of being natural/genuine (that is, not contrived). The delicacy of the accompanying arrangement helps to solicit feelings of compassion towards the protagonist, the bass providing a sensitive counter melody in its high register while the guitar and piano gently articulate the harmony in crotchets. The explanation of what the protagonist can see – 'There's a boat on the reef with a broken back' – is given emotional impact as the vocal soars up an octave from its previously confined position to an upper auxiliary note (being the 6th) for the word 'reef', before employing a 9-8 suspension to emphasize the word 'broken'. The harmony is also significant here: having helped to convey the rather melancholic tone of the song's opening through the use of Aeolian mode – chords i, i7d, VI, IIIb (Am, Am/G, F, C/E) – there follows a sudden shift to the ascending melodic minor to provide a major chord IVb (D/F♯) which adds further emphasis to the words 'broken back'. The change in harmonic language also offers the possibility of progress but this is effectively denied by an immediate return to the confined, Aeolian identity of the first half of the verse wherein the protagonist offers a final reiteration of his ability to 'see', supported by unison ascending movement in the accompanying instruments (chords F, G, Am). Despite this return, the song maintains an air of unpredictability: a change of metre to $\frac{3}{4}$ meaning the final beat of the vocal phrase concludes over the seemingly premature return of the introductory guitar riff whose rise and fall of pitch appears to allude more strongly now to the song's numerous references to water.

---

[32]     An anacrusis is a note or notes (often referred to as a pickup) preceding the first downbeat.

The second verse continues to reinforce the suggested insight of the protagonist as he speaks of a joke he knows and once imparted. A descending, lower-register bass and the addition of kit help to maintain the strength of direction, while the melodic repetition works to stress the words 'joke', 'know it' and 'very well', breeding a sense of familiarity. The joke itself is apparently old, having been told 'long ago' – a fact that is subtly underpinned by a delayed resolution of the previously used 9-8 suspension. Unlike verse one, the change in metre to $\frac{3}{4}$ is now replaced by two bars of $\frac{2}{4}$ and this, along with repeated use of high-register and fast-paced vocal, results in a distinct change in mood. In particular, the way in which verse two concludes appears somewhat erratic, and less measured than previous phrases; the vocal itself becomes more accented and hence seemingly aggressive in its delivery; and the musical tension at this point in the song is also heightened through ascending, unison movement in the accompaniment. The subsequent return to $\frac{4}{4}$ is again relatively unexpected, but this time there is no melodic resolution as the vocal stresses the minor 7th before closing on the 4th. Given the previous conveyance of sincerity and encouragement of empathy, such gestures imbue the final phrase 'take my word I'm a madman don't you know?' with a distinct lack of authenticity and a palpable feeling of sarcasm, even anger.

While the first two verses establish themes of insight and mystery, and set the seeds for a possible questioning of the labelling process (who is mad/sane), it is not until the third verse that the protagonist actually identifies himself with the character of the fool. The first vocal phrase is soft yet clearly audible and follows the same pattern as previous verses: 'Once a fool had a good part in a play'; but it is the ensuing question – 'If it's so would I still be here today?' – that is especially poignant. The arch phrase shape again lends these words a certain prominence, and the use of major chord IV augments the questioning feel, encouraging listeners to ponder the relevance of the protagonist's differing circumstances. The reference to plays is suggestive of Shakespeare's employment of the fool character, but the notion of a fool inhabiting a 'good part in the play' possibly pre-dates this, as Otto points out:

> Perhaps the first signs of a jester in English drama were in some of the Vice characters, such as Fancy and Folly in John Skelton's *Magnificence* (1515). Folly carries a jester's bauble and can be dressed in motley and mistaken for the fool of the play, whereas in fact it is he who makes fools of the others. Like the stage jester, the Vice character was a favourite with the audience, and the part was often played by the best actor in the troupe.[33]

The better-known fools of Shakespeare's plays – Touchstone in *As You Like It* (1599), Feste in *Twelfth Night* (1602) and *King Lear*'s Fool (1606) – all exhibit attractive qualities that constitute a positive response to the parts in question. With particular reference to the Fool in *King Lear*, Derek Russell Davis writes: 'He

---

[33]     Otto, p. 205.

represents sanity, insight and self-criticism – the antithesis of the King's madness […] His is the cause of the stupid against the clever, the weak against the strong.'[34] In 'Madman Across the Water', the comparison with such literary fools provides a means to pinpoint the protagonist's identity while implying a less favourable situation, a part no one would voluntarily play or wish to applaud.

The avoidance of literal repetition on the repeats of verses is a testament to John's skilful manipulation of melodic construction, and once again the verse ending is extended in a way that suggests building frustration. The protagonist comments on the strangeness of the reactions he receives from others, in particular the way in which they find him amusing while at the same time using his humorous behaviour as evidence of insanity. The vocal is noticeably animated at this point, entering on the second semiquaver of beat two and utilizing semiquaver rhythms to ascend a minor 7th interval from its starting point. In addition, the kit engages in some vigorous embellishment, filling all available space between the vocal utterances to achieve a seemingly claustrophobic feel. This marks an important moment in the song's progression as its subdued, ballad-style opening is overtaken by the more powerful, rousing and unpredictable feel characteristic of much theatre rock. The change of metre to $\frac{2}{4}$, forceful vocal delivery, off-beat start and fast rhythmic pace convey a frantic feel, while the suggested strangeness ('It's quite peculiar in a funny sort of way') is expressed through the emphasis on the major 6th (note E above the G chord) and minor 7th (note G above the Am chord). An immediate repetition of phrase then cements the sense of frustration for the concluding line – 'They think it's very funny everything I say' – the end of which utilizes a vocal fall in pitch redolent with weariness.

From the above analysis, it is possible to conclude that John's protagonist is an artificial[35] or knowing fool who bears witness to his own powers of insight, referring to a boat on a reef with a broken back ('I can see it very well') as an unexplained euphemism for impending doom. With the reference to the joke he told long ago comes the suggestion of age-old wisdom, and he uses sarcasm as a means of drawing attention to the labelling process he has been subjected to ('Take my word I'm a madman don't you know?), effectively daring the listener to see him differently. Such questioning of apparent truths was, according to Auslander, a recognized characteristic of seventies glam rock which 'mounted an assault on the

---

[34]     Derek R. Davis, *Scenes of Madness: A Psychiatrist at the Theatre* (London, 1995), p. 159.

[35]     Otto's description of the need to pass an Act to contain the number of artificial fools in fifteenth-century Scotland provides evidence to illustrate the general belief that foolishness gave one permission to speak truthfully: 'The feigning of folly could be a profitable business, and in fifteenth-century Scotland there was such a proliferation of artificial fools that the Act for the Away-Putting of Feynet Fools was passed on 19 January 1449, meting out such gentle punishments as ear nailing and amputation to those who tried to pass themselves off in court as genuine fools.' Otto, p. 36.

whole idea of the "natural" so dear to the counterculture'.[36] Through its emphasis on theatricality, glam possessed the ability to challenge notions of normative behaviour, suggesting instead that all social identifications are constructs. The particular challenge proffered in 'Madman Across the Water' appears to align with such an approach, and parallels may be identified between its encouragement to question society-driven labels and the anti-psychiatry theories of Thomas Szasz, who, in the same year that John's song was released, wrote:

> Most people who are considered mentally sick (especially those confined involuntarily) are so defined by their relatives, friends, employers, or perhaps the police – not by themselves. These people have upset the social order – by disregarding the conventions of polite society or by violating laws – so we label them 'mentally ill' and punish them by commitment to a mental institution.[37]

The dramatic potential of the song is furthered during the transitional bridge where John adopts the voices of others, the language used and form of address appearing to suggest parental figures talking among themselves about their allegedly insane son:[38] 'Get a load of him he's so insane, you better get your coat dear it looks like rain.' The melody moves from harmony tones (3rd and 5th) onto the 9th for the word 'him', as if pointing an accusatory finger to identify the outsider. Emphasis is also given to the word 'insane', which has a markedly long rhythmic duration[39] and is embellished through the use of a musical turn that effectively conveys the notion of instability (see Example 5.1). The vocal delivery for the subsequent phrase then becomes more staccato, the rhythmic construction noticeably detached; an octave leap in the melody between the words 'coat' and 'dear' is especially melodramatic; and the pronunciation of the word 'dear' (dee-ah) sounds unequivocally posh, losing the relaxed American accent previously adopted. Such features lack the sensitive expression found within the melodic gestures of the verse sections and appear to suggest a sense of unfeeling indifference, even emotional detachment. The move away from first person is underpinned by a shift in harmonic content as the phrase begins on the relative major chord (C) before coming to rest on the dominant chord (E) of A melodic minor. While such gestures have the possibility to connote increased strength and the promise of closure, here they simply serve to detail the different circumstances, and perhaps social status, of the characters – a fact that is evident from the final three chords accompanying the words 'looks like

---

36    Auslander, p. 67.

37    Thomas Szasz, *Ideology and Insanity: Essays on the Psychiatric Dehumanization of Man* [1970] (London, 1973), p. 84.

38    The song's use of parental voices is similar to that found in the Beatles' 'She's Leaving Home', although the sentiment expressed lacks the same sense of anguish.

39    The harmony at this point pauses for the first time on chord V as if to support the sense of examination, thereby encouraging listeners to ponder the significance and accuracy of the vocal statement.

rain'. At this point, instead of the usual conclusion employing chords F, G Am (all verse sections end in this manner), the harmonic phrase comes to rest on the tonic major, implying that the other characters do not share the protagonist's plight; their context is, in fact, the absolute antithesis of his own.

Example 5.1 'Madman Across the Water' transitional bridge (vocal)

The listener is made to wait until the two-part chorus before discovering the full extent of the protagonist's plight. Low-pitched, arco strings enter alongside an ominous, resonating bass sound to mark the beginning of this sectional change. The subject position remains that of the other characters, their presumed identity as the protagonist's parents becoming stronger as two voices in harmony deliver the lines: 'We'll come again next Thursday afternoon, the in-laws hope they'll see you very soon.' The unstoppable and menacing routine of the visits is imaginatively brought to life through the compelling nature of the accompanying musical gestures as percussion (sounding like the horse's hooves effect of two coconut halves being hit together), busy quaver movement in piano and heavily accented rising and falling string phrases introduce a feeling of increased drive. The apparent sense of tension is enhanced through the harmonic uncertainty surrounding the 6th degree of the A minor scale as the phrase begins by progressing to the brighter major IV chord of the ascending melodic minor (moving from chord IIIb C/E to chord IVb D/F♯) before returning to the VI–VII–i (F, G, Am) progression of Aeolian: the, by now, characteristic musical signature of the protagonist's sorrow.

Unlike the protagonist's phrases, which enter gently via the preparatory device of an anacrusis, the visitor's phrases begin on the second semiquaver of beat one, producing an interrupted effect akin to a musical backlash against the accompanying sound sources. The repeated semiquavers, the first three on the same pitch, appear suggestive of the insistence to return ('We'll come again'), while accented non-harmony tones (4–5 appoggiatura over the D chord; the 7th above the F chord; and 6th above the G chord) add to the uneasy atmosphere before allowing a moment of pause on the 5th of Am (see Example 5.2). The pause itself is significant as melodic, harmonic and rhythmic activity ceases for an entire bar, ensuring the effectiveness of the following repeat of phrase which functions as a last musical metaphor for the parent's imminent revisit. Like the second half of the transitional bridge, the vocal delivery here lacks emotion, with no embellishments or melismas, and the vocal tone has a harder edge, once again marking it as distinct from that of the protagonist.

Example 5.2 'Madman Across the Water' two-part chorus (vocal)

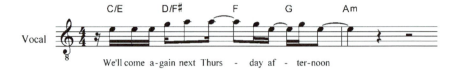

Part two of the chorus introduces a noticeably lighter texture – sustained, warm strings and piano in a higher tessitura – indicative of a further change of scene. An Fmaj7 chord highlights the reinstatement of the protagonist's speaking voice; and the vocal becomes softer in both tone and dynamic as it appears to seek an empathetic response to the beginning of a question: 'Is it in your conscience that you're after' (the use of melisma and downward pitch inflection on the last word signifying a return to the more emotive delivery of before). The sense of calm is, however, short-lived as a sudden unison ascending quaver phrase in the accompaniment finishes abruptly to ensure maximum impact for the protagonist's angry end of phrase: 'another glimpse of the madman across the water?' The vocal at this point is loud and powerful and involves an unexpected, shouted leap up a minor 6th, the surprise effect of which is enhanced via the re-use of off-beat semiquaver rhythm witnessed in the first half of the chorus. The word 'madman' is again marked as Other through the use of non-harmony tones E (7th) and D (6th) over an F chord, and the eventual melodic closure on the word 'water' is subverted through a dramatic fall in pitch and reverb effect. At this point, during mixing, the original vocal track would have been brought down while the reverb return was brought up, increasing the send to the reverb to ensure it sounds thicker and more continuous. The resulting sound effect conjures up the impression that the protagonist is falling away only to return in the form of an echo (no longer whole), and this underlines his apparent place of isolation.

Having established the differing character types of the fool inherent in each song, it is useful to explore the way in which their particular settings suggest certain historical contexts and how these, in turn, shape the kind of social critique offered. As stated previously, 'The Fool on the Hill' draws on the natural fool identity and, as the fool himself is not incarcerated, appears to suggest a historical setting before what Michel Foucault terms 'the great confinement'[40] of the seventeenth century. The fact that the fool occupies a vantage point from which to observe the world is in keeping with the suggestion of his uncommon powers of (in)sight. Being motionless on a hill also implies that his solitary existence is chosen and not inflicted; the physical barrier (the hill) is a natural one as opposed to a systematic, artificial one (such as an asylum or hospital). The song's setting demonstrates a certain affinity then with the existence of madmen in the fifteenth century described by Foucault as leading an 'easy, wandering existence'. Admittedly,

---

[40]     Foucault, p. 38.

the townspeople would be likely to drive them away but they were permitted to 'wander in the open countryside, when not entrusted to a group of merchants and pilgrims'.[41] Most important to Foucault's conceptualization of this period is his assertion that a dialogue exists between unreason and reason where 'madness is an undifferentiated experience, a not yet divided experience of division itself'[42] and that, while madmen may have been imprisoned in certain cities, madness was not yet defined as a mental illness and, as such, no treatment was insisted on.[43]

Foucault also identifies the proliferation of characteristics integral to the fool identity observed in 'The Fool on the Hill', in particular the notion of fool as truth-sayer, detailing how towards the end of the Middle Ages:

> In farces and *soties*, the character of the Madman, the Fool, or the Simpleton assumes more and more prominence [...] If folly leads each man into blindness where he is lost, the madman, on the contrary, reminds each man of his truth [...] he utters, in his simpleton's language which makes no show of reason, the words of reason.[44]

In speaking of wisdom, Foucault offers a further observation concerning the fool's uncommon knowledge – one which bears an affinity with Laing's belief in the schizophrenic's understanding of the inner world:

> This knowledge, so inaccessible, so formidable, the Fool, in his innocent idiocy already possesses. While the man of reason and wisdom perceives only fragmentary and all the more unnerving images of it, the Fool bears it intact as an unbroken sphere: that crystal ball which for all others is empty is in *his* eyes filled with the density of an invisible knowledge.[45]

Moreover, there is an affinity here in terms of language – the Beatles' lyric 'eyes in his head see the world spinning round' becoming more obviously associated with Foucault's description of the fool's 'eyes filled with the density of an invisible knowledge'.[46]

But the historical context is not quite so simple to pinpoint, for there is a particular problem with citing the Beatles' song so neatly within Foucault's pre-

---

[41]    Ibid., p. 8.

[42]    Ibid., p. xi.

[43]    Foucault cites the example of cities like Nuremberg which 'contained great numbers of madmen – many more, in any case, than could have been furnished by the city itself. These madmen were housed and provided for in the city budget, and yet they were not given treatment; they were simply thrown into prison.' Ibid., pp. 9–10.

[44]    Ibid., p. 14.

[45]    Ibid., p. 22.

[46]    Ibid.

seventeenth-century utopia.[47] The difficulty lies in the actual lack of dialogue that takes place between the fool (representative of so-called madness/unreason) and others (representative of sanity/reason). Each verse provides observations concerning other people's attitudes towards the fool and the fool's response (or non-response) to such, building up to an eventual point of reversal and revelation in verse four.

The progression (in terms of lyric) is as follows:

1. The first verse establishes other people's disinterest in establishing any kind of social contact with the fool but also asserts that the fool's isolation is not solely informed by others, for it is also his choice to remain silent: 'nobody wants to know him, they can see he's just a fool / and he never gives an answer'.

2. The second verse reveals how the fool is impervious to people's attitudes towards him – not caring if they listen or not, making sounds but not for the purpose of communicating with others: 'nobody ever hears him, or the sound he appears to make / and he never seems to notice'.

3. Verse three details people's false assumptions/suspicions of the fool – they can tell what he wants to do despite never hearing him – and this mistrust leads to dislike. The fool's detachment is again reiterated as his emotions are never displayed externally, which in turn allows others to justify their disaffection for him: 'nobody seems to like him, they can tell what he wants to do / and he never shows his feelings'.

4. In verse four a clever point of reversal is revealed. This time, the fool's response/thoughts are described first, the only time the listener is given any information regarding his opinion and the revelation that he *knows* (not sees or tells) that the others are the fools (hence his disinterest in their view of *him*). This revelation is followed by the apparently banal repetition of 'they don't like him', which again demonstrates the reasoning (or lack of it) for the fool's social exclusion – he's just a fool who they don't hear: 'and he never listens to them, he knows that they're the fool / they don't like him'.

---

[47]    It is worth noting that Foucault's work has received a number of criticisms in relation to the historical observations it contains. The very suggestion of an earlier age when it was possible for madness and reason to engage in amiable dialogue is criticized by certain writers: see, for example, Peter Sedgwick, *Psycho Politics: Laing, Foucault, Goffman, Szasz, and the Future of Mass Psychiatry* (New York, 1982). Kathleen Jones claims that Foucault 'exerted a massive influence on sociological thought through an analysis deliberately based on emotive images rather than on logical argument', and she cites his reference to the Ship of Fools as one such example. Kathleen Jones, *Asylums and After: A Revised History of the Mental Health Services: From the Early 18th Century to the 1990s* (London, 1993), pp. 170–75.

The relative freedom afforded the Beatles' fool, yet distinct lack of dialogue between supposed reason and unreason, means the song fails to align with Foucault's own version of history surrounding the eventual conceptualization of madness as a medical illness. The two themes actually combine Foucault's suggested tolerance of madmen pre-seventeenth century with his attested silencing of them that occurred with the advent of asylums. Given Foucault's observations concerning developments within the world of art, literature and philosophy that predicate a shift towards the literal confinement of unreason, one could argue that the Beatles' song is perhaps suggestive of a point in history which Foucault would no doubt view as pivotal – the end of the Renaissance, a period in which he asserts madness 'comes to the fore' only to be 'tamed':

> The Middle Ages had given madness a place in the hierarchy of vices [...] In the Renaissance, Madness leaves this modest place and comes to the fore [...] By a strange act of force, the classical age was to reduce to silence the madness whose voices the Renaissance had just liberated, but whose violence it had already tamed.[48]

And yet, such an argument is undermined by the primary reason Foucault gives for the effective silencing of madness – that the medicalization of madness was born out of the act of confinement itself: 'the science of mental disease, as it would develop in the asylum, would always be only of the order of observation and classification. It would not be a dialogue.'[49] And thus one may conclude that, while drawing on themes central to Foucault's work, 'The Fool on the Hill' is set in a fictional age, a time where dialogue had already ceased despite the relative (physical) freedom of the friendless fool.

In total contrast, John's protagonist (the madman across the water) is afforded no such liberty. As the song develops, allusions to mythical and physical acts of separation are mixed in such a way that the reality of his confinement in a mental asylum becomes increasingly clear. Following the drama of the two-part chorus, the undulating introductory motif returns, its rolling feel (now enhanced by constant use of tom fills on beats two, three and four) evoking the numerous lyric references to water that arguably serve as a metaphor for the perceived barrier between sanity and madness. In fact, such allusions effectively support Foucault's observation that 'water and madness have long been linked in the dreams of European man',[50] and one is reminded of his own account regarding the prominence of the Ship of Fools in the literature and iconography of the fifteenth century.[51] The fact that John's madman is 'across the water' (the act of his separation being conveyed through the aforementioned use of reverb effect) also aligns with the mythical

---

48    Foucault, pp. 24, 38.
49    Ibid., p. 250.
50    Ibid., p. 11.
51    See Foucault, pp. 7, 8, 10, 11, 13.

belief in the madman's ability to journey to concealed worlds, again perceptively articulated by Foucault:

> on water, each of us is in the hands of his own destiny; every embarkation is, potentially, the last. It is for the other world that the madman sets sail in his fool's boat; it is from the otherworld that he comes when he disembarks. The madman's voyage is at once a rigorous division and an absolute Passage.[52]

While Foucault acknowledges the undesirable aspects of madmen being forced to embark – whether literally or metaphorically – on Ships of Fools, it is the latter reality of the mental hospital that he accuses of restraining the extreme and inner journey of possibilities madness could symbolize or indeed offer the individual. Speaking of what he terms the 'classical experience of madness', he writes:

> Oblivion falls upon the world navigated by the free slaves of the Ship of Fools. Madness will no longer proceed from a point within the world to a point beyond, on its strange voyage; it will never again be that fugitive and absolute limit. Behold it moored now, made fast among things and men. Retained and maintained. No longer a ship but a hospital.[53]

It is in this, some anti-psychiatrists would argue still present, age of division and restraint that John's madman finds himself confined.

Serving as a musical metaphor for the emotional excess that madness commonly represents and the suppression of its limits through physical confinement, an active instrumental section featuring strings utilizing strong bowing, accented patterns, semiquaver flourishes and marked syncopation is positioned between the end of first chorus and recapitulation of verses one and two; the return to the contrasting, sombre verse material signifying that there is no possibility for such displays of vibrancy to affect change in the madman's circumstances. As if to confirm this, further evidence of the protagonist's captivity is provided in the extended bridge section which, like the first, involves an initial change of metre to $\frac{2}{4}$, forceful high-pitched vocal delivery and fast rhythmic gestures to convey the lyric 'The ground's a long way down but I need more' – the sense of distance being signified by intervallic augmentation in the accompanying string gestures. The subsequent question 'Is the nightmare black or are the windows painted?' provides further information concerning the protagonist's surroundings and is more resigned in feel, occupying as it does a lower and more confined use of pitch register. The image conveyed is that of a prison where high walls and blackened windows guarantee no possibility of escape or contact with external reality and, as such,

---

[52]    Ibid., p. 11.

[53]    Ibid., p. 35. Foucault goes on to identify the new role madness was to occupy in supporting notions of true reason: 'Tamed, madness preserves all the appearances of its reign. It now takes part in the measures of reason and in the labor of truth.' Ibid., p. 36.

parallels may be drawn between the song's content and the writings of many anti-involuntary confinement critics.

Of particular relevance, Lindsay Prior's work identifies ways in which the actual architecture of mental hospitals was intended to emphasize the presumed demarcation between reason and insanity. With reference to his own study hospital, which was designed and constructed between 1900 and 1920, Prior notes that: 'As with many similar asylums elsewhere it was deliberately planned so as to divorce its inmates from the everyday demands of mainstream metropolitan life – its outer walls and its gate lodge, in particular, functioning to emphasize a boundary which at that time was believed to exist between sanity and madness.'[54] Further to this, the added obstruction of blackened windows may be likened to Valeriy Tarsis's controversial novel *Ward 7* wherein, based on his real-life experience of being confined as a political prisoner in a Russian mental hospital in 1962, he describes the asylum's internal features as follows: 'The window panes were opaque, immovable and invariably curtained, in order to make sure of obliterating the street with its young poplars, flower-beds, cats and passers-by, and with it the very notion of life going on outside.'[55] As in 'Madman Across the Water' then, there is reference to a deliberate separation, a physical division perceptible to both sane and 'mad' persons alike that corroborates Foucault's observation regarding the likely intention behind the medicalization of madness: '*homo medicus* was not called into the world of confinement as an *arbiter*, to divide what was crime from what was madness, what was evil from what was illness, but rather as a *guardian*, to protect others from the vague danger that exuded through the walls of confinement'.[56] This view is equally shared by Szasz, who, on the subject of seventeenth-century madhouses, points out that 'when these institutions were founded, they were not considered medical or therapeutic facilities. Rather, they were regarded as prison-like structures for the confinement of socially undesirable persons.'[57] The fact that John's song makes no mention of medical treatments or doctors further promotes the idea of the asylum being a place of custody as opposed to cure.

The 'others' Foucault refers to as being in need of protection are represented in 'Madman Across the Water' in a demonstrably negative light as the protagonist's parents (see earlier discussion of verse three and chorus). The extent of the harmful impact their visits inflict on the protagonist is revealed in the final stages of the song where he asks in apparent desperation: 'Will they come again next week – can my mind really take it?'

The answer to his initial question is then cruelly confirmed by a repetition of chorus ('We'll come again next Thursday afternoon'). It is for this reason that

---

[54]     Lindsay Prior, *The Social Organization of Mental Illness* (London, 1993), p. 25.

[55]     Valeriy Tarsis, *Ward 7: An Autobiographical Novel*, trans. K. Brown (London, 1965), p. 18.

[56]     Foucault, p. 205.

[57]     Thomas Szasz, *The Manufacture of Madness* [1970] (London, 1973), p. 155.

the song may be considered supportive of anti-psychiatry theories that identify various damaging links between the family and madness – a trait that Foucault, Cooper and Laing appear to share.

In his chapter entitled 'The Birth of the Asylum', Foucault refers to the way in which, from the nineteenth century onwards, stature is given to any social organization headed by a male through the way in which madness comes to be linked with notions of the family:

> The prestige of patriarchy is revived around madness in the bourgeois family. [...] Henceforth, and for a period of time the end of which is not yet possible to predict, the discourse of unreason will be indissociably linked with the half-real, half-imaginary dialect of the family. So that what, in their violence it was once obligatory to interpret as profanations or blasphemies, it would henceforth be necessary to see as an incessant attack against the Father.[58]

Foucault argues that the identified mad came to be perceived as children in need of direction, citing Samuel Tuke's York Retreat as an instigator of such thinking:

> For this new reason which reigns in the asylum, madness does not represent the absolute form of contradiction, but instead a minority status, an aspect of itself that does not have the right to autonomy, and can live only grafted onto the world of reason. Madness is childhood. Everything at the retreat is organized so that the insane are transformed into minors.[59]

Cooper's criticism of mental hospitals and universities is also relevant to our understanding of the song's potential meaning, and develops Foucault's observation into a scolding denouncement:

> Both institutions are rife with phoney concern of a confused paternalistic-maternalistic sort on the part of the 'guardians' that operate against the 'guarded'. Both are fair mothers (the alma mater) with breasts full of the old poison, tranquillizers in every conceivable form, everything from the right pill for the right patient to the right job for the right graduate.[60]

As has been documented in earlier chapters, and unlike Foucault, both Cooper and Laing were responsible for advancing theories of family-induced madness; and, again, in 'Madman Across the Water' we find evidence of their ideas filtering through into popular song of the early 1970s. Indeed, the parents' dismissal of the protagonist and their failure to recognize either his potential wisdom or the harmful effects of their unproductive visits bear a striking similarity to the critique offered

[58]   Foucault, pp. 253–4.
[59]   Ibid., p. 252.
[60]   Cooper, *The Death of the Family*, p. 63.

in the same year (1971) by Ken Loach's film *Family Life*[61] – a film purportedly influenced by conversations with Laing and radical psychiatrist Mike Riddal.[62]

The film was based on the television play *In Two Minds*, written by David Mercer, directed by Ken Loach and broadcast on the BBC in 1967 as part of the TV series *The Wednesday Play* (1964). According to reviewer Janet Moat:

> Mercer's play caused a sensation. Senior psychiatric experts fell over themselves to claim that Kate (Anna Cropper) was not schizophrenic but merely hysterical and depressed – like a vast proportion of the population, who exhibited similar symptoms. [...] The controversy was such that he [Mercer] appeared on the TV arts programme *Late Night Line Up* (BBC, 1964–72) to deny that he had any particular theory or practice in mind, but fellow dramatist Dennis Potter, writing in the *New Statesman*, pointed out that the play 'completely supported the arguments and theories of R.D. Laing, who believes that schizophrenia is more a particular style of communication than an organic disease of the brain'. Mercer had drawn on Laing's book, *Sanity and Madness in the Family* for the play, and was thus accused of making propaganda and not art.[63]

Given the impact of the play and the subsequent exposure of its idea in film format, it is likely that, by demonstrating the extensive influence of Laing's and Cooper's work, it too played an important role in introducing anti-psychiatric ideas to the general population. While there is no biographical evidence to suggest that lyricist Bernie Taupin was influenced by Mercer's work, 'Madman Across the Water' and *Family Life* contain striking similarities in relation to their portrayal of oppressive family relations.

With respect to the film version, the lead protagonist, Janice Baildon (played by actress Sandy Ratcliff), struggles to meet her family's expectations of 'normal',

---

[61]     *Family Life* (1971) directed by Ken Loach; screenplay by David Mercer; produced by Tony Garnett, EMI Films. USA release date: October 1971 (New York Film Festival); UK release date: December 1971.

[62]     In an interview with Tony Garnett and Ken Loach for the radical paper *7 Days*, and in response to the question 'How did you come to make *Family Life*?', Tony Garnett made the following reference to writers associated with anti-psychiatric theories: 'Well, actually it goes back to when I was at University [...] reading psychology in a desultory way [...] Then I came across Erving Goffman's book, *The Presentation of Self in Everyday Life*, which just knocked me over. [...] Then I struck up a friendship with David Mercer whose own reading had gone through all these changes as well, and then meeting Ronnie Laing, and talking to him, and then it all came together.' When asked how many people discussed the film, Garnett acknowledged the influence of Mike Riddal: 'Mike Riddal was very helpful. He played the progressive psychiatrist in Family Life but he's not an actor; he's a progressive psychiatrist.' *7 Days* (12 January 1972), sourced from *Jump Cut*, 10–11 (1976), pp. 43–5.

[63]     Janet Moat, Review of *In Two Minds*, British Film Institute, screen online (2003), retrieved 21 July 2005 from http://www.screenonline.org.uk/tv/id/557285/index.html.

'respectable' behaviour, and the ensuing conflict results in an eventual diagnosis of schizophrenia and medical intervention – hospitalization, electroconvulsive therapy (ECT) and tranquillization. The portrayal of family relations demonstrates the pain and frustration both sides endure, and yet Janice's gradual descent into catatonia is undoubtedly represented as being a result of both her family's and psychiatry's failed attempts to cure her of a natural desire for independence. In fact it is a relatively innocent flouting of her parent's rules (failing to arrive home at the allotted time one evening) that prompts their search for medical assistance, and the desire for it to offer some form of moral chastisement:

> Mother: Your father and I have decided you have to see a doctor.

> Father: It's not a bloody doctor she needs, it's the police. No self-respecting person would behave the way you have. There must be something wrong with you child.

And later, when at first Janet is placed in the care of a non-interventionist psychiatrist who believes in exploring the social roots of his patients' problems, her mother shows concern about the relative freedom of the ward:

> Mother: No pills, not sedated or tranquillised?

> Father: What about the discipline doctor? How do you teach them right or wrong?

Just as the label of madness is questioned in John's song ('Take my word I'm a madman don't you know?'), Janice's boyfriend asks what it is to be normal and suggests that it involves being both inert and compliant, traits that are instilled in each of us by our families:

> Boyfriend: Is normal sane? Passive, in their place … And that's what families are: bloody training camps to get you to do the same.

When Janice returns to the mental hospital she is put under the care of a traditional psychiatrist, who confirms the idea of existence as:

> Doctor: Getting married, having relationships.

> Janice: I'm mad then?

> Doctor: Well, you *are* ill.

Both texts, through their questioning of what it means to be normal and the suggestion that deviation from such results in a label of madness, align fully with

Laing's theory regarding the accepted, but misguided, belief that alienation from one's own self connotes sanity:

> The 'normally' alienated person, by reason of the fact that he acts more or less like everyone else, is taken to be sane. Other forms of alienation that are out of step with the prevailing state of alienation are those that are labelled by the 'normal' majority as bad or mad.[64]

The suggestion is that traditional psychiatry is called upon to correct deviant behaviours in order that the patient may return to a life of bland acceptance. (In *Family Life*, following Janice's first bout of ECT treatment, she is shown packing chocolates into boxes on a production line as 'Every day is a happy day' sounds from a factory radio.) In order to demonstrate this viewpoint further, both texts portray the protagonist's parents as being unable to relate to their offspring ('They think it's very funny everything I say'), preoccupied instead with what are trivial matters ('You better get your coat dear, it looks like rain').[65] In 'Madman Across the Water', the protagonist's charge that it is his parents' visits that are the cause of his mental decline is equally born out in *Family Life*, where visiting day simply provides an additional opportunity for Janice's parents to encourage compliance with their views. The following dialogue takes place after an incident involving Janice being instructed by a staff nurse to end a friendship with a fellow, male patient. Her angry reaction, whereupon she breaks a chair, provides justification for the nurses to tranquillize her:

> Father: After all these years now are you beginning to realise who's been right, us, or do you still think you're right?
>
> Janice: I don't know
>
> Father: You don't know? (looks to mother) She doesn't know (who then sighs) You only attacked the staff nurse with a chair, that's all, and you say you don't know?
>
> Mother: Then there's this boy, what's going on there? We're very concerned and worried about him.
>
> Janice: I didn't do anything with that boy.

---

[64]     Laing, *The Politics of Experience*, p. 24.

[65]     Richard Yates's 1961 novel *Revolutionary Road* portrays a comparable scenario in which the identified 'mad' man, John Givings, reveals the unspoken tragedy of mass conformity in a torrent of insightful accusations directed at the lead protagonists. Like John's character, Givings's relationship with his parents is one of apparent frustration and contempt.

After some further interrogation Janice's parents relent momentarily before warning that a failure to comply will result in prolonged confinement:

> Mother: Don't look so miserable, we're not *really* getting at you. Cheer up.
>
> Father: Look love, try and behave yourself for God's sake will you? And you'll have to collaborate with them because if you don't you could be in here forever.
>
> Janice: No, sometimes I think it's if I do co-operate that's how I'll be in here forever.

The fact that Janice, at one point, returns willingly to the mental hospital to escape her domineering mother and father – and John's protagonist openly anguishes over the potential return of his parents – reveals the extent of the breakdown in their family relations. While both are fictional characters, Janet Gotkin's autobiographical novel *Too Much Anger, Too Many Years* (1975) reveals a similar desperate bid for autonomy, where parting from her parents after she is committed to a mental institution brings unabashed relief:

> 'Thank God', I heard my own true self say. 'Thank God I won't have to see them for two weeks.' Even the clay of the death pit would be a relief after that closed web […] I gave a last look at my parents, a sombre and pathetic pair, mourning my demise prematurely, I thought. It was with relief that I allowed Mrs Rooney to guide me out of the room.[66]

The negative parental representations alongside the desire for understanding and autonomy in 'Madman Across the Water' ensure it adheres to one of rock's traditional themes of rebellion (as articulated in numerous earlier songs such as The Who's 'My Generation' and The Doors' 'The End'). At the same time, its psychiatric context provides a sense of distinctiveness and dramatic opportunity as the stakes are that much higher when the threat is that of involuntary confinement in a mental hospital. While 'The Fool on the Hill' exhibits a similar critique of society's unwillingness to accept difference, the song never reveals the exact identity of those who dislike and alienate the fool. There is certainly no inference that they are his relations; and, as it is not until the first chorus that the musical gestures suggest that the summation of the 'fool' offered in verse one is both misleading and inadequate, the listener is initially more likely to identify with the suspicious onlookers than the mysterious, solitary figure of the fool. This, of course, serves a purpose, for it exposes the listeners' own propensity for fearing difference. At the same time, elsewhere in the song it necessitates the use of a

---

    [66]    Janet Gotkin and Paul Gotkin, *Too Much Anger, Too Many Tears: A Personal Triumph over Psychiatry* (New York, 1975), pp. 78–9.

variety of musical gestures that can function to promote a compassionate response to the fool's circumstances.

Numerous developments in the instrumental arrangement aid the narrative progression of 'The Fool on the Hill' (helping to create a sense of build towards verse four) while at the same time encouraging an empathetic response from the listener regarding the fool's situation. In the second verse, for example, an added electro-acoustic guitar engages in a call and response with the vocal, playing small, arch-shaped, consonant phrases to produce a lighter mood than that generated in verse one. The lyric at this point describes the fool in a way that playfully contradicts previous observations: 'well on the way, head in a cloud', the inference being that, while not outwardly progressive (remaining static on a hill), the fool is nevertheless inwardly progressive (engaged in a form of inner journey). During the second half of verse two, and in response to the lyric 'man of a thousand voices talking perfectly loud' (which again imparts a sense of the fool's unearthly powers), the flutes' counter melody strengthens the aforementioned lightening in mood – their entry being more rhythmically active and their ensuing harmonies occupying a higher pitch range in comparison to the first verse. Narrative concept aside, the flutes' development performs an important compositional function, ensuring that musical interest is maintained despite the amount of literal phrase repetition occurring in the vocal melody (see Example 5.3). Their melodious embellishments also mean that important words, alongside the repeated revelation chord (return to tonic major), receive the necessary stress – the chromatic, semiquaver sextuplet in the final bar of the second chorus is a precise example of this.

Example 5.3   'The Fool on the Hill' flute development

Sympathy for the fool is also encouraged via the juxtaposition of solo recorder section and vocal in verse three. Here, the recorders play a four-bar solo which, through a proliferation of triplet figures, slides between notes, gradual ascent in pitch and alternating tonic-dominant bass line, adds an amiable, naïve quality to the song that contrasts harshly with the negative sentiment of the following vocal: 'and nobody seems to like him, they can tell what he wants to do'. To underpin this alteration of mood the arrangement becomes more static: the bouncy bass line and recorders cease while the piano quaver figures are articulated in a more legato fashion, resulting in a distinctly plaintive feel.

The pinnacle of the song (verse four) is approached via a repeat of chorus containing further subtle developments in the flute accompaniment. The character of this final verse is distinguished by the amount of freedom and exuberance it exudes. The alternating bass movement of the recorder solo returns to allow a resurgence of momentum, while the vocal breaks with past melodic motives to offer a jovial extemporization in which the simplicity of the binary (major/minor) opposition – that which informs the form of the song and symbolizes both the different sides of the fool's nature and the conflict that exists between him and others – is ridiculed. The vocal teasingly alternates between the major 3rd (F♯) and minor 3rd (F), the very notes responsible for determining the major or minor tonality. The high-spirited feeling is endorsed by the correspondingly high pitch of the vocal and use of melisma on the word 'Oh', the major minor alternations eventually coming to rest on the note G – the highest pitch of the song. In subsequent bars, the theme of alternation continues as repeated tonic to dominant quaver movement in the vocal effectively reminds listeners of the fool's ability to see the world spinning 'round and round and round and round and round' (Example 5.4).

Example 5.4  'The Fool on the Hill' verse 4 (vocal extemporization)

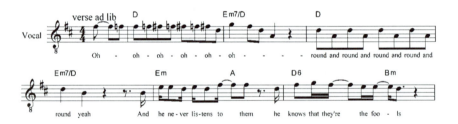

The exact moment at which the song discloses its second and perhaps most significant revelation (the first being witnessed during the initial refrain) occurs during the second half of verse four. Here, for the first time, listeners are informed by the vocal observer of the fool's own thoughts regarding others: that 'he never listens to them, he knows that they're the fool'. Emphasis of this part of the narrative is again ensured through the high pitch register of the melody which, for three bars, concentrates on the pitches D, E, F♯ and G (the highest, concentrated pitch range of the song) and employs many accented non-harmony tones (for example, an F♯ appears against the dominant chord of A to evoke a certain uncomfortableness surrounding the words 'to them' and 'like him'). The descending contour of the phrase 'he knows that they're the fool' and falling slide on its final word suggest an element of tiredness, even lament (see Example 5.4). As such, the vocal observer, through his compassionate treatment of the fool, reveals not only his own powers of perception but also a powerful critique of society's unwillingness to accept difference. It could also be argued that the song's more subtle approach to the issue of alienation (not situating the fool within a context of psychiatric treatment) actually reinforces the real issue of society's predilection for labelling and exclusion: that it is, as Thomas Scheff identifies, based on the identification of enduring rule-breaking (in other words, the fool flouts what is considered acceptable behaviour in public):

> Each culture tends to reify its definition of decency and reality, and so provides no way of handling violations of its expectations in these areas. The typical norm governing decency or reality, therefore literally 'goes without saying' and its violation is unthinkable for most of its members. For the convenience of the society in construing those instances of unnamable rule-breaking which are called to its attention, these violations may be lumped together into a residual category: witchcraft, spirit possession, or, in our own society, mental illness.[67]

As Foucault rightly declares: 'On all sides, madness fascinates man. The fantastic images it generates are not fleeting appearances that quickly disappear from the surface of things';[68] and one could argue that this accounts, at least in part, for both the Beatles' and Elton John's interest in exploring its thematic potential. But alongside such exploration comes the potential for exploitation, a fact that has led many writers to document the unsavoury tradition of observing the Other for the purpose of private (or in this case, potentially mass) titillation.[69] So could either song be criticized for a lack of sensitivity in this regard? While the Beatles' fool is being observed by the singer, there is no suggestion that this is in any way undesirable, for the fool remains detached and impervious to such voyeurism. Moreover, because the singer is commenting on the opposing relationship between the fool and those around him, his own relationship to the character remains undisclosed; indeed there is certainly no suggestion that he regards the fool as a spectacle for amusement.

By questioning the motive for the protagonist's parents' continued visits ('Is it in your conscience that you're after another glimpse of the madman across the water?'), John's song clearly draws on the once common act of so-called madmen

---

[67]     Thomas Scheff, *Being Mentally Ill: A Sociological Theory* (London, 1966), p. 34. Scheff continues to outline the link between such rule-breaking and the potential labelling of mental illness: 'In this discussion, the diverse kinds of rule-breaking for which our society provides no explicit label, and which, therefore, sometimes lead to the labelling of the violator as mentally ill, will be considered to be technically *residual rule-breaking*'. Ibid.

[68]     Foucault, p. 23.

[69]     See, for example, Andrew Scull, *The Most Solitary of Afflictions: Madness and Society in Britain, 1700–1900* (New Haven and London, 1993), pp. 51–4. See also Thomas Szasz, *Insanity: The Idea and its Consequences* (New York, 1987), p. 179, and Szasz, *Cruel Compassion: Psychiatric Control of Society's Unwanted* (New York, 1994), pp. 118–19.

and madwomen being displayed for the amusement of the general public,[70] but in a way that plainly denounces such behaviour. Foucault points to the irony of such displays following the confinement of 'mad' persons in mental asylums –the fact that madness was effectively silenced while at the same time being served up as a form of theatrical attraction – and this subject is painfully explored in the final scenes of *Family Life*, where a silent Janice is exhibited by an insensible psychiatrist to his less than attentive medical students as a classic case of 'extreme mutism'. The setting is admittedly not theatrical in the sense that the spectators are medical students, but the fact that Janice is asked to sit on a high chair at the front of a lecture theatre and is spoken about as if she isn't there attests to the fact that her existence has become one of inertia and absence, her only role now to serve as a demonstration for the training of future psychiatrists within the medical model of psychiatry (her doctor making it clear that: 'there is no discernable connection between her various symptoms and her environment'). John's protagonist is also not displayed to the general public; but the lack of meaningful dialogue between him and his visitors leads him to believe that their only motive is one of morbid fascination, hence his call to their consciences. The final vocal phrase of the last chorus, 'madman across the water', seems exaggerated both in terms of its descent and return (via reverb effect) as once more the suggested departure and resulting echo signify the madman's isolation from the supposed world of reason. The subsequent dissonance of a string cluster chord implies a sense of unease at his departure before all parts unite in a final rendition of the instrumental interlude, the basis for which is the undulating introductory motif. The song fades on this motif, with no further vocal utterances – the rise and fall of motif seemingly evoking the departing 'Ship of Fools'.[71]

---

[70]    Foucault writes that: 'As late as 1815, if a report presented in the House of Commons is to be believed, the hospital of Bethlehem exhibited lunatics for a penny, every Sunday. Now the annual revenue from these exhibitions amounted to almost four hundred pounds; which suggests the astonishingly high number of 96,000 visits a year [...] Here is madness elevated to spectacle above the silence of the asylums, and becoming a public scandal for the general delight.' Foucault, pp. 68–9. The Victorian asylums continue to excite public fascination, with references to them found in various contemporary song/ album titles (see, for example, James Blunt's *Back to Bedlam*, 2005, and Kasabian's *West Ryder Pauper Lunatic Asylum*, 2009).

[71]    The phrase itself was employed on at least two other occasions in the 1970s by noteworthy bands. In the previous year, The Doors' song 'Ship of Fools' had appeared on their 1970 album *Morrison Hotel*. The ship (a likely drug reference) is depicted as offering an escape from the dangers of the real world: 'Come on baby, now we're going home. Ship of fools, ship of fools. The human race was dyin' out. No one left to scream and shout. People walking on the moon. Smog will get you pretty soon.' The phrase also appeared as the title of a later track by The Grateful Dead, by which time its use had become more akin to the original meaning in Sebastian Brant's moralistic tale: 'Though I could not caution all, I yet may warn a few: Don't lend your hand to raise no flag atop no ship of fools' (appears on the album *From the Mars Hotel*, released June 1974).

In conclusion, Elton John and Bernie Taupin achieve a questioning of definitions of sanity and madness by contrasting the mythical aspects of the artificial fool's powers of wisdom with the mundane and unfeeling features of his visitors. The suggestion is one of family conflict – a theme capitalized on by Laing and Cooper in their attempts to demonstrate the sometimes rational reaction of supposed schizophrenic persons to their impossible family situations, and brought to wider public attention through the film release in the same year of *Family Life*. The actual critique of the madman's confinement was perhaps a little outdated given the advent of deinstitutionalization and a move towards community care, but it nevertheless provides a useful means of illustrating and condemning the historic barrier thought to exist between madness and sanity.[72] Despite its apparent lack of psychiatric context, 'The Fool on the Hill' offers an equally robust critique of social exclusion, focusing on our seemingly innate dislike of difference. The mythical aspects of the natural fool's unearthly abilities are contrasted with the presumptuous and hostile features of those around him, and two points of revelation attest to the fool's superior state of mind. Both songs thus offer empathetic, yet differing, accounts of the fool's demise while at the same time securing a certain sense of victory through their protagonists' challenge to blind conformity. Moreover, an insightful critique of social segregation – analogous to Foucault's theory concerning the lack of dialogue between reason and unreason – lies at the heart of each, guaranteeing their continued relevance.

---

[72] Pilgrim and Rogers argue that: 'The use of the Victorian asylums for warehousing the insane was a mechanism for bringing about a break in the dialogue between reason and unreason on the one hand, and society and the disturbed on the other. In the contemporary era, where mental hospitals are in decline, the narrative of loss and difference is preserved in the status of becoming a patient.' David Pilgrim and Anne Rogers, *A Sociology of Mental Health and Illness* (Buckingham and Philadelphia, 1999), p. 80. Their argument thus attests to the continued relevance of the content found in both *Madness and Civilization* and 'Madman Across the Water'.

# Chapter 6

# Conclusion

Having identified the various ways in which anti-psychiatric ideas are embodied both verbally and musically within discrete songs, the greater part of this conclusion aims to examine the extent to which the analysed texts are interconnected in terms of their constituent themes and processes. In general this is intended to demonstrate that such anti-psychiatric stances were not merely coincidental, but a particular feature of the historical period in question. A number of additional songs and artists, drawn from a variety of styles and periods, are alluded to in order to strengthen this argument and point to possible avenues for future investigation and analysis. The final sections of this conclusion offer possible reasons as to why the links between popular music and anti-psychiatry occurred and then subsequently diminished. Some general observations are also included concerning the appeal of madness as a topic for musical exploration.

Prior to an in-depth examination of commonalities in relation to characterization, alienation, notions of reversal, psychiatric treatment, confinement and distinct musical approaches, it is useful to consider interrelationships as more precise objects of critique and, where relevant, the particular historical periods from which they are derived. As the only artist to have personally undergone psychiatric treatment, Lou Reed perhaps unsurprisingly references, and questions, the more contemporary medical treatments of electroconvulsive therapy (ECT) and the major tranquillizers as opposed to outdated treatments such as surgical lobotomy. Moreover, 'Kill Your Sons' is one of the few anti-psychiatric songs of the 1970s to avoid criticism of involuntary, long-term hospitalization: meaning that Reed's protagonist evades the potential label of enduring victim, and the focus remains firmly fixed on the central, and arguably more up to date, issues concerning the injurious effects of electroshock 'treatment' and possible inefficacy of drug therapy.

While being relatively unique in the specificity of its psychiatric relevance, Reed's song nevertheless shares a common theme with all other subjects of previous chapters: a questioning of the kind of behaviour that constitutes mental normality and conversely mental abnormality; in fact, all appear to advocate the notion of an alternative reality which, in turn, would appear central to their popular appeal. Bowie's protagonist points to the alienation inherent in society and implies that his medical treatments (specifically lobotomy) are intended to recondition him to accept an agreed and acceptable version of reality: 'Day after day, they take some brain away, then turn my face around to the far side of town, and tell me that it's real, then ask me how I feel'. Pink Floyd's protagonist in 'Brain Damage' similarly implies the act of enforced mental readjustment: 'You raise the blade, you make the change, you rearrange me till I'm sane', while *The Dark Side of the Moon* album as a whole serves to criticize conventional notions of normality through its questioning of the concepts of time and individual purpose. The insightful fool in the Beatles' 'The Fool on the Hill' inhabits an alternative reality in which he remains both detached and impervious to the petty concerns of his critics, while Alice Cooper's protagonist embarks upon a surreal journey during the final verse of 'The Ballad of Dwight Fry' (although the suggestion here is that it is an undesirable consequence of his enforced captivity, and perhaps only an imaginary escape from the reality of his confinement). For Reed, and Elton John, accepted concepts of normality are exposed as fake by detailing the inconsequential, irrational and mechanized behaviour of their protagonists' supposedly sane relatives. While John's protagonist bears witness to his own powers of insight, expounding prophesies of future misfortune, Reed advocates the ability to dismiss a conventional, routine existence by adopting a delinquent persona in which the very means of psychiatric control (drug therapy) is effectively mocked.

Reed and Alice Cooper identify strongly with social control theories, positioning their protagonists within a family setting designed to showcase their anti-disciplinarian personae. Reed's family critique imbues his song with an acute sense of irony given its title and chorus lyric 'kill your sons', while the inferred family unit in Cooper's song suggests a failure to live up to traditional role expectations of both husband and father. In a less confrontational manner, Elton John's protagonist becomes the victim of not only physical confinement but also of the unrelenting family visits he is made to endure, asking in eventual desperation: 'Will they come again next week, can my mind really take it?'

It is worth noting that John's and Bowie's implied setting of long-term involuntary confinement, along with Bowie's references to surgical lobotomy, are less relevant to a critique of contemporary psychiatric practice, drawing instead on pre-1950s themes (pre-deinstitutionalization and the advent of the major tranquillizers). The actual sites of confinement are analogous to eighteenth- and nineteenth-century depictions of mental asylums: Bowie referring to 'mansions cold and grey' positioned on the 'far side of town',[1] while John's song, albeit less specifically, details a place with high walls and blackened windows. Cooper's reference to an intensive care ward where his protagonist endures a comparatively short stay ('I was gone for fourteen days') suggests an experience more in keeping with contemporary practices where a patient would likely receive a period of observation followed by outpatient drug therapy. However, his allusion to the physical restraint of a straitjacket, and noticeable omission of drugs references, undermines this clear-cut assumption and serves to stress, and once again question, the custodial function of the psychiatric hospital. A more detailed examination

---

[1]   Although it should be noted that some such places existed well into the twentieth century: De la Pole psychiatric hospital outside Hull, for example, was just such a mansion: opened in 1883 and not closed until 1998.

of how certain texts commonly approach and utilize the issue of psychiatric confinement will be provided in a separate section of this conclusion. Suffice it to say, there are numerous possible reasons why such outdated themes and practices have continued to resonate within popular cultural idioms, and these will also be addressed at a later point.

While the songs previously featured vary in terms of the particular anti-psychiatric ideas they exhibit – and each draws on a slightly different, and often nebulous, combination of medical, social and cultural beliefs surrounding madness – their predilection for questioning normality and posing alternative realities results in a further shared characteristic: a strategy of critique based on the act of reversal. The proposition that so-called 'sanity' is in fact madness and vice versa results in clearly identifiable moments of revelation – points at which traditional conceptions are reversed – which serve to challenge the medical model of psychiatry and its constituent methods of diagnosis and treatment. In Bowie's 'All the Madmen' and Alice Cooper's 'The Ballad of Dwight Fry' it occurs at the point of chorus; for Pink Floyd's *The Dark Side of the Moon* it takes place during both 'Brain Damage' and 'Eclipse'; in Reed's 'Kill Your Sons' and Elton John's 'Madman Across the Water' it occurs during the episodes critiquing the protagonists' relations; and in 'The Fool on the Hill' two elements of revelation occur during the chorus and final verse. The lyrical content fulfils an important role at such points, signalling a potential denial of listener expectations; however, it is principally the manipulation of musical elements that provokes an understanding of the reversal process. A more detailed exploration of the aforementioned issues – alongside analysis of interrelationships with reference to characterization, alienation, psychiatric treatment and confinement – reveals further commonalities relevant to an understanding of popular music's adoption of an anti-psychiatric stance.

## Characterization

Songs involving a variety of overt theatrical gestures and the artist's adoption of a character role that is distinct from their usual performing persona (in other words unique to that particular musical text) enable a potential questioning of psychiatric diagnosis based on the notion of role play. Conventional signifiers of 'mad' behaviour typically take on an exaggerated form, only to be cast aside in evidence of the singer's ability to 'play' a role, thus revealing what Szasz termed the 'myth of mental illness'.[2] Such an approach is perhaps best illustrated in Bowie's and Alice Cooper's use of multiple vocal style/tone wherein the notion of 'playing' the part of a madman implies that madness itself is a mere fabrication which, in turn, prompts a questioning of the establishment that purports to diagnose and cure it.

---

[2]     Thomas Szasz, *The Myth of Mental Illness: Foundations of a Theory of Personal Conduct* [1961] (London, 1972).

Bowie's seemingly calculated manipulation of vocal delivery (shifting between chest voice, falsetto and spoken passages) and the variation in the production of his voice (use of excessive plate reverberation, double tracking, single, unaffected voice, fast tape delay and extreme panning) convey a distinct element of theatricality; and yet in 'All the Madmen' it is the positioning of such devices in relation to the lyric text, and their connection to other musical parameters, that evokes a sense of 'invented' madness. Considering the lyrics in isolation, the kinds of behaviour conventionally considered indicative of mental disturbance (a belief in one's ability to fly, self-harming, talking to inanimate objects) appear to be re-enforced rather than challenged. However, the assertive rhythmic and melodic nature of the vocal (see analysis of the bridge sections of 'All the Madmen' in Chapter 1), controlled use of repetition, playful undertones and effective signal processing suggest a more complex and ultimately challenging engagement with behaviour typically deemed 'mad'. Moreover, the fact that certain behaviour is only threatened ('I *will* scream, I *will* break my arm, I *will* do me harm') indicates not only a conscious awareness of its likely effect – a diagnosis of madness – but most crucially proof that it is all simply an act he is able to control, a role he is prepared to 'play'.

Alice Cooper's protagonist in 'The Ballad of Dwight Fry' demonstrates a similar ability to flit in and out of a madman role in an evidently conscious, predetermined manner. The initial recount of his stay in an intensive care ward conveys a perceptible sense of abnormality (through ungainly use of pitch, laboured rhythmic phrasing, low register, half-spoken tone) that is liable to support a belief in his need for psychiatric aid. However, the rapid employment of higher-pitched chest voice, increasingly directed melodic phrasing and snarled accusation regarding the ward being a 'danger zone' reveal Fry's ability to merely 'play' the role of the madman. In fact, any suggestion of real (as opposed to enacted) insanity is portrayed as being a direct consequence of his enforced confinement; that is to say, it is a natural and understandable product of mistreatment as opposed to being an actual mental disease: 'See my only mind explode, since I've gone away'. The shift to present tense (implying this is an ongoing process) during the chorus passages and evident strength of musical gestures impart a sense of confidence and sincerity that not only assist in the communication of this message, but equally attest to the protagonist's state of reason.

Clearly, both Bowie's and Alice Cooper's manipulation of character may be seen as directly illustrative of Szasz's insistence that 'mental illness is not something a person *has*, but is something he *does* or *is*'.[3] As Bruce Wilshire identifies, 'Theatre is the art of imitation that reveals imitation',[4] and in the aforementioned musical examples the protagonist's ability to wilfully adopt and subsequently cast aside behaviours conventionally regarded 'mad' reveals the

---

[3]     Szasz, *The Myth of Mental Illness*, p. 275.

[4]     Bruce Wilshire, *Role Playing and Identity: The Limits of Theatre as Metaphor* (Bloomington and Indianapolis, 1991), p. ix.

theatrical nature of madness itself, as Szasz asserts: 'mental illness is an action not a legion [...] it is also an act, in the sense of a theatrical impersonation'.[5] To a lesser degree, Elton John's principal protagonist in 'Madman Across the Water' also points to problems surrounding the recognition and diagnosis of madness, utilizing sarcasm as a means of drawing attention to the labelling process he has been subjected to ('Take my word I'm a madman don't you know?').

While it would appear that this strategy of transparent role play is most prevalent in Bowie's and Alice Cooper's particular brand of theatre rock, it is important to recognize that Reed's and Elton John's employment of character roles elicits an equally powerful challenge to ostensible truths concerning the form and nature of madness by revealing the fake, self-serving and mechanized behaviour of allegedly 'sane' persons (those not committed or undergoing psychiatric treatment). Elton John's varied vocal delivery, in which he essentially manipulates tone and dynamic as opposed to using spoken voice or pronounced signal processing, is utilized to portray multiple character roles which again imbue the song with an essential theatricality. The noticeable difference in tone and contrasting way in which melodic phrases are constructed make it possible to distinguish between the voice of the alleged 'madman' and his supposedly 'sane' visitors (see analysis of bridge and chorus sections in Chapter 5); but most significant to the argument in question, the musical and lyrical representations of the latter are decidedly negative and create an underlying tension that serves to destabilize notions of both madness and sanity. A comparable strategy is utilized in 'Kill Your Sons', although it is not until the first person narrative of the third verse that Reed introduces the character of defiant adolescent – by which point the critique of his purportedly 'sane', but clearly dysfunctional, family is complete and his own unaffected, audacious disposition seems in far less need of psychiatric treatment.

The use of characterization in Pink Floyd's 'Brain Damage' is rather less straightforward in that the protagonist initially adopts the position of distant observer before becoming directly embroiled in the narrative action and recounting his own diagnosis of insanity, enforced treatment and confinement. As in Bowie's and Alice Cooper's songs, there is a flirtation with stereotypical 'mad' behaviour and a deliberate attempt to convey the sense of menace all too often associated with it – 'Got to keep the loonies on the path' (see analysis of verses one and two in Chapter 3). Once the protagonist reveals his own vulnerability to accusations of insanity ('the lunatic is in *my* head'), the treatment he is forced to undergo (psychosurgery and confinement) is administered not in an attempt to affect a cure, but as a means of eliminating his potential threat to the social order: 'you rearrange me till I'm sane/lock the door and throw away the key'. Despite the reassuring chorus gestures which propagate the value of personal endeavour and stress the importance of individual expression, the protagonist remains essentially a victim of the system – sacrificed as proof of psychiatry's concealed social function.

---

[5]     Thomas Szasz, *Insanity: The Idea and its Consequences* (New York, 1987), p. 212.

Prior to 1968 there is certainly evidence of other popular music artists utilizing 'mad' characters in their songs, two of the most notable cases being Napoleon XIV's 'They're Coming To Take Me Away Ha Haaa!' (1966) and Jimi Hendrix's 'Manic Depression' (1967). However, the cause of the protagonist's madness in both instances is their inability to conquer love loss and, while offering some form of challenge to the medical model in the sense that their conditions are not conceptualized as actual biological illnesses/diseases, there is no obvious evidence of an anti-psychiatric stance. Rather, these texts demonstrate different influences in which a perceived link between love and madness is combined with an acceptance of a medical diagnosis. David Jones points out that 'the connection between love and madness is hardly new' and quotes Shakespeare's *As you Like It* – 'Love is merely madness'[6] – in evidence. Of particular relevance, however, is Jones's qualitative research, where interviews with the relatives of people suffering from serious mental illness revealed a tendency to 'suppose that the illness was caused through the person having had relationship difficulties or the trauma of unrequited love', demonstrating 'the point at which mainstream psychiatric models departed most from the beliefs of [the] interviewees'.[7] Thus, it may be argued that musical texts disseminating a causal link between relationship breakdown and madness are drawing on, and in turn reinstating, largely popular, as opposed to medical, opinion.

Napoleon XIV's unrelenting, rhythmic, half-spoken vocal line and snare drum accompaniment are suggestive of an unstoppable march to what the protagonist affectionately terms the 'funny farm'. His unsettled, excitable delivery is addressed directly to an ex-love whom he pleaded with not to leave because he'd 'go beserk [sic]'; the conclusion to the first verse confirms this forewarning: 'You left me anyhow and then the days got worse and worse and now you see I've gone completely out of my mind.' Aside from the facile portrayal of his mental breakdown, the various attempts to convey lyrical humour (revealing his past love to be a 'mangy mutt' and concluding the song with an inane joke) and consistent use of slang terms for both mental illness and psychiatric hospitals (flip my lid/ funny farm/happy home) appear decidedly opportunist. Being a novelty song, one would anticipate a certain amount of musical and lyrical quirkiness, but in this instance its effect is to reinforce notions that madness manifests itself in entirely observable ways – through bizarre, inane, uncontrolled behaviour that is ultimately in need of containment. Sander Gilman's theory regarding our evident need to identify madness as 'difference' is relevant here, for the function of such

---

6     Shakespeare, *As You Like It*, Act 3, Sc. 2, ll. 420–26. Quoted in David W. Jones, *Myths, Madness and the Family: The Impact of Mental Illness on Families* (Basingstoke, 2002), p. 87.

7     Jones, *Myths, Madness and the Family*, p. 87. In the same text, Jones concludes: 'It may be that this reflects a deeply held belief that such relationships are somehow fundamental to mental health, and the understanding (not necessarily conscious) that the observance of sexual boundaries defines mental health in some way', p. 91.

stereotypical conceptions is to create a compelling illusion of 'madness' from which we may differentiate ourselves as 'normal':

> The banality of real mental illness comes in conflict with our need to have the mad identifiable, different from ourselves […] This moment when we say, 'they are just like us,' is most upsetting. Then we no longer know where lies the line that divides our normal, reliable world, a world that minimizes our fears, from that world in which lurks the fearful, the terrifying, the aggressive.[8]

'They're Coming To Take Me Away Ha Haaa!' thus serves to represent an unmistakable, and hence reassuring, border line between the 'mad' and the 'sane', the appeal of which, as Susan McClary demonstrates, may be traced back to the 'mad' scenes of operas such as Donizetti's *Lucia di Lammermoor* (1835).[9]

Hendrix's 'Manic Depression', while devoid of such insensitive clichés, similarly identifies love loss as instrumental in the protagonist's mental suffering – 'Woman so weary, the sweet cause in vain. You make love, you break love. It's all the same. When it's over, when it's over mama. Music sweet music. I wish I could caress, caress. Manic depression is a frustrating mess' – the melancholic sentiment entirely in keeping with the stylistic codes of what is essentially a $\frac{3}{4}$ blues. There is, however, no perceptible musical engagement with the title's subject matter, giving the distinct impression that the lyrics 'a broken heart' could, without major consequence, have replaced the potentially more loaded term 'manic depression'. Despite the use of medical terminology, the reference to a classified mental illness serves little purpose other than to stress the extent of the protagonist's sadness. The song lacks the theatrical complexities of many later works dealing with a similar subject matter, and instead demonstrates an artist appropriating medical terminology with no discernible intention of exploring, or indeed questioning, its wider significance. A comparable example from the same year is Willie Dixon's 'Insane Asylum' (1967), although here a musical duet with Chicago blues singer Koko Taylor enables the traditional narrative of 'man saves woman' to underpin the story of a 'little girl' driven to an 'insane asylum' because without her man's love she 'ain't nowhere'. The lyrical text does offer some critique of psychiatric confinement as evidenced in the male protagonist's reaction on discovering his lost love – 'And then sorrow struck my heart. Tears began to stream down from my eyes. The only woman that I ever loved in my whole life, out here in a place, in a condition like this' – but, again, the musical text remains seemingly unresponsive to the potential exploration of issues of both diagnosis and psychiatric treatment.[10]

---

[8]  Sander Gilman, *Seeing the Insane* (New York, 1982), p. 13.

[9]  See Susan McClary, *Feminine Endings: Music, Gender, and Sexuality* (Minneapolis, 1991), p. 92.

[10]  The song was covered in flamboyant fashion by Diamanda Galas as part of her 'Malediction and Prayer: Concert for the Damned' tour and released as a live recording on the album *Malediction and Prayer* (1998).

Perhaps the earliest mainstream popular song to utilize the character of the madman while demonstrating elements of anti-psychiatric thinking is The Move's 'Cherry Blossom Clinic' (1968), which features a protagonist who, in an apparent attempt to evoke a degree of realism, introduces his circumstances in a spoken introduction replete with appropriate sound effects (snare raps suggestive of footsteps, a heavy door opening and slamming shut, followed by a key turning in a lock): 'It was one morning when I woke up, and then I found out that they'd signed some papers, and that I was gonna be kept in a bed owing to the state of my mind.' As in the aforementioned Bowie and Pink Floyd songs, there is a perceptible alignment with theories advocating psychiatry's hidden social function – 'I found out that the authorities had said, um, that I'd gotta have special food fed to me for my thoughts' – and each chorus ends with a dramatic textural change to three-part vocal harmony and sparse guitar accompaniment for the phrase 'Lock me in and throw away the key', highlighting the protagonist's principle concern of long-term confinement. The song's conclusion contains a further affront to the psychiatric establishment's curative ability as the, now committed, protagonist reveals his own pessimistic evaluation of events: 'Probably feel better when I'm dead'; and it may be argued that such elements are representative of the form in which anti-psychiatric ideas first filtered through into popular music.

That said, the extent of the critique found in 'Cherry Blossom Clinic' remains tempered by its overt commercial nature wherein the upbeat, sing-along style arguably diminishes the seriousness of the aforementioned ingredients. The verses are similar in sound and delivery to The Move's third single, 'Flowers in the Rain' (1967), and the lyric content depicts the protagonist's visions/delusions in a way that appears entirely in keeping with their previous fondness for the psychedelic: 'Sunbeam from flowered skies, twenty thousand butterflies. Glorify my bed in deep maroon, turn from hot to very cool, though it seems incredible, I could ride a bike around the room.' In other words, the madman persona may have simply offered a further opportunity for the band to indulge in the fantastical, childlike imagery characteristic of their previous work. The most notable musical gesture (aside from the previously mentioned three-part vocal harmony) to have a direct bearing on the interpretation of lyric is used to underpin the last words of the phrases 'I was going off my head' and 'They must think I'm going mad'. In each case, the full band plays a unison triplet rhythm that alternates chromatically and repeats over two bars to provide an ominous moment of pause in which the manifest fear of 'madness' may be pondered. The fact that the re-release of the song, aptly titled 'Cherry Blossom Clinic Revisited' (1970), prompted *Rolling Stone* reviewer John Mendelsohn to describe it as 'an adaptation of a charming song about confinement in a mental hospital' with 'orgasmic choruses' further attests to its altogether polite and generally unthreatening nature.

If 'Cherry Blossom Clinic' marks the first, albeit tentative, steps towards the incorporation of anti-psychiatric thinking as an integral part of constructing one's 'mad' character, the work of singer-songwriter Kevin Coyne may be considered representative of its more complete absorption. Two works in particular –

'Asylum' (1969) and 'Our Jack' (1970) – feature first person accounts by so-called 'mad' protagonists whose insightful assessments of their, not dissimilar, predicaments serve to question the validity of their diagnoses and treatment. The character portrayed in 'Asylum' is very similar to that later portrayed in Elton John's 'Madman Across the Water' in that his repeated, unanswered questions – 'Can you hear me? Can you see me? Do you notice me when you're riding by?'[11] – appear to support Foucault's claim with respect to the silencing of madness that occurred as a result of the 'Great Confinement'.[12] Water acts as the metaphorical barrier between John's protagonist and the rest of the world and, in turn, functions to symbolize the division of the 'mad' and the 'sane'; the blackened windows, high walls and lack of meaningful dialogue between him and his visitors further imply his acute physical and emotional detachment. Coyne's character describes a similar form of isolation, the metaphorical barrier in this instance being high park fences, while the featureless room in which he lives – 'I live in a yellow room with yellow walls, yellow house with yellow doors' – and lack of response to his persistent questioning affirm his suspected non-existence.

Coyne's allegedly 'mad' character, 'Our Jack', is allowed a voice midway through the song, whereupon his withdrawal from society – at first inflicted upon him by his doctor and sanctioned by his parents – is eventually self-imposed as a result of his decision to 'put out' his 'fire' and 'hide away in some great room for a year and a day and a day and a day'. The song is of a more theatrical nature than 'Asylum', featuring multiple characters to construct the unhappy story of a son who suffers a breakdown because he cannot meet his parents' expectations with respect to his modest career aspirations. His treatment, considering he is the only one to understand the adage 'better to be happy than have money', is clearly represented as unnecessary and unduly manipulative. Despite the fact that Coyne's characters mutually display characteristics that serve to question their 'mad' identity, it should be noted that neither offers any form of overt challenge to rectify their circumstances or indeed weaken the power of those who hold them captive. In this sense, while encouraging a questioning of psychiatry's function and methods, Coyne's characters bear a similarity to Pink Floyd's protagonist in 'Brain Damage', presenting a damning account of their experiences while remaining essentially powerless victims.

Two further songs receiving commercial success in the early 1970s – Black Sabbath's 'Paranoid' (1970) and The Kinks' 'Acute Schizophrenia Paranoia Blues' (1971) – reveal the growing interest in the construction of self-confessed

---

[11]    A large amount of reverb is applied to these vocal questions in the opening of the song which helps to evoke the protagonist's state of distance and hence isolation from those he attempts to address. The reverb is removed once the protagonist begins explaining his surroundings, whereupon the sudden closeness functions to emphasize his account of captivity.

[12]    Michel Foucault, *Madness and Civilization: A History of Insanity in the Age of Reason*, trans. R. Howard (London, 1997), p. 38.

'mad' characters, although, as with the previously discussed songs by Hendrix, Napoleon XIV and Willie Dixon, there is little evidence of an anti-psychiatric stance from within either the musical or lyric texts. What is evident, however, is that these songs do at least encourage a questioning of society's attitudes towards those who deviate from what is deemed acceptable, 'normal' behaviour. Black Sabbath's 'Paranoid' is clearly important in terms of the way in which it functions to tranquillize fears of difference which may all too readily be interpreted as some form of mental abnormality. Its adolescent appeal is secured through its acknowledgement of boredom and an inability to recognize the seemingly natural route to a state of 'grown-up' contentment: 'All day long I think of things but nothing seems to satisfy, think I'll lose my mind if I don't find something to pacify [...] I can't see the things that make true happiness.' The common belief that insanity is detectable simply from a person's look is effectively challenged –'People think I'm insane because I'm frowning all the time' – while, unlike Hendrix's and Dixon's admission of mental breakdown being caused by love loss, Sabbath's protagonist bears no such romantic notion – 'Finished with my woman 'cause she couldn't help me with my mind' – ensuring that the causes of his mental anguish remain self-contained yet resolutely outside the bounds of the medical model (there is no reference to biological illness or psychiatric intervention).

The Kinks' song is more accepting of a medical judgment – 'I've been to my local head shrinker to help classify my disease. He said it's one of the cases of acute schizophrenia he sees' – but does at least draw attention to the stigma and resulting isolation that typically accompanies such a diagnosis: 'Even my old dad lost some of the best friends he ever had. Apparently his was a case of acute schizophrenia too.' The aforementioned lyric equally aligns with genetic theories of madness which, as Jones comments, 'have placed the origins of mental illness within families [and] have deep historical roots. Morel's nineteenth-century theory that insanity was the product of degenerate reproduction (that is, children produced by those with mental infirmity would be prone to mental illness) is a good example.'[13] While the verses provide ample evidence (within the lyric content) of the protagonist's increasing paranoia, the choruses attempt to lighten the mood by introducing a form of communal purging – 'Schizophrenia, schizophrenia, I've got it, you've got it, we can't lose. Acute schizophrenia blues' – that derides the fear typically associated with a psychiatric diagnosis. In terms of the musical text, neither song contains musical gestures that appear specifically linked to the subject of madness; 'Paranoid' exhibits a sound that is in keeping with the rest of Black Sabbath's repertoire at that time, and The Kinks' 'Acute Schizophrenia Paranoia Blues' offers no perceptible musical engagement with the subject matter of its title.

It is thus possible to argue that the songs featured in the previous five chapters mark an important development in the ascension of the 'mad' character within popular music, as each asserts its own particular challenge to the psychiatric

---

13    Jones, *Myths, Madness and the Family*, p. 17.

establishment through musical and verbal texts that are inextricably linked to convey a sense of personal endeavour and defiance. The apparently mutual objective of both lyric and musical gesture serves to imbue the texts with an essential validity that dismisses doubts concerning the possibility of insensitive exploitation, while the theatrical mode of expression permits a more complex insight into what it means to be labelled and 'treated' as 'mad'.

## Madness and the Family

Popular songs displaying a level of antipathy for the family unit, and most typically parental figures, were not unheard of prior to the early 1970s. Frank Zappa's 'Mom & Dad' (1968) provides one such example where the title's subjects are portrayed as emotionally indifferent and preoccupied with surface appearances:

> Ever take a minute just to show a real emotion
> In between the moisture cream and velvet facial lotion?
> Ever tell your kids you're glad that they can think?
> Ever say you loved 'em? ever let 'em watch you drink?
> Ever wonder why your daughter looked so sad?
> It's such a drag to have to love a plastic mom & dad[14]

From my previous analysis it would appear, however, that during the late 1960s and early 1970s it was increasingly common for such songs to possess a psychiatric context where family members are accused of conspiring with doctors to have their offspring confined and 'treated' by the medical profession. Such links between notions of the family and psychiatry were not new, as Jones explains: 'Ideas about psychiatry and family life have, over the last few centuries in the West, evolved together because they are both institutions in which it is hoped people's emotional lives might be contained and controlled';[15] and this points to the suitability and appeal of such subject matter to an ostensibly young rock audience keen to assert their own sense of individuality and possible resentment for what society expects and demands of them.

As detailed in previous chapters, both Reed and Elton John position their protagonists as sons in conflict with their respective family members whose supposed 'normality' is effectively challenged by providing evidence of their irrational and emotionally ambivalent behaviour: Reed's protagonist's father breaks a table with an axe, while John's protagonist's parents make light of his mental state before proceeding to comment on the weather: 'Get a load of him, he's so insane. You better get your coat dear, it looks like rain.' Moreover, each

---

[14]     Frank Zappa and the Mothers of Invention 'Mom & Dad' from the album *We're Only In It for the Money* (Verve/MGM, 1968).

[15]     Jones, *Myths, Madness and the Family*, p. 12.

song appears to align, at a deeper level, with specific anti-psychiatric theories that, while drawing on the historical relationship between madness and the family, suggest different ways in which that relationship may be critiqued. By exposing the façade of the idyllic family unit, Reed, for example, promotes the theory that psychiatric treatment is more likely a result of social judgement as opposed to concrete medical evidence; and, by implication, uses the subject of the family, and particularly the traditional foundation of marriage, to question all society's institutions. As such it is possible to identify parallels between his stance and that advocated by R.D. Laing and David Cooper, both of whom attempted to expose the concealed function of such establishments which, in Laing's words, were 'to promote respect, conformity, obedience [...] to promote a respect for work: to promote a respect for "respectability"'.[16] Alternatively, Elton John identifies more strongly with theories that expound the potential injurious effects of the family on its associate members' mental health; in other words theories which locate the root causes of a person's mental breakdown within the family unit itself: 'Will they come again next week? Can my mind really take it?' His stance is thus more akin to the work of the 'Family Therapy Movement', a group of therapists working in the mid-1940s–1960s who, according to Jones, 'had the common goal of hunting for the roots of schizophrenia in the behaviour and communication styles of the immediate family (usually the parents) of the identified patient'[17] and provided some influence on the early writings of both Laing and later Cooper.[18] In addition, the circulation of such family-based theories in both anti-psychiatric writing and popular culture at the time – see previous chapters for references to texts such as *Family Life* (1971) – arguably influenced Alice Cooper's decision to provide a paternal identity for the protagonist in 'The Ballad of Dwight Fry' where, although no accusations of family-induced madness are apparent, the family setting implies a list of responsibilities and a behaviour model that the character appears at a loss to fulfil – hence his commitment to a psychiatric care ward.

Further songs from the period actively linking ideas of the family and madness reveal yet more angles from which their long-established relationship may be questioned: in the previously mentioned songs – 'Cherry Blossom Clinic' by The Move and Kevin Coyne's 'Our Jack' – the protagonists' parents take it upon themselves to contact the medical profession and agree to their sons being sectioned without consulting them. The Move's protagonist simply wakes to discover 'they'd signed some papers', while the parents of hapless victim 'Our Jack' call the doctor after witnessing their son's strange behaviour and, following a vague yet undeniably common diagnosis – 'I think he's got something, I think it's schizophrenia or something' – conclude 'if we put him in you know where, I think

---

[16]     Ronald D. Laing, *The Politics of Experience* [1967] (Harmondsworth, 1978), p. 26.

[17]     Jones, *Myths, Madness and the Family*, p. 18.

[18]     See references to Laing and Esterson, *Sanity, Madness and the Family* and Cooper, *The Death of the Family* in Chapters 2 and 4.

he'll be out in a fortnight'. In both songs the sons' behaviour is portrayed as, at most, fanciful and immature, and in Coyne's song a perhaps understandable result of the boy's inability to assert his own desires in relation to his future career. Neither son exhibits behaviour that could be deemed threatening to others or themselves, and as such the implication is that the parents are seeking help from the psychiatric establishment simply to rejuvenate a sense of waning parental authority: the very title of Coyne's song establishing the boy's lack of autonomy and inescapable belonging to his parents – '*Our* Jack'. The songs thus draw on traditional fears surrounding involuntary confinement and the role families have historically played in committing unwanted or uncontrollable relatives to psychiatric establishments. Moreover, as witnessed in Reed's 'Kill Your Sons', both imply a social as opposed to medical justification for the sons' diagnoses.

In his later song 'Mad Boy' (1972), Coyne is able to widen this accusation to inculpate the whole of society, whose repeated accusations – 'It's in his brain, it's in his brain' – and directions – 'fetch the doctor, fetch the doctor' – provide an indication of the pressure the wider public exert on individual families in order to maintain the desired sense of social order. The underhand intention behind such interference is made clear in the song's final moments where, as soon as the doctor is confirmed to have 'done his job', the final directive – 'Put him out to grass in the park. Put him out, no more trouble, no more difficulty with his mother' – makes clear the real purpose and justification for the 'mad' boy's 'treatment'. This awareness of societal pressure to be nothing but conventional equally informs Shel Silverstein's 'The Ballad of Lucy Jordan', first recorded by Dr Hook and the Medicine Show in 1973 before coming to greater prominence via Marianne Faithfull's 1975 version. In a similar vein to the Rolling Stones' 'Mother's Little Helper' (1966), the female protagonist becomes overwhelmed, and disillusioned, by a realization of her mundane existence as mother and housewife, and the fact that she will never 'ride through Paris in a sports car with the warm wind in her hair'. While lacking any real notion of psychiatric critique, Silverstein's song nevertheless draws on the same theories of family-induced madness witnessed in Elton John's 'Madman Across the Water' – although here the fact that the protagonist is female allows for a more specific interrogation of traditional gender roles which, in this instance, are portrayed as a source of unbearable constraint leading to the protagonist's eventual mental breakdown (Lucy climbs onto a rooftop and is eventually led down 'to the long white car that waited past the crowd').

It would thus appear that the aforementioned popular songs of the late 1960s and early 1970s not only demonstrate an interest in linking ideas of the family and madness, but do so in such a way as to cast suspicion and contempt on the motives, or at least practices, of each. Such derision is, however, not overly explicit to the extent that the songs convey a sense of out and out protest; rather the verbal narrative and supporting musical gestures (see previous musical analysis of 'Madman Across the Water') are cleverly constructed to provide snapshots of relevant dialogue and, typically, a scenario where the protagonist is positioned in apparent opposition – both physically and mentally – to their principal family members. Physically, the protagonist is characteristically portrayed as a victim, involving confinement and/or treatment of some kind, whereas mentally the converse occurs as they are revealed to possess greater insight, sense and passivity than all corresponding authority figures (parents, spouses, doctors). In this way, listeners become aware of the implied criticism at the same time as taking pleasure in the narrative progression of events; while most will have had little or no experience of psychiatric involvement, all will have experienced the curtailing of personal emotions and desires understood to be an inevitable part of growing up and family life in general, and it is this universal experience that assures the relevance and appeal of the songs in question. Connecting ideas about psychiatry with those of the family thus ensures not only a degree of individuality, but greater accessibility too.

### The Allure of the 'Mad' Fool

Chapter 5 explored the way in which the Beatles' 'The Fool on the Hill' and Elton John's 'Madman Across the Water' draw on two different yet related fool identities: the 'natural' and the 'artificial'. These are not isolated cases, however, for Bowie's 'All the Madmen' equally subscribes to certain essential characteristics of foolery: the lyrical puns of the two-part bridge section and the fact that the entire song utilizes a premise of reversal as its means of facilitating a questioning of definitions of madness and sanity suggest the adroit antics of an artificial or knowing fool designed to expose the folly of the purportedly sane. Further examples from the same period indicate that the fool identity was perhaps more commonly employed at this time than previously recognized, and an interest in exposing apparent 'truths', coupled with what would appear to be an increased fascination with concepts of madness, may have been the catalyst for such.

Released a year after 'The Fool on the Hill', the Small Faces' song 'Mad John' (1968) bears some striking similarities to the former both in terms of its subject matter and general execution.[19] Unlike the Small Faces' usual psychedelic R'n'B repertoire, it is a gentle, folk-style ballad with a lilting $\frac{6}{8}$ feel which, reminiscent of the Beatles' use of acoustic recorders and flutes, manages to convey an atmosphere of simplicity and innocence that in turn enhances the 'innocent' and 'childlike' qualities of its protagonist, 'mad' John. The lyric content also helps promote such

---

[19]     Folk music singer-songwriter Tom Paxton released a similarly titled song, 'Crazy John', in 1970 which takes John Lennon's protest for peace as its central concern, identifying Lennon's altruistic vision and resulting isolation: 'Crazy John, you tell them, but they don't want to know. They never can hear you, John, they have no desire. They're beginning to fear you, John, and their hate's getting higher.' In a similar vein to 'The Fool on the Hill', John is portrayed as a victim of his own free-will and insight; it constitutes a form of 'craziness' the singer openly covets: 'Crazy John, I want to be crazy too'.

characteristics, beginning in nursery-rhyme fashion – 'There was an old man who lived in a green wood' – before going on to describe 'mad' John as an innocent child of nature who would 'sing with the birds in the morning' and 'laugh with the wind in the cold hand of night'. While John is not literally termed a 'fool' in the song, the final verse identifies him as 'a wise one' and, as such, he appears to possess all the required features of the 'natural' fool identity. As in 'The Fool on the Hill', this conclusion is also imaginatively brought to life by means of detailing the acrimonious nature of his relationship with others, where people revile him because he lives 'the life of a tramp' while all he does in return is offer them love. Moreover, the suspicion of others is similarly portrayed as small-minded and cowardly, the lyrics revealing how mothers say to their children 'Beware of Mad John' while people comment from behind their curtains 'He's not quite right'. The story eventually reveals that it is, in fact, *they* who are the eventual victims of the scenario for, because their hatred of John generates no ill feelings in return, they become frightened of him. In this way, they are responsible for their own fate – 'shaking from behind their curtains' – and an appealing sense of contrast is thus constructed between their own self-inflicted sense of captivity and the relative freedom – 'the sun was his friend, he was free' – of 'mad' John.

Musically, further parallels may be drawn as the dialectical opposition between major and minor harmony (witnessed in the tonic major to tonic minor relationship of verse and chorus in 'The Fool on the Hill') is used to convey the two contrasting views of the song's protagonist. The verses detail 'mad' John's natural existence while providing an account of people's mistrust, hatred and eventual fear of him. As such, the modal A Aeolian harmony (i, III, iv progression) offers a suitably subdued, even plaintive, feel that is noticeably removed at the onset of the chorus. Beginning with a positive affirmation of John's behaviour – 'John had it sussed' – the chorus involves a corresponding move to the tonic major chord (A major) followed by a cycle of fifths (Dsus2, G, C, Fmaj7, Bm, E). The effect of this harmonic gesture provides a stronger sense of purpose and movement towards the final statement – 'he was free' – whereupon a move up a semitone to the chord of F breaks away from the functional movement to underpin the feeling of liberation. The contrast in vocal enunciation between the two sections also contributes to the change in mood, with the chorus adopting an exaggerated cockney accent that is evidently less formal in delivery than preceding verses and seemingly invites a sing-along response. Aside from this rather transparent articulation of form, emphasis is given to the lyric 'beware of Mad John' as the vocal becomes harder and louder in tone and dynamic, and the instrumental texture cuts abruptly on the word 'John' – as if to separate him from his precursor of madness – before a lone bass fill leads into verse two. 'Mad John' and 'The Fool on the Hill' thus contain many common features, a final one of which may be found in the free vocal sections towards the end of each song, where the Small Faces' 'Ay-diddle aye di' lyrics evoke the same sense of freedom and playfulness as McCartney's vocal ad-lib melisma sung to the single syllable 'Oh'.

Procol Harum's 'In the Autumn of My Madness' (1968) was released in the same year as 'Mad John' and, with its concentration on the relationship between notions of truth and madness, appears to act as a forerunner to Elton John's 'Madman Across the Water'. The use of word play and implied age-old wisdom are clearly present – 'When all my thoughts are spoken, save my last departing birds, bring all my friends unto me and I'll strangle them with words'; but most relevant is the suggestion of the enlightened madman who admits to the burden of his increased awareness and knowledge – 'the things which I believed in are no longer quite enough, for the knowing is much harder and the going's getting rough'. However, while Elton John's protagonist is termed 'insane' by others, and cleverly mocks the label of 'madman', Procol Harum's protagonist implies that madness is a particular process one undergoes in order to attain increased awareness or insight, the 'Autumn' of his madness inferring that the process is reaching its end; his knowledge has reached its pinnacle and now he must contend with the harsh reality of 'knowing'. In this respect, parallels may be drawn between 'In the Autumn of My Madness' and Pink Floyd's *The Dark Side of the Moon*, for both draw on similar ideas surrounding the relationship between madness and wisdom, the roots of which can clearly be traced back to notions of both the natural and artificial fool.

As outlined in Chapter 5, suggestions of a link between mysticism and madness – the belief that madness enables access to hidden truths and a glimpse into humanity's future fate – are present in both 'The Fool on the Hill' and 'Madman Across the Water'; and it is interesting to note the impact this has on the song's protagonists, in that both fools are unable to share their wisdom and insight with those around them. The Beatles' protagonist chooses a form of self-imposed detachment and is effectively ostracized by others, while Elton John's protagonist's attempts to convey forewarnings which are belittled by accusations of madness. The absurdity of this dilemma is imaginatively explored in Thin Lizzy's song 'The Hero and the Madman' (1973), which delivers a comic book style fantasy via its melodramatic, half-spoken (in an evidently staged American accent), half-sung verses. As in the aforementioned songs, there is a suggestion of the madman's mystical powers, which are disregarded by those around him: 'The madman climbed the steeple spire, "Go higher" said the crowd from down below. "But the World's on fire" cried the madman from the steeple spire. "You're a liar" cried the crowd from down below. So the madman climbed the steeple spire and let a crystal ball tear fall on the crowd below.' Attention is then drawn to this dichotomy in the subsequent chorus, with its repeated question – 'Oooh, are you the hero or the madman?' – identifying the way in which the foretelling of unwanted 'truths' may just as easily be interpreted as an act of madness as an act of heroism. A certain amount of menace is also attached to the word 'madman' via a noticeable change in vocal delivery while upward bass movement to a non-harmony note seemingly enhances the element of uncertainty.

Later, references to the character of the 'mad' fool appear less frequently within popular music; although two songs from the band Madness are worthy of note because of the way they so clearly rejuvenate the 'natural', innocent fool identity witnessed in the previously discussed songs by the Beatles and the Small Faces. The first of these, 'Madness (Is All in the Mind)' (1985), involves a protagonist who lives in the moment – 'You'll never find me in a hurry, because I live my life day by day' – and dismisses accusations from others that he is mad, claiming that madness is simply a state of mind (presumably that of those doing the labelling): 'People say I'm crazy but I'm not that way inclined, I know what I know and I'll happily show that madness is all in the mind.' Although by this point the band had already moved away from the more explicitly ska roots of their early work, the carefree attitude and whimsical rhymes of this song complemented their established happy-go-lucky image, and the title track of their subsequent album, *Mad Not Mad* (1985), continued this tradition, featuring another play on the band's name. 'Mad not Mad' points to the potential multiple meanings of the term 'mad', as the protagonist, reminiscent of a nursery-rhyme character, claims that he is 'mad' (presumably in a good way: carefree, simple, innocent) but 'not mad' (presumably in a bad way: a danger to himself or others). The chorus encourages listeners to ponder their own understanding of the term, but the light-hearted sentiment of both musical and lyric texts diminishes the song's ability to seriously question the potential misuse of the word: 'Would you dance with a madman, madman, madman? Over the hills and far away, arm in arm, mad not mad.' Rather than demonstrating and thus critiquing other people's suspicious and unkind treatment of those who fail to conform to the actions and behaviour of the majority, the song, like the Kinks' 'Acute Schizophrenia Paranoia Blues', infers that a sense of group solidarity is all that is needed to survive. Appropriation of the commonly understood euphemism for impending madness – 'going round the bend' – and the act of self-labelling – identifying himself as a 'madman' – are, nevertheless, crucial to diminishing the power of any would-be name callers: 'Hello crazy gang, goodbye with a bang. What are we but our friends sailing round the bend. In love through thick and thin, I know it will all win.'

A similar adoption of the term 'fool' occurs in Green Day's song 'Basket Case' (1994) with the protagonist identifying himself as 'one of those melodramatic fools, neurotic to the bone no doubt about it'. Despite the fact that there is no evidence of the character traits identified in previous examples, the song does at least capitalize on comparable feelings of insecurity regarding what comprises normal/sane and irregular/paranoid behaviour. And yet it seems that the adoption of a 'mad' fool identity had, by this point, become a less popular means of exposing society's penchant for identifying and isolating individuals failing to conform to accepted behaviour models. The aforementioned songs of the 1960s and 1970s set the lonely figure of the fool in opposition to those around him, and their portrayal of his infinite wisdom continues to prompt questions concerning the motives and behaviour of those intent on ascribing labels of madness. The general desire for, and acceptance of, more overtly theatrical musical styles at this time arguably played a role in the selection of such thematic material, whereas future, harder, more aggressive musical styles exhibiting an interest in themes of madness appear to prefer less mythical figures on which to base their protagonists.

## Alienation and the Madness of War

The concept of alienation appears in two different, yet related, modes in the previous chapters. The first is clearly relevant to the above conclusions pertaining to the fool's (mis)treatment, in that 'The Fool on the Hill', 'Madman Across the Water' and 'Mad John' all reveal society's capacity for alienating the individual deemed at variance with the majority. Moreover, this form of selective alienation is of wider significance to an exploration of anti-psychiatric ideas in popular music because it points to the possibility of such texts advocating psychiatry's potential to enact concealed forms of social conditioning. For example, it is by recognizing society's predilection for such treatment of individuals who have 'disregarded the conventions of polite society' that Szasz is able to construct his theory concerning the covert function of psychiatry wherein he argues 'social deviance [has been] renamed "mental illness"'.[20] Aside from its obvious relevance to the way in which both fools are given a label of madness in 'Madman Across the Water' and 'Mad John', it is a theory that has evident bearing on our understanding of the protagonist's treatment in 'All the Madmen', 'Kill Your Sons' and 'The Ballad of Dwight Fry' (see Chapters 1, 2 and 4 for details).

The second mode of alienation, articulated with apparent candour in Bowie's 'All The Madmen' and Pink Floyd's *The Dark Side of the Moon*, concerns the arguably more prevalent, yet ostensibly obscure, mode of alienation believed by anti-psychiatrists Laing and Cooper to be inherent within society itself.[21] In fact, Laing's assertion that 'The condition of alienation, of being asleep, of being unconscious, of being out of one's mind, is the condition of the normal man'[22] may be regarded as one of the most important ideas to receive attention within the aforementioned works by Bowie and Pink Floyd, where traditional conceptions of madness and sanity are similarly reversed on the grounds of society's widespread state of disaffection.

Both modes of alienation have received further attention within numerous other popular songs, although only those exhibiting an apparent anti-psychiatric stance are of relevance here. The first form of selective alienation may be identified within two songs of the late 1960s previously discussed: The Move's 'Cherry Blossom Clinic' features a protagonist who recognizes his own state of isolation,

---

[20]     Thomas Szasz, *Ideology and Insanity: Essays on the Psychiatric Dehumanization of Man* [1970] (London, 1973), p. 67.

[21]     See Chapters 1, 3 and 5 for references to R.D. Laing's theory of man's estranged state and Chapters 2 and 3 for references to David Cooper's warning concerning the dangers of blind conformity.

[22]     Laing, *The Politics of Experience*, p. 24.

lamenting 'From the corner of my eye, callous friends just pass me by', while Kevin Coyne's protagonist in 'Asylum' repeatedly asks if others can hear him, yet tellingly receives no reply. Both examples portray their protagonist's alienated state as being a direct result of their enforced captivity. Like the protagonist in 'Madman Across the Water', they have already experienced an initial process of estrangement – a consequence of being identified as in some way 'different' from the majority – before succumbing to the more permanent state of alienation brought about by their confinement in a psychiatric institution. As such, both demonstrate an affinity with Foucault's theory concerning the lack of dialogue between reason and unreason, the advent of the asylum and resulting medicalization of madness having reduced it to silence (see Chapter 5 for a comprehensive overview of this in relation to 'Madman Across the Water'). Conversely, the protagonists featured in 'The Fool on the Hill' and 'Mad John', while undoubted victims of the same particularized alienation, have yet to find themselves in an enforced state of physical detachment. Indeed, these two characters readily adopt a form of self-alienation – standing motionless and alone on a hill/living alone in the woods – that is linked to an awareness of their apparent wisdom and, as the songs progress, becomes increasingly suggestive of society's own ills.

The second mode of (widespread) alienation appears to feature more frequently as a subject for exploration throughout popular music discourse, and songs utilizing a detectable anti-psychiatric context – which usually imply that such alienation is a form of sickness within society – have an apparent ability to accentuate its negative effects. King Crimson's '21st Century Schizoid Man' (1969) is one such example where heavily distorted vocals (the unnatural effect of which is comparable to Lou Reed's use of vocal equalization in the choruses of 'Kill Your Sons') sing of a bleak future in which 'Schizoid man' is seemingly emotionless and unable to relate to others. Despite the popular belief that the word 'schizoid' is in some way connected to schizophrenia, in medical terms it is understood to be a personality disorder characterized by a lack of interest in social relationships, and emotional coldness. By linking images of war and death (the lyrics contain references to napalm and funeral pyres) to concerns over the potential misuse of brain manipulation – 'neurosurgeons scream for more at paranoia's prison door' – and consumerism – 'Nothing he's got he really needs' – the effects of mass alienation culminate in a frightening vision of where humankind might be heading.

It is this same inference that madness is, in fact, a social condition principally characterized by mass alienation that appears in grindcore/death metal band Napalm Death's songs 'Mass Appeal Madness', 'Mentally Murdered' and 'Walls of Confinement', all of which appear on their 1991 album *Death by Manipulation*. As in the aforementioned '21st Century Schizoid Man', and equally reminiscent of Pink Floyd's anti-consumerist stance in 'Money', Napalm Death's 'Mass Appeal Madness' provides a powerful social critique where the desire for material wealth and infamy equates to a lack of ethics and personal beliefs: 'Cash styled deadhead, no conscience or opinions. Material gain bar happiness means shit [...] Mass appeal madness eats your brain. [...] Public eyes see fit your second face.

Freakshow – fooling those who imitate'. In this instance, mass alienation is not simply a result of emotional coldness but, in line with Laing's beliefs, involves people adopting a false self which is tantamount to a lack of individuality. Similarly, their critique of social institutions in the song 'Mentally Murdered' – 'As the free thought you were born with becomes externally polluted. Lose sight of your ideals in their brain washing institutions [...] Living up to others' expectations takes hold of your assiduity. Mentally murdered!' – demonstrates a certain affinity with David Cooper's accusations regarding the tranquillizing effects of educational institutions, the family and psychiatry which he used to substantiate calls for 'an external, mass-social, and internal, personal and private, divorce from all the mechanizations of capitalist imperializing society'.[23] All such mechanizations then lead to a state of disaffection whereupon the protagonist acknowledges that the 'walls of confinement' are not the physical ones posed by the psychiatric hospital but the mental ones resulting from other people's distorted sense of self: 'Before my eyes I see a wall 12,000 miles high and the same amount wide. Within that wall are faces of people to whom I once could relate. Now communicating seems hard when there's an ego barrier to break through ... Biased in conclusion, trapped in seclusion. To the outside – exclusion.'

The Eels' songs 'Mental' (1996) and 'My Descent into Madness' (1998) are equally focused on thoughts of mass delusion and estrangement. In common with 'Madman Across the Water' and 'Fool on the Hill', 'Mental' – which appeared on the album *Beautiful Freak* – highlights people's inability to accept difference and their recourse to labelling in order to protect an inert acceptance of what they believe acceptable and 'true'. Unlike the previously discussed character of the fool, the protagonist in this instance is searching for 'just a little truth' and it is his disillusionment with the media in particular that earns him his stigmatizing label – 'They say I'm mental 'cause I'm not amused by it all'. The later song, 'My Descent into Madness', adopts the same morose lyric sentiment as that witnessed in the opening of Bowie's 'All the Madmen', with the protagonist observing, from his place of confinement inside 'ward nine', the depressed and lonely state of the town's inhabitants: 'Springfield's looking pretty dusty today. I see their dreams coming undone. The view from inside ward nine affords this much; a town teeming with the unloved.' Rather than enhancing the melancholic lyric content, the song's undulating, high-register bass riff has a purity and smoothness of tone that, alongside the repeated IV–I (G, C) chord movement, warm organ texture and minimal string counter-melody, appears reminiscent of the (misleading) sense of calm evoked during the A sections of Pink Floyd's 'Breathe', and is thus suggestive of the town's ignorance concerning the reality of their limited existence. A similar strategy of undermining this evocation of sublime acceptance and calm (witnessed in 'Breathe's B section) is also evident as the final chord movement of the verse is both non-functional and unresolved, the B♭, F, A♭, Gm, D♭ progression serving to disrupt the previous fluency/predictability to add further poignancy to the vocal's

---

23    Cooper, *The Death of the Family*, p. 139.

ironic request to be locked in his ward – 'Close the window and lock it so it's good and tight'. While the chorus then reasserts the predictable IV–I chord movement and enhances the saccharine textures of the verses through the addition of sleigh bells and a naïve-sounding 'la la la la la la la la' vocal motif, the middle section reveals the same reversal strategy as that witnessed in the chorus sections of 'All the Madmen' as the protagonist invites the listener to 'come visit me tonight at eight o'clock and then you'll see how I am not the crazy one'. At this point the contrasting texture, which cuts to vocal and bass with heavily filtered, barely audible strings, implies a certain detachment from that previously synonymous with 'the outside', and appears to evoke the setting of the protagonist himself – suggesting either the ward's capacity to muffle sounds from the outside world, or perhaps the deadening of his senses through medication. Whatever the exact intention behind this textural and timbral manipulation, the placid, predictable nature of the verse and chorus musical gestures, juxtaposed with the protagonist's revelations concerning both the townspeople and his own state of disaffection, create an undeniably sinister atmosphere where, once again, an individual 'mad' man is apparently at odds with the supposedly 'sane' interests and beliefs of the majority. The song thus combines both modes of alienation, for the reality of the 'unloved' masses – their 'dreams coming undone' – is shown to be no more favourable an existence than that of the confined protagonist.

The same derision of one's social environment is apparent within Green Day's widely acclaimed epic 'Jesus of Suburbia' (2004) as the protagonist questions his sanity from within a setting where mass alienation is, once more, characterized by a lack of genuine experience – 'a land of make believe that don't believe in me' – and love – 'City of the damned, lost children with dirty faces today. No one really seems to care.' The proposition that madness is a social condition is also explored within Los Angeles hip hop group Psycho Realm's song 'Psycho City Blocks/ Psychic Interlude' (1998), which employs terminology commonly associated with mental illness to provide a scathing account of the violence and crime that characterizes the LA urban environment: 'We come from psycho cities and blocks. We're raised by gunshots low life in hip hop.' While not criticizing the psychiatric establishment as such, in the final verse the protagonist has evidently succumbed to the adverse influence of his social environment and acknowledges his own madness through a confession of brutal behaviour: 'Clearing the mind but my soul is mad. Tendency to act real bad […] Yeah, we the fuckin crazy youth from the streets. You see me […] delivering a metal rainstorm.' In this way the medical model is, in effect, challenged, for madness – defined by 'psycho' behaviour – is considered a product of a person's external, social environment and circumstances as opposed to a malfunction of internal biology.

The conceptualization of madness in terms of violent behaviour is, of course, not new; the late 1960s anti-war protests in particular fuelled analogies of madness and war (see the quotations from Marcuse and Laing in Chapter 1) and the previously discussed King Crimson's '21st Century Schizoid Man' and Pink Floyd's 'Us and Them' demonstrate the influence such rhetoric had on popular music. Later songs such as Ozzy Osbourne's 'Crazy Train' (1980) and Fun Boy Three's 'The Lunatics Have Taken over the Asylum' (1982) apply the same method of critique to the cold war period. While Osbourne sings of the madness of the 'us and them' philosophy – 'Crazy, but that's how it goes, millions of people living as foes' – and even implies that such a legacy of violence is causing his own mental anguish – 'Heirs of a cold war that's what we've become. Inheriting troubles I'm mentally numb. Crazy I just cannot bear' – Fun Boy Three adopt an anti-politician stance akin to that witnessed in Pink Floyd's 'Brain Damage': 'No nuclear the cowboy told us, and who am I to disagree? Cos when the madman flips the switch, the nuclear will go for me. The lunatics have taken over the asylum.' Here the expressionless/ deadpan delivery of Terry Hall and use of a single repeated note for the refrain (which eventually descends chromatically midway through the word 'asylum') help to convey the sense of restriction, monotony and bleakness resulting from the madness of politicians who are accused of wanting to strip away people's basic human rights, as indicated in the final, extended refrain: 'Take away my right to choose […] take away my point of view […] take away my dignity.' Like 'Brain Damage', the word 'lunatic' is levelled at those in political power;[24] but the fact that they are taking over the 'asylum' implies a wider social critique where the majority are also accountable for their relative position of acceptance and apathy.

## Criticism of Psychiatric Treatments

The denigration of three principal forms of psychiatric treatment – lobotomy, drugs and ECT (also commonly referred to as EST or electroshock therapy) – is apparent within three of the songs featured in previous chapters, although each maintains a discrete approach in terms of its method of criticism and degree of descriptive detail. Bowie's 'All the Madmen' makes reference to all three types of treatment, two of which (Librium and EST) are mentioned only fleetingly while being effectively mocked via the use of lyrical and musical puns (see analysis of the bridge section in Chapter 1). The use of humour alongside the protagonist's claimed ownership – 'Just *my* Librium and me and *my* EST makes three' – serves to trivialize the negative, and possibly corrective, associations of such treatment and forms a method of critique that negates the need for detailed description of

---

[24]     The word 'lunatic' once referred to a medical diagnosis whereby the afflicted person suffered temporary bouts of madness that were influenced by the phases of the moon. Its more commonly recognized usage was within criminal law where the term referred to someone of proven unsound mind. Once the diagnosis was made, it determined that the accused was unable to comprehend the nature of their crime, but also meant a loss of their civil rights. The use of the term 'lunatic' in the song thus implies that politicians are performing criminal acts that rightly deserve some punitive treatment by way of a reduction in their civil liberties; the irony of the final refrain is thus enhanced as it is in fact they who are enforcing sanctions upon the general public.

either the treatments themselves or their adverse side-effects. The act of lobotomy is initially belittled in the same way, before a change of tone in the final verse recounts the serious allegation that parts of the brain are removed in order for the protagonist to acknowledge a preferred 'reality'.

Pink Floyd's 'Brain Damage' concentrates its criticism solely on the extreme act of lobotomy but lacks the level of dissidence witnessed in 'All the Madmen'. Nevertheless, both texts utilize musical gestures designed to accentuate the clinical act of surgery, and both imply that the intention behind such is to facilitate the rearrangement of the protagonist to a preferred mental state. While neither song makes a direct reference to who is conducting the operation, the difference between Bowie's reference to 'they' – 'they take some brain away' – and Pink Floyd's more direct accusation of 'you' – 'You raise the blade, you make the change' – is interesting, for the latter arguably has more impact in terms of encouraging feelings of mass culpability. Moreover, the title of the song 'Brain Damage' develops the indictment concerning the after-effects of lobotomy from one of mind-manipulation to that of both physical and mental impairment.

As already explained, Reed's 'Kill Your Sons' differs from the above songs ostensibly through its concentration on contemporary forms of treatment and the amount of detailed medical information included with respect to types of drugs and specific after-effects. EST is the primary target of Reed's criticism and, unlike Bowie's and Pink Floyd's songs, the perpetrators are immediately identified, and their authority undermined, by the initial lyric – 'All your two-bit psychiatrists are giving you electric shock'. The psychiatric context is thus firmly established before the ensuing verses and chorus widen the charge of mental harm to that of the protagonist's parents – 'Don't you know you're gonna kill your sons?' Accusations concerning the debilitating memory loss and slowness of mental functioning following electroshock are conveyed via detailed recollections that, while undoubtedly drawing on Reed's own personal experience, encourage listeners to place themselves in the undesirable position of patient: All *your* two-bit psychiatrists are giving *you* electro shock. But every time *you* tried to read a book, *you* couldn't get to page seventeen 'cause *you* forgot where *you* were.' As detailed in Chapter 2, various musical gestures assist in evoking the harmful after-effects of EST, and the song's initial, despondent character is only slightly counteracted by the humorous way in which the protagonist's relations are ridiculed. Following this, the second form of treatment to receive attention in the song initiates not only a change in mode of address but also a change in the method of critique, for here the protagonist recollects his personal experience of drug therapy involving the major tranquillizer Thorazine; and his admission of how much fun it was – like Bowie's use of puns – quashes the potential for its administration to be regarded as a form of chastisement for 'bad' behaviour. Despite the apparent blasé manner in which the experience is recalled, Reed nevertheless includes information regarding its harmful consequences, with lyric references to choking alongside the deliberately compromised melodic construction and vocal delivery (see Chapter 2 for analysis), implying not surgical lobotomy but the arguably less gruesome, yet equally debilitating, form of chemical lobotomy.

Looking to other artists, the Ramones' song 'Teenage Lobotomy' (1977) is a further example from the 1970s that combines Bowie's use of frivolous humour alongside Reed's celebration of youth delinquency to affect a 'no brain, my gain' mentality that is perhaps more menacing than the allusion to lobotomy itself. With evident irony, the protagonist boasts of becoming the ultimate delinquent as a direct result of medical intervention, the after-effects of which enable him to attain a higher degree and the love of all the girls: 'I guess I'll have to tell 'em that I got no cerebellum. Gonna get my PhD, I'm a teenage lobotomy yeah! [...] All the girls are in love with me, I'm a teenage lobotomy yeah!'[25] In the song's opening, the word 'lo-bo-to-my' is rhythmically chanted by the group members to initiate a feeling of celebratory consensus. The $\frac{6}{4}$ time signature of the introduction; subsequent move to $\frac{4}{4}$ for the verse; and return to $\frac{6}{4}$ during the instrumental breaks provides an unpredictable, lurching feel that, alongside the powerful rawness of the guitar riffs, augments the general feeling of menace. The largely shouted lead vocal, being simple in terms of its melodic construction (following the chord changes in predictable fashion) and relatively up-front in the mix, ensures the lyrics and their evident message of defiance are clearly audible throughout.

Similar tactics are used to deride methods of psychiatric treatment in the Ramones' later songs 'Gimme Gimme Shock Treatment' (1977), 'Go Mental' (1978) and 'Psycho Therapy' (1983). In the latter, the behaviour of a 'teenage schizoid' with 'glowing eyes' is comically magnified to denigrate perceived connections between teenage delinquency and mental illness. Pranks, muggings, burglaries, even murder are threatened by a protagonist who appropriates and flaunts harmful labels intended to capture and punish his misdemeanours: 'I'm a teenage schizoid ... a teenage dope fiend ... a kid in the nut house ... a kid in the psycho zone'; and, as in Reed's 'Kill Your Sons', psychiatric medication – in this case the barbiturate Tuinal – is venerated for keeping him 'edgy and mean'.[26]

Drug therapy, and its potential to result in what is sometimes referred to as 'chemical lobotomy', finds particular critique in the 1970s songs of Kevin Coyne 'Our Jack' (1970) and the Doctors of Madness' 'I Think We're Alone' (1976). The former includes a section where the protagonist's father, in an effort to reassure his wife that they have done the right thing by having their son sectioned, demonstrates his firm faith in psychiatric medication – 'There's not much wrong that a few pills can't put right.' The prescription of the pills and his assumption concerning their efficacy are then brought into doubt as the story unfolds to reveal the social, as opposed to biological, reasons behind the son's diagnosis and treatment (see

---

25    Lobotomy does not actually target the cerebellum, but the term is reasonably well known as an important area of the brain, and the resulting point of rhyme produces one of the key lyrical hooks of the song.

26    The song was later covered by Skid Row and appears on their cover versions EP *B-Side Ourselves* (1992).

earlier section on madness and the family for further details). In 'I Think We're Alone', the Doctors of Madness employ a different approach in which the mental suffering of the protagonist is implicit yet its cause remains a mystery. Here, the sense of despair is concentrated on the failure of the medical profession to either identify or cure his mental anguish. In fact, the implication is that the tests and pills merely exacerbate his sense of despondency: 'but the doctors know best, so I've taken the pills and I've taken the tests but they don't seem to understand [...] strangled by doubt again [...] They just make me feel like I'll never get out. So now I'm looking around for a rope [...] it's the only way out.'

Today, the term 'lobotomy' remains synonymous with brain death, although its ability to generate feelings of fear and revulsion is often capitalized on, not to condemn past psychiatric practices but to warn of the various current means of mind manipulation – be they chemical, political or institutional, which may result in a similar loss of personal identity. Swedish death metal band Mental Crypt's 'Chemical Lobotomy' (1999) lacks the rebellious spirit of Reed's 'Kill Your Sons', but nevertheless attempts to detail the no-win situation experienced by those prescribed psychiatric drugs – 'Perishing in agony, the breakdown of my senses. With chemical lobotomy I ignore the consequences' – only to find that their mental suffering is replaced by chemical dependency and a lack of self-control: 'Addicted to this fatal saviour. Agony will send me to my grave. No control of destiny. Consumed by drugs I meet my final day.' The psychiatric context is less evident within Sepultura's 'Lobotomy' (1989), where the title merely provides an analogy for the brain/emotional death affected upon the protagonist by a 'system' created to 'lie and deceive'. The resigned and depressed fate depicted in Mental Crypt's song is also avoided in favour of threats of brutal revenge in which the protagonist acknowledges that his feelings of revulsion outweigh those of empathy as the injustice he has been dealt renders him oblivious to self-blame: 'Eye for an eye, you receive your just reward. Now I'll live my life with indifference. I've tortured without remorse, I've slaughtered without fear. Brain killing brain. Brain killing brain.'

Despite the continued practice of ECT, references to it within post-1970s popular song are less common than the aforementioned treatments of lobotomy and pills. That said, one song that plainly upholds the challenging sentiment of Reed's 'Kill Your Sons' is Eels' 'Electro-Shock Blues' (1998), where a comparable catalogue of memory loss and reconditioning is suggested by the fact that the protagonist feels compelled to 'write down "I am okay",' only to end the first verse with the sombre admission, 'I am not okay'. Use of equalization on the vocal produces a similar telephone effect to that witnessed on 'Kill Your Sons' (albeit without the heavy distortion), and the apparent lack of reverb suggests a state of detachment as opposed to proximity. In contrast to this, the repetitive two-bar accompaniment utilizes alternating piano notes drenched in reverb and a keyboard sample which, having its own ambience, indicates the position of the sample's trigger to connote a permanent sense of stasis that effectively underpins the lyric content in verse two: 'Another day, another day. Not another day.' While the actual act of electroshock is not detailed, the word 'blues' in the title, having no apparent musical reference, implies a lament regarding its usage; and the opening lyric 'Feeling scared today' conveys the fear of its application, a fear that can only be assuaged through the use of drugs: 'Pink pills feel good, finally understand, take me in your warm embrace.' The unchanging, minimal nature of the song, and detached, melancholic vocal are integral to its anti-psychiatric stance for, despite the comfort afforded by the drugs, neither they nor the electroshock have the capacity to change the protagonist's position of unending monotony and depression. The inference that such psychiatric treatment could be prescribed as some form of punishment – as was the case in both 'Kill Your Sons' and 'All the Madmen' – is not evident, but its ability to cast doubt on the efficacy and thus moral grounds for such forms of intervention remains clear.

## Criticism of Involuntary Psychiatric Confinement

As detailed earlier, the actual sites of psychiatric confinement portrayed by the songs featured in previous chapters are plainly varied, and yet all appear united in their condemnation of involuntary internment. References to cold, grey mansions; cellars dark and grim; care wards described as danger zones; locked doors; high walls and blackened windows all serve to invoke feelings of negativity and dread concerning the act of, and experience of, psychiatric confinement. Kevin Coyne's descriptions emanating from the same period are similarly bleak, for in 'Asylum' the protagonist describes how all internal features are yellow, while outside it is always dark, the fences are high and the gates are closed. In 'House on the Hill' (1973) – 'the place where they always give you pills' – conditions are likewise uninviting: 'the rooms are always chilled, they're never cosy'.

Despite the period of deinstitutionalization that occurred from the 1950s onwards, analogies to prisons are used by both Alice Cooper and Elton John as a means of stressing the involuntary aspect of their protagonists' plight – 'The Ballad of Dwight Fry' effectively augmenting this through references to straitjackets and sirens which, in turn, advocate theories of psychiatric policing as opposed to medical cure. While it appears that depictions of psychiatric confinement become less common in popular song from the 1980s onwards, two notable examples – Ozzy Osbourne's 'Diary of a Madman' (1981) and Eels' 'My Descent into Madness' – adopt a similar strategy of critique. Like Cooper, with his references to being 'inside' as an 'inmate' and confined in a straitjacket, Osbourne utilizes the popular euphemism for doing prison time – 'walk the line again today' – while Eels' protagonist describes how 'The jacket makes me straight so I can just sit back and bake'.

Perhaps more disturbingly, Pink Floyd's 'Brain Damage' invokes the fear of being identified as a 'no-hope' case, involving permanent seclusion with little hope of cure or release – 'You lock the door and throw away the key' – a situation not uncommon for those having undergone surgical lobotomy. Three years earlier,

The Move had included an almost identical lyric in 'Cherry Blossom Clinic' – 'Lock me in and throw away the key' – while, as previously detailed, the song's introduction contains sound effects of a door slamming and locking before the protagonist recounts being told he was 'going to be kept in a bed'. Similar evidence of enforced confinement is manifest within Alice Cooper's protagonist's anxious pleas for release (see analysis of the first interlude section, Chapter 4); Kevin Coyne's protagonist's admission in 'Asylum' – 'I'm captured here'; and Ozzy Osbourne's description of perpetual captivity and its psychological effects in 'Diary of a Madman' – 'Screaming at the window, watch me die another day. Hopeless situation, endless price I have to pay.' In the latter song, the chorus harmony also helps convey a sense of captivity as the A Aeolian phrase descends only to alternate between chords VII and VI before returning to its starting point (Am, G, F, G, F, G, Am). The use of minor mode and lack of progression, as in Elton John's 'Madman Across the Water' (which employs the same F–G–Am progression), thus evokes a state of melancholic intransience that serves as a fitting metaphor for the protagonist's lack of freedom. The result of all such references is that listeners are encouraged to question the custodial function of the psychiatric hospital and, as such, all the aforementioned songs share an affinity with Szasz's unremitting claim that 'detention of persons in mental institutions against their will is a form of imprisonment'.[27]

The actual effects of involuntary confinement as indicated in the above songs are comparatively diverse. Perhaps the most unique among them is Bowie's 'All the Madmen' where, in spite of its bleak opening, the protagonist demonstrates a clear desire to remain in his state of captivity, for he is convinced that all the 'madmen' are sane while only the 'sad men' roam free and will eventually 'perish'. The reality of his internment is thus bound up within a more complex reversal process in which the 'mad' possess true reason and the psychiatric hospital affords a place of refuge. That said, the song does not advocate the internment of all supposedly 'mad' men and 'mad' women; rather it acknowledges the improbability of curing society's ills and suggests a union of like-minded, enlightened souls – even if such a convergence must occur within the confines of a psychiatric hospital. A suggested solidarity among those interned not only helps communicate such a message – 'Day after day, they send my friends away […] I'd rather stay/play here with all the madmen' – but also aligns with Goffman's theory concerning the effect of the 'total institution' where 'sometimes special solidarities extend throughout a physically closed region' and residents 'have a lively sense of common fate'.[28]

Alice Cooper's 'The Ballad of Dwight Fry' advocates a similar sense of collective identity whose roots are found not only in the shared experience of

---

[27]    Szasz, *Ideology and Insanity*, p. 113. The title of Chapter 9 within this book provides further evidence of Szasz's abhorrence for such psychiatric intervention: 'Involuntary Mental Hospitalization: A Crime Against Humanity', p. 113.

[28]    Erving Goffman, *Asylums: Essays on the Social Situation of Mental Patients and Other Inmates* [1961] (London, 1991), p. 59.

captivity, but also in the perception that the place of confinement represents a threat to one's person: 'I made friends with a lot of people in the danger zone'. The song's critique is firmly centred on the psychiatric establishment itself and, contrary to the reversal strategy evident in Bowie's song, implies that the protagonist is driven insane by his experience of enforced confinement – 'See my only mind explode since I've gone away' – both inside the intensive care ward and in the confines of a straitjacket. Loss of weight, lack of sleep and a confused sense of time are identified as initial side-effects, while the increasingly frantic yet unacknowledged pleas for release (see analysis of first interlude section, Chapter 4) are indicative not of mental illness but the fear of continued captivity. The same accusation is inferred within Ozzy Osbourne's 'Diary of a Madman' where any hope of cure is extinguished by the detrimental impact of the protagonist's internment – 'Sanity now it's beyond me [...] manic depression befriends me' – with the end lyric consisting of a final appeal for release: 'Set me free!'

Kevin Coyne's songs 'Our Jack', 'Asylum' and 'Mad Boy' offer yet more perspectives on the issue of confinement and its potential impact on those labelled 'mad'. The protagonist in 'Our Jack', like Bowie's protagonist, decides to relinquish his freedom – although the reasons for such are a product of resignation as opposed to valour because, as he is prevented from pursuing the life he chooses in the outside world, he resolves to give up on life altogether: 'Put out my fire, hide away'. The protagonist in 'Asylum', while well aware of his impoverished circumstances and their negative impact – 'I'm waiting here, I'm captured here, and the gates are closed. I can't stand no more' – lacks the defiant spirit of either Bowie's or Alice Cooper's protagonist; however, Coyne's portrayal of the instigators of the boy's commitment in 'Mad Boy' is extremely effective in revealing the possibility for psychiatric confinement to be utilized as a means of disposing of society's unwanted: 'Put him out to grass in the park [...] he can't make it any more, any more, any more, any more'.

All the preceding examples question whether or not such restrictive action is either necessary or moral; but depictions of involuntary psychiatric confinement within popular music do not always demonstrate such compassion. The later 1980s in particular revealed an interest in exploring the rightful imprisonment of the criminally insane where diagnoses of madness were linked to acts of violence, and the act of confinement provoked only threats of retribution. The onset of such material may have been influenced by the growth in literature concerning both real and fictional accounts of the motivational impetus, actions and subsequent punishment of serial killers[29] – see, for example, Ann Rule's *The Stranger Beside Me: Ted Bundy: The Shocking Inside Story* (1980); Ted Schwarz's *The Hillside*

---

[29]     American metal band Macabre epitomize the extreme product of this influence, with tales of individual serial killers manifest in their lyric content. Among the songs featured on their first EP, *Grim Reality* (1987), were 'Serial Killer', 'Son of Sam' and 'Ed Gein'. It is a theme they have continued to exploit: 'Jeffrey went to the Black & Decker Store and bought himself a drill and a saw' ('Drill Bit Lobotomy', 2003).

*Strangler: A Murderer's Mind* (1981); Terry Sullivan and Peter Maiken's *Killer Clown: The John Wayne Gacy Murders* (1983); and Thomas Harris's *Red Dragon* (1981). American thrash band Slayer provided the first notable example of this type in the song 'Criminally Insane', which appeared on their 1986 album *Reign in Blood*. Here an exploration of the kind of power serial killers aim to wield over their victims is presented through the protagonist's boasts of violence – 'For my victims no tomorrow' – and threatened breakout – 'escape for me has fast become a game'. The disclosure of the pain his commitment causes – 'Branded in pain, marked criminally insane. Locked away and kept restrained' – is not intended to secure sympathy as the ensuing lyric is both remorseless and chilling: 'But what have I done? I have yet only just begun to take your fuckin' lives!' The level of tension and aggression builds throughout this section of the song as the shouted, yet clearly enunciated, vocal begins with rhythmic variation on a single pitch – drawing attention to key words such as 'criminally' and 'insane' – before slowing to crotchet stabs that gradually ascend in pitch to a climactic semiquaver burst: 'take your fuckin' lives!' In response to this gesture, the guitars and drums deliver two unison semiquaver stabs of their own that serve as a fitting metaphor for the threatened violence and its intended decisiveness. The same punctuation technique, this time featuring the full line-up, is used at the end of each chorus, where the protagonist's command over his victims is underlined in the final phrase: 'I'll make you follow.' The staccato, semiquaver stabs and quaver rests that separate them serve to mark the song's sectional boundaries and offer some contrast to the frenetic distorted guitar riffs; but most importantly they augment the hostility inherent within the vocal tone and lyric content by way of the suddenness with which they dissect the horizontal time axis. The opening to the song provides further evidence of dramatic time manipulation, beginning as it does in a half-time feel that is disrupted midway through the third bar with an unexpected kick drum on the sixth demisemiquaver of beat 2, signalling a move to double-time that, when later the protagonist describes his situation – 'Quarters for the criminally insane, the sentence read for life I must remain' – becomes further energised via the use of snare hits on the half-beat.

English goth-rock band Fields of the Nephilim's 'Vet for the Insane' (1987) and American death metal band Autopsy's 'Critical Madness' (1989) are also songs which feature the subject of violent madness and its physical containment. 'Vet for the Insane' begins with a subdued, picked guitar foundation that lends an ominous undertone to the low-pitched, menacing commands of the protagonist who repeatedly whispers the word 'relax' before revealing a past brutal act: 'Flowers in your kitchen they weep for you. I'm gonna shred them all to pieces, like I did to you.' The chorus becomes higher in pitch and more melodic as the protagonist progresses from threats to appeals for help – 'In this asylum I cry for you. I want to go home ... help me, I want to go home' – appeals which fail to elicit sympathy as the song ends with a somewhat clichéd reinforcement of his unstable mind (a repeated phrase that evokes the taunt of childhood teasing, accompanied by an out-of-tune music box). Autopsy's 'Critical Madness' equally draws on a number of 'mad' stereotypes in its effort to link madness and violence – the killer hears voices: 'Mind snapped thoughts of death, demented voices in his head'; commits psychotic murder: 'Bloody killing spree, brain fed eternally, psychotic mission of death, critical madness'; suffers a '*violent* breakdown'; and is justly incarcerated: 'No hope for a normal life, insane asylum is your home.'

Playing, or as in 'Critical Madness' portraying, the role of a serial killer diagnosed criminally insane does not necessarily condone the actions of such persons; indeed parts of Slayer's lyric are demonstrative of the protagonist's awareness regarding the consequences of his actions – 'The path I chose has led me to my grave'; and while escape and retribution are planned, they remain a fantasy as opposed to a reality. Clearly, the construction of madness is entirely different from that demonstrated within the previous chapters and, while an in-depth examination of such is beyond the scope of this book, suffice it to say that differences in genre and associated cultural codes largely determine this outcome. Thrash and death metal are, in part, identified through their interest in exploring apocalyptic themes; and playing the part of the interned, criminal 'mad' man is a means of promoting traditional codes of masculinity through visual and aural signifiers of power, aggression and resolve.[30] The act of confinement in such situations thus provides a means of heightening the perceived levels of tension and frustration inherent within the musical text, and is not, I would argue, intended as a means of questioning the curative potential or moral rectitude of psychiatric confinement.

## Musical Depictions of Madness and Identified Commonalities

Techniques used to signify the Otherness of madness within the musical texts explored in previous chapters appear to conform to one universal strategy involving compositional devices that may be interpreted as constituting a form of opposition to conventional, functional and logical musical processing. In particular, chains of signifiers that are in some way non-compliant with listeners' comprehension and expectations of utilitarian musical devices serve to function as representative of the marginalized, irrational identity of madness. Much of this is dependent on an awareness of stylistic conventions where any musical gesture not adhering to established codes may be regarded as standing in evident opposition to the norm; however, at a deeper level more subtle manipulations such as a lack of directed harmonic/melodic phrasing or irregular rhythmic phrasing, while not necessarily at

---

[30]        The appeal of adopting a serial killer persona is perhaps best understood if one considers the personality traits of fictionalized characters such as Dr Hannibal Lecter, who first appeared in Thomas Harris's novel *Red Dragon* and became the focus of its sequel, *The Silence of the Lambs* (New York, 1988). Often described as an anti-hero, Lecter is highly intelligent, incisive, manipulative, indomitable and capable of extreme acts of brutality against those who impinge upon his freedom or in some way offend him.

odds with stylistic convention may – especially in conjunction with an appropriate lyrical word or phrase – be deemed to evoke those feelings of unease, confusion and abnormality associated with traditional conceptions of madness.

Both 'All the Madmen' and 'Brain Damage' begin with harmonic and melodic gestures designed to convey the Otherness of madness prior to revealing unexpected points of reversal wherein strongly directed, functional passages appear in support of the lyrical references to the actual sanity and, in the case of 'Brain Damage', the need for self-assuredness of those labelled different from the majority and supposedly in need of psychiatric treatment. Similarly, the use of non-chord tones in 'Madman Across the Water' for the key words 'him' and 'madman' and the minor vi chord underpinning the word 'fool' in 'The Fool on the Hill' effectively convey the outsider identity of the 'mad' fool before other gestures (the revelation chord in 'The Fool on the Hill'; the expressive melodic gestures of Elton's 'mad' man set against the clipped, impassive ones of his 'sane' relatives) illicit sympathy for their positions of exclusion.

'The Ballad of Dwight Fry' adopts a somewhat different position from the aforementioned songs, in that Fry is the only protagonist to be represented as being at some point genuinely mad. True, the initial manipulation of vocal tone and melodic phrasing appears demonstrative of the character's ability to flit in and out of the madman role, but the real indictment against involuntary psychiatric confinement can only be achieved by representing the protagonist's resulting mental disintegration (as witnessed in the second instrumental interlude and final verse). The song's opening is characterized by musical gestures – ungainly use of pitch, laboured rhythmic phrasing and disturbed, low register, half-spoken tone – that may be recognized as constituting a sense of abnormality in relation to the protagonist's ability to express both himself and his circumstances. Moreover, this understanding is compounded by the subsequent introduction of normative vocal gestures more in keeping with the song's predominant hard-rock style – more fluent, sung phrasing, occupying a higher register and strained chest voice – which serve to suggest the ease with which the former musical peculiarities suggestive of madness may be fabricated. The later 'real' evocation of Fry's degeneration into madness follows repeated claims concerning the detrimental mental effects of his captivity – 'See my only mind explode since I've gone away' – and is represented without the use of vocal in an atonal guitar solo where dissonance resulting from seemingly random pitch bends in half-time provide the principal means for evoking a sense of disorientation and perceived lack of rationality. Madness is thus conceived not as a biological disease, but as a breakdown resulting from external pressures; it is not something that is merely visible in the actions and spoken words of its supposed victims (which can be either misconstrued or deliberately fabricated), but manifests itself as an internal breakdown of the senses (represented sonically in 'The Ballad of Dwight Fry' without the use of vocal and lyric projection).

Given the way in which all songs explored in the previous chapters have been proven to share ideas that may collectively be termed 'anti-psychiatry', it is worth identifying musical commonalities which may provide clues as to their suitability for the exploration and communication of such subject matter. The songs' opening passages in particular not only set the scene for the questioning of psychiatric practices but, most importantly, provide an initial insight into the musical approaches that will be employed in such a task. Bowie, Alice Cooper, Pink Floyd and Elton John all create unusual, atmospheric openings for their songs, often conveying ominous undertones which encourage a series of questions pertaining to their protagonists' situations: Why are his friends locked away?/Where is daddy?/ Who is the madman across the water? In addition, such introductions indicate the extent to which textural and timbral manipulation will be important to the way in which a sense of drama is put across within the main body of the songs. Initial and subsequent choices of instrumentation are also crucial to the musical expression of mood: the fact that Bowie, Alice Cooper and Elton John all employ relatively sparse opening textures featuring a strummed, acoustic guitar accompaniment for their protagonist's initial statements encourages not only feelings of intimacy and genuine experience, but also supports the sense of an unfolding musical journey where more powerful timbres and dense textures eventually emerge to convey a variety of emotional states. All songs adhere to what is conventionally understood to constitute a basic rock ensemble – with drums, bass, guitars and lead vocal providing the essential timbral ingredients; but many then build onto this a number of unusual sound sources – for example, Bowie's and the Beatles' use of recorders; Pink Floyd's use of sound effects; Alice Cooper's use of metallophone; the Beatles' use of finger cymbals; Pink Floyd's and Bowie's use of synthesizers – that, alongside other musical signifiers, help to communicate a sense of mystery and peculiarity, both of which traditionally encapsulate notions of abnormality. Further to this, the instrumental roles are often more varied than would be the case in songs whose function is principally to encourage listeners to dance; and the numerous instances of word-painting – for example, the use of high-register bass working in metaphorical opposition with Bowie's claim to be 'as heavy as can be'; the use of driving percussion to accompany the relative's promised return in 'Madman Across the Water' – reveal an imaginative approach to atmospheric and timbral detail. Extreme textural contrasts – used to striking effect in 'The Ballad of Dwight Fry', 'Us and Them' and 'Madman Across the Water' – and the incorporation of spoken voice by Bowie, Alice Cooper and Pink Floyd further demonstrate an interest in bringing the subject matter to life in a way that is both enlightening and thought-provoking.

At a time when music production techniques were rapidly advancing, one might assume their use to be largely indicative of the desire for a certain novelty factor; however, with the exception of 'The Fool on the Hill', whose production remains understated throughout, all other songs explored in the previous chapters feature what could be considered flamboyant technological effects that appear entirely purposeful in the sense that they enhance and strengthen the potential meaning of the concomitant musical ideas. Lou Reed's use of vocal equalization and analogue tape delay, for example, encourages a more concentrated listening response and assists in highlighting the all-important title lyric. Noticeable reverb effects are applied to the lead vocal in the opening of 'All the Madmen' and at the end of each chorus of 'Madman Across the Water' to signify their protagonists' state of isolation, while the excessive reverb applied to the final lyric of 'The Ballad of Dwight Fry' – 'insane' – works alongside a dramatic descending glissando to infer Fry's permanent fall into the abyss of madness. Reverse reverb is applied to the introductory acoustic guitar riff in 'Madman Across the Water' and, as with the use of reversed guitar chords in the second instrumental interlude of Alice Cooper's song, serves to provide an unnerving sense of suspense and anticipation regarding what will follow. Extreme panning appears to increase the lavish and elated feel of the final chorus and ending of 'All the Madmen', while in 'Us and Them' its application to the word 'Them' is used to evoke a sense of threatening encirclement. In terms of sound effects, Alice Cooper's insertion of an explosion pinpoints the literal detonation of Fry's mind, whereas Pink Floyd's innovative use of sound effects throughout *The Dark Side of the Moon* helps to convey the album's basic tenets regarding the passage of time and man's unthinking existence.

Musical analysis within the previous chapters has demonstrated how discrete musical elements such as harmony, melody, rhythm and production work in conjunction to produce a variety of extra-musical effects. However, for the purpose of identifying commonalities in musical approach, it is perhaps more comprehensible to continue to examine such elements in isolation, bearing in mind that they may be only one in what is effectively a chain of signifiers responsible for encouraging a particular interpretation of the musical text. Harmony, for example, has an evident impact on one's interpretation of melodic construction; however, there are three discrete usages of harmony that deserve independent comment. The first concerns the employment of non-functional progressions (modes and chromaticism) which may be used to symbolize the unfamiliar and imbue the musical text with a sense of unease (see, for example, the use of Phrygian in the opening verse and two-part bridge sections of 'All the Madmen' and the use of chromaticism in 'The Ballad of Dwight Fry'). Aeolian harmony is often used to help convey a melancholic mood (the move from E major to E Aeolian during Alice Cooper's verse progression and the use of Aeolian progression in 'Madman Across the Water' are two such examples), while the use of repeated non-functional progressions, and in particular the use of Dorian mode, is utilized to convey a lack of direction or perceived closure (see, for example, Pink Floyd's use of Dorian harmony in 'Breathe' and the opening to 'The Ballad of Dwight Fry').

The second use of harmony worthy of comment concerns the employment of functional diatonic and major mode progressions to express a sense of strength, assuredness and direction; and, from a formal perspective, these tend to arrive at significant points – typically choruses – within the musical text. 'All the Madmen' employs a functional, A major progression to convey a determined message in support of the protagonist's desire to stay with all the madmen and vouch for their sanity; the chorus of 'Kill Your Sons' breaks away from the verse's stagnant cycle of repetition, utilizing functional harmony to serve as a metaphor for the predicted act of killing; Pink Floyd's 'Eclipse' and 'Brain Damage' both employ functional harmony to help create a feeling of emotional peaking, with the Lydian inflections in the chorus of 'Brain Damage' adding a further element of encouragement/ striving; and 'The Ballad of Dwight Fry' utilizes E Mixolydian minor during its choruses to contrast with the relative ambiguity of the verses and, due to its brighter feel, support the revelation that it is actually the protagonist's treatment that is driving him 'insane'. Spells of functional harmony are also used to provide support for apparent truths within the lyric text that are later revealed to be false. (The use of a ii, V, I progression underpinning the lyrics 'nobody wants to know him, they can see he's just a fool' in 'The Fool on the Hill' and the alternating tonic, dominant progression reinforcing the sentiment 'Got to keep the loonies on the path' in 'Brain Damage' are both examples of this device.)

The third harmonic device of note concerns the shift between tonic major and tonic minor to establish a sense of dialectic opposition representative of 'us and them'. In 'The Fool on the Hill' this manifests itself between discrete sections whereby the major verse is set against a chorus in tonic minor; in 'Madman Across the Water' the change in subject position during the transitional bridge is underpinned by a harmonic shift to the relative major indicative of his relatives' strong position (not sharing his plight, they are thus major while he remains characterized with a minor identity); and in 'Us and Them' the lyrics 'us' and 'me' are accompanied by the tonic major while 'them' and 'you' are juxtaposed in the relative minor.

In addition to the aforementioned harmonic devices, melody equally informs potential interpretations of the lyric text via the expressive use of non-harmony tones, manipulation of melodic contour and rhythmic construction. Numerous instances of word-painting enliven the lyric text and encourage an emotive response from the listener (see, for example, the use of appoggiaturas to stress the protagonist's detachment from his friends in 'All the Madmen'; the poignancy of the descending phrase accompanying the words 'sun going down' in 'The Fool on the Hill'; and the descending repetition of the word 'run' to signify the mounting distance between sons and parents in 'Kill Your Sons'). The placement of non-harmony tones in relation to the lyric text is also significant in that their weak relationship to the accompanying chord (they are neither the root, 3rd nor 5th) suggests a lack of security that impacts on one's reading of the accompanying word(s): for example, the use of the 9th, 7th and 6th informs the Other identity of the protagonist in 'Madman Across the Water'; and the fall from tonic to the 7th provides an element of uncertainty alongside the words 'EST' and 'lobotomy' in 'All the Madmen'. Noticeable contrasts in melodic construction perform a similar function to the varied use of harmony described above, perhaps the best example being that found in 'The Ballad of Dwight Fry' where the uncomfortable and unwieldy character of phrases used to describe Fry's mental state suddenly give way to more directed, conventional phrases that establish the notion of conscious role play (similar examples occur in 'All the Madmen' between the sigh-like contour of the verse and more directed, sing-along chorus melodies; and the amorphous quality of verse and more determined chorus melodic statements in 'Kill Your Sons'). Finally, the manipulation of melodic rhythm also impacts on one's interpretation of potential meanings: in the songs 'Brain Damage' and 'The Ballad of Dwight Fry' the rhythmic fluency of the vocal delivery appears unnecessarily compromised to convey the protagonists' confused mental states; the metre changes in 'Madman Across the Water', while adding an air of unpredictability, also help establish the contrasting moods that encourage a critical reading of the protagonist's relatives; and the adherence to structured time during the 'I wanna get outta here' passage in 'The Ballad of Dwight Fry' is crucial to conveying an apparent sense of rationality and hence justification for the protagonist's frantic appeals for release.

All compositional elements thus appear to demonstrate, to varying degrees, a sense of the adventurous through which it becomes possible to convey contrasting and sometimes conflicting moods. The articulation of form and structure in Bowie's, Alice Cooper's and Elton John's songs – where two-part choruses, multiple bridge and instrumental sections allow for unpredictable plot developments – further attest to such. Moreover, the fact that the surrounding songs on each respective album are arguably less audacious in terms of musical complexity suggests that, in each case, the topic of madness performs a crucial role in permitting and dictating such musical experimentation.

## Suggested Reasons for the Interest in Madness and Anti-Psychiatry

While evidence attesting to the social significance of the aforementioned songs is simply conjectural, in the case of 'The Ballad of Dwight Fry' Alice Cooper's later description of it as 'the definitive Alice song' suggests he clearly believes it to be representative of quality. Similarly, Bowie's insertion of 'All the Madmen' into the set of his 1987 *Glass Spider* tour implies its continued significance to him as a means of showcasing his early theatrical exuberance. For the same reason that the 'mad' aria became an almost mandatory part of opera in the nineteenth century, the topic of madness offers artists such as Bowie, Alice Cooper and Elton John the opportunity to explore a variety of intense emotions which, in order to be successfully conveyed, necessitate a high level of musical skill. As demonstrated in the previous section, their songs thus provide a veritable stage from which to exhibit a wide range of musical talents in terms of both composition and performance. Moreover, the theatrical element of the aforementioned artists' musical style – involving the depiction of multi-faceted characters – enables an ostensibly complex construction of madness to be portrayed in which the incorporation of anti-psychiatric ideas becomes paramount. As detailed in previous chapters, the employment of theatrical role play is significant here for it not only nullifies the potential threat of artists themselves being deemed 'mad' but also serves to destabilize conventional notions of what is believed to constitute 'sane' and 'insane' behaviour.

Aside from providing the ideal thematic backdrop from which to showcase artists' musical abilities, the topic of madness holds a certain attraction because of its association with all things unconventional, and in the case of Reed and Alice Cooper this manifests itself in an apparent desire to *play* the deviant. It is also the case that real-life encounters with the psychiatric establishment may prompt and shape an artist's musical evocation of such, as has been previously suggested in the case of Bowie, Reed and Pink Floyd, where its exploration may even be regarded as potentially therapeutic. The appeal of portraying a character deemed 'mad' by others may also be explained with reference to ideas linking madness, creativity and genius which, as Roy Porter identifies, have a long history giving rise to one of the few instances where being labelled 'mad' might be judged an expression of regard:

> Greek thinkers advanced the idea of divine madness in the artist, 'inspired' (literally 'filled with spirit') or touched by a divine 'fire'. Notably in the *Phaedrus*, Plato spoke of the 'divine fury' of the poet, and works attributed to Aristotle (384–322 BC) sketched the profile of the melancholy genius, whose solitary discontent fired his imagination to produce works of originality. Such views were revived in the Renaissance by Ficino and other humanists; to dub a poet 'mad' was, in the conventions of the age, to pay him a compliment.[31]

Numerous writers have attempted to account for such connections[32] and Lionel Trilling's essay 'Art and Neurosis' (1950) is particularly relevant to certain ideas expounded in the previously examined songs, namely the linking of madness with an ability to reveal hidden truths, and the reversal of conventional notions of madness and sanity:

---

[31]     Roy Porter, *Madness: A Brief History* (Oxford, 2003), p. 66.

[32]     Writing in the 1970s, Anthony Storr notes: 'It seems probable that the idea that genius is somehow allied to madness did not originate in observing that creative people had more neurotic or psychotic symptoms than anyone else, but in the feeling that both creative people and mad people had mental experiences which the ordinary person found incomprehensible or did not share'. Anthony Storr, *The Dynamics of Creation* (Harmondsworth, 1991), p. 263. More recently, Dean Simonton offers the following theory: 'In general, creativity requires the cognitive ability and the dispositional willingness to "think outside the box"; to explore novel, unconventional and even odd possibilities; to be open to serendipitous events and fortuitous results; and to imagine the implausible or consider the unlikely. From this requirement arises the need for creators to have such traits as defocused attention, divergent thinking, openness to experience, independence and nonconformity. Let us call this complex configuration of traits the "creativity cluster." Because some psychopathological symptoms correlate with several of the characteristics making up the creativity cluster, moderate amounts of these symptoms will be positively associated with creative behavior.' Dean K. Simonton, 'Are Genius and Madness Related? Contemporary Answers to an Ancient Question', *Psychiatric Times*, 22/7 (31 May 2005), sourced from www.psychiatrictimes.com.

The myth of the sick artist, we may suppose, has established itself because it is of advantage to the various groups who have one or another relation with art. To the artist himself the myth gives some of the ancient powers and privileges of the idiot and the fool, half-prophetic creatures, or of the mutilated priest [...] By means of his belief in his own sickness, the artist may the more easily fulfil his chosen, and assigned, function of putting himself into connection with the forces of spirituality and morality; the artist sees as insane the 'normal' and 'healthy' ways of established society, while aberration and illness appear as spiritual and moral health if only because they controvert the ways of respectable society.[33]

Of course many psychiatrists have also sought to debunk the suggested link between madness and genius; for example, with specific reference to music, W.H. Trethowan writes 'the vulgar notion of the mad genius is an overstatement'[34] and Szasz feels compelled to remind us that 'Our ideas about genius, madness, and the existence of a close relationship between them are modern inventions [...] Genius and madness are value terms, not medical or scientific terms.'[35] Yet, as Porter notes, 'The breakdowns (sometimes followed by suicide) of such creative figures as Antonin Artaud, Nijinsky, Woolf, Sylvia Plath, and Anne Sexton further fuelled the mad/genius debate'[36] and the idea of madness being the price of extreme creativity or scientific brilliance remains a frequently reinforced cultural stereotype.[37] This is not to suggest that the previously mentioned popular musicians

---

[33]     Lionel Trilling, *The Liberal Imagination* (New York, 1950), p. 162. In 1998 an article in *Q* Magazine explored the theory that rock'n'roll may drive its stars insane, suggesting that there is a particular pressure on artists to identify with such subject matter: 'In Rock'n'Roll culture, the disproportionate value lent to music supposedly touched by strife, conflict and madness warps the picture further. As long as *Closer*, *In Utero* and *The Holy Bible* are lionized, the image of rocker as a forsaken creature will survive and the pressure on artists to emulate these dark benchmarks will continue.' 'How Pop Life Drives Stars Insane: The Psychic Dangers, and Mental Casualties', *Q*, 147 (December 1998), p. 88.

[34]     William Trethowan, 'Music and Mental Disorder', in Macdonald Critchley and R.A. Henson (eds), *Music and the Brain* (London, 1978), pp. 399–400. Trethowan also takes issue with how commonly the, in his view erroneous, term is dispensed: 'The concept of the mad genius has not, furthermore, been confined to composers, but has been liberally applied to painters, poets and playwrights, to scientists and inventors, to all those, in fact, who have that particular quality of mind which lesser men are apt wrongly to regard as visionary; but after all is said, there appears to be no firm evidence that mental instability is conducive to creativity.' Trethowan, p. 400.

[35]     Thomas Szasz, 'The Mad-Genius Controversy', *The Freeman*, 55 (December 2006): 22–3.

[36]     Porter, *Madness: A Brief History*, p. 66.

[37]     The films *Shine* (Fine Line Features, 1997) – about the mental breakdown of classical pianist David Helfgott – and *A Beautiful Mind* (Dreamworks, 2001) – about the Nobel prize-winning mathematician John Forbes Nash Jr who was diagnosed with schizophrenia – are two such examples.

thought of themselves as actual geniuses, but that the often cited link between madness, creativity and genius lends the role of the 'mad' man a certain allure based on the premise that their creativity sets them apart (and above) ordinary people.

Despite Porter's reference to Woolf, Plath and Sexton, his observation that 'the glamorization of the gloomy genius had traditionally been a male preserve'[38] may help to explain why representations of 'mad' *men* as opposed to 'mad' *women* are found so much more frequently in popular music. While it is not the intention of this book to provide an in-depth exploration of issues of gender and madness within popular music – for this subject arguably warrants a comprehensive study of its own – the research herein strongly suggests that, in this particular cultural sphere, madness is predominantly the territory of male composers and performers. Indeed, there appears to be a comparative lack of songs written or performed by female artists that portray 'mad' women and, as indicated in my introduction, I located only three examples from the time period of the songs examined in the preceding chapters that may be identified as in any way embodying ideas of anti-psychiatry from a woman's perspective.[39] What is interesting is that this is in total contrast to the many representations of 'mad' women that occur within classical music, specifically opera, where, as McClary notes, 'madwomen show up rather more prominently than one would expect'[40] – the principal reason being that:

> The socially perceived differences between male and females were [...] often mapped onto the differences between reason and unreason. Both official institutions (law and medicine) and also cultural enterprises such as literature were engaged in constructing and transmitting such formulations. And as the

---

[38]     Porter, *Madness: A Brief History*, p. 87.

[39]     Clearly there are women artists whose songs present insights into 'us and them', although few appear to identify themselves as 'mad' women within their song lyrics. Thus it may be that women's madness is, on the whole, dealt with by female artists in a more subtle and, perhaps understandably, wary manner. One exception to this, according to McClary, is Diamanda Galás who, she claims, 'seizes the signs of dementia in order to give voice to political outrage'. McClary, *Feminine Endings*, p. 111. Other more recent song examples include 'Medication' by Garbage (1998), 'Opheliac' by Emilie Autumn (2006) and 'Runs in the Family' by Amanda Palmer (2008). There may well be more such examples, but this is an area that ultimately demands further research.

[40]     McClary demonstrates how the madness of female protagonists is 'delineated musically through repetitive, ornamental, or chromatic excess, and how normative procedures representing reason are erected around them to serve as protective frames preventing "contagion"'. McClary, p. 81. In contrast to this, the musical demarcation of madness within the popular songs examined here shows no signs of utilizing 'protective frames', for, as has been illustrated, the majority enact a reversal process where such 'normative procedures representing reason' instead become emblematic of the myth of madness.

frequency of operatic madwomen indicates, music likewise participated in this process.[41]

Much academic research has been conducted with respect to the apparent over-representation of women's 'madness' in both medical and cultural spheres (see Chesler, 1972; Showalter, 1987; Busfield, 1991) and Jane Ussher's observations are especially pertinent regarding the perpetual menace the label of madness holds for all women:

> I am publicly called 'neurotic' or 'hysterical' by senior men at work if I speak out or criticize. It's a common pattern. Women members of the British Parliament are continuously hectored and pathologized when they speak. Intelligent educated men still use the threat of the label of madness very cleverly, with no shame. It silences many of us. We are all in danger of being positioned as mad. Forming part of what it is to be a woman, it beckons us as a spectre in the shadows.[42]

It is therefore possible that the conspicuous nature of the many types of madness linked to women and femininity[43] means the role of the 'mad' woman is too perilous a prospect for most female popular musicians to embrace; perilous in the sense that it may be impossible for a woman to inhabit the role of madness without that role being interpreted as in some way an authentic part of her basic mental constitution. Even if this were not the case, artistic representations of madness can sometimes unwittingly reinforce such connections, as McClary warns: 'the more art gives us vivid representations of sexually frenzied madwomen, the more society as a whole (including scientists) takes for granted the bond between madness and femininity'.[44] And within popular music, Charlotte Church's song 'Crazy Chic' (2005) is a prime example wherein she readily admits that the object of her love infatuation has caused her to become 'unglued', 'not logical', 'not

---

[41]    McClary, p. 81. Porter similarly observes that, 'from the mid-nineteenth century, women have come to dominate the cultural stereotyping of mental disorder – and they have been disproportionately the recipients of mental treatments, both within and beyond custodial institutions'. Porter, *Madness: A Brief History*, p. 87.

[42]    Phyllis Chesler, Women and Madness (New York, 1972); Elaine Showalter, *The Female Malady: Women, Madness, and English Culture, 1830–1980* (New York, 1985); Joan Busfield, *Men, Women and Madness: Understanding Gender and Mental Disorder* (Basingstoke: Palgrave Macmillan, 1996). Jane Ussher, *Women's Madness: Misogyny or Mental Illness* (Hemel Hempstead, 1991), p. 6.

[43]    According to Porter, 'Depressive, hysterical, suicidal, and self destructive behaviour [...] became closely associated, from Victorian times, with stereotypes of womanhood in the writings of the psychiatric profession, in the public mind, and amongst women themselves.' Porter, *Madness: A Brief History*, p. 88.

[44]    McClary, p. 84.

sane', 'crazy', 'stupid', 'whacked out', 'a crazy chick' who admits to needing 'therapy' and 'professional help'.

With respect to the way in which psychiatric diagnoses themselves may be thought of as gendered, Pilgrim and Rogers observe that 'if women are seen prejudicially as being illogical, then men are seen as dangerous'.[45] And this distinction is important, for as Ussher reminds us:

> Men are 'mad' too [...] but [...] often men's madness takes a different form in our society. It may have different roots. It certainly exists within a different framework from that of women's madness, within a different discourse: it has a different meaning [...] men may be mad – but are likely to be positioned as bad. They are likely to manifest their discontent or deviancy as criminals.[46]

This being the case, the role of the 'mad' man may accentuate certain masculine traits that may be perceived as advantageous to the male rock artist, for being positioned as 'bad' in the context of one's rock persona is arguably more attractive than being perceived as simply 'safe' or, as might be the case for female artists adopting the 'mad' woman role, 'irrational'. For those men who are, in reality, labelled 'mad' there is, however, an undesirable consequence to such stereotyping, as Pilgrim and Rogers reveal:

> The affixing of diagnostic labels which imply 'dangerousness' and the focus on the behavioural consequences of a person's state of mind has corresponding consequences [...] men are more likely to be dealt with at the 'harsh' end of psychiatry. Thus, once a label has been affixed, overall as a group, men are in some respects dealt with more punitively than women.[47]

So, male performers' interest in madness and the resulting questioning of psychiatric treatment may also, in part, be explained by an awareness of psychiatry's more severe handling of men in general. Given Pilgrim and Rogers' assertion that 'in attempting to make women more visible, some feminist scholars may have made men relatively invisible [so that] types of madness which were linked to men and masculinity are ignored',[48] it would appear that the male artists featured in the preceding chapters have actually helped bring men's madness into the public arena as an often neglected topic for exploration and discussion.

A further point regarding gender and its relationship to madness within the context of popular music concerns McClary's observation that 'images of hyper-

---

[45]     David Pilgrim and Anne Rogers, *A Sociology of Mental Health and Illness* (Buckingham and Philadelphia, 1999), p. 60.

[46]     Ussher, pp. 9–10.

[47]     Pilgrim and Rogers, p. 57.

[48]     Ibid., p. 61.

masculine madness are extremely prevalent today in heavy metal',[49] for it is perhaps no coincidence that thrash, death and black metal – all of which have their roots in heavy metal – contain songs which capitalize on the aforementioned association of men's madness with illicit behaviour by detailing acts of severe violence (see the previous discussion of Slayer and Autopsy).[50] It is also worth noting that anti-psychiatry ideas are extremely rare within the majority of such songs, although claims that their references to violent madness are purely gratuitous are somewhat simplistic and reactionary because – alongside allusions to war, genocide and religion – these often serve as the basis for potent social critique. Conversely, in the early 1970s, Bowie, Lou Reed, Alice Cooper and Elton John all promoted images that were either androgynous or distinctly feminized;[51] and, for this reason, their 'mad' protagonists may be more comparable to many of opera's 'mad' men who, McClary states, are 'almost always of two sorts: their madness is either a manifestation of guilt [...] or of wounded or insufficient masculinity; i.e. they have become "like women" and thus participate in feminine excess'.[52] The musical adventurousness witnessed in the 'mad' songs of Elton John, Bowie and Alice Cooper certainly suggests a possible connection with the characteristic immoderation of McClary's second character type. Moreover, Catherine Clément's observation that: 'their song, whether sad or amusing, is like women's song. Dreadful in their madness or brilliant in their gaiety, they escape the

---

[49]   McClary, p. 190.

[50]   Further examples are 'Unsane, Insane and Mentally Deranged' (2001) by death metal band Murder Squad in which the protagonist offers insights into his own depravity: 'Sick mind at work, bewildered and in a trance, reach for your insides, to touch to feel and tear your soul apart'; 'Witness my Madness' (2003) by death metal band Scent of Flesh in which water and madness are metaphorically linked ('drowned into the sea of madness') before the protagonist confirms his identity as a serial killer: 'Because of me someone will die again, it is my way of life to be your pain. Witness my madness'; 'Septic Schizo' (1987) by Sepultura in which the protagonist commits self-violence: 'What I see in front of me is only the reflection of my insanity [...] My head throws itself against the wall, making my blood flow free of me'; and 'The Beast of Madness' (2002) by black metal band Ragnarok where madness and murder are equated with the devil: 'Look into my demon eyes. Watch me arise [...] I am the face of madness and pleasure. I am the face of death and terror. Say my name and you will die.'

[51]   See Todd Hayne's overview of glam rock: 'Bowie, Roxy, Iggy, Reed – had all been part of this brief chapter in pop history ... the result of a unique blending of underground American rock with a distinctly English brand of camp theatricality and gender-bending.' From the Foreword written by Haynes in Barney Hoskyns, *Glam! Bowie, Bolan and the Glitter Rock Revolution* (London, 1998), p. x. See also Auslander's premise that there was 'nothing "natural" about glam rockers androgynous personae, which were clearly and overtly constructed as bricolages of bits of masculine and feminine gender coding'. Philip Auslander, *Performing Glam Rock: Gender and Theatricality in Popular Music* (Ann Arbor, 2006), p. 67.

[52]   McClary, p. 190.

game of man-and-woman and, one by one, become heroes of deception'[53] seems especially poignant given Bowie's and Alice Cooper's penchant for manipulating conventional notions of madness and sanity.

Having identified a number of possible reasons for popular music artists' interest in the subject of madness, there remains the more specific question of why anti-psychiatry ideas in particular should filter through into songs of the late 1960s and early 1970s. Looking first to the anti-psychiatry movement itself, it is perhaps significant that all of its chief commentators were male; and, as Colin Jones identifies, 'given the largely unproblematized versions of gender roles to which Laing and others adhered: anti-psychiatry – like much of the 1960s counter-culture – was very largely boy's stuff, a guy thing'.[54] Again, this may help to explain the propensity of male artists willing to adopt such ideas into their music; but Jones's reference to the counter-culture[55] is equally pertinent, for all of the artists in the preceding chapters were musically active – albeit some in an embryonic form – during the late 1960s[56] when music 'was thought to say things of cultural and political significance, to have a message',[57] and thus any visible links between anti-psychiatry and the counter-culture could account for their awareness of anti-psychiatry ideas. To this end, and in support of such connections, John Henzell claims that: 'the concept and practices that underlie radical therapy and anti-psychiatry [...] were part and parcel of the whole range of "alternatives" that came into being during this period as objections to the state, orthodox professional practices, and the imprisoned frames of mind that were felt by many to compose

---

[53]     Catherine Clément, *Opera, or the Undoing of Women*, trans. B. Wing (London, 1989), p. 120.

[54]     Colin Jones, 'Raising the Anti: Jan Foudraine, Ronald Laing and Anti-Psychiatry', in Marijke Gijswijt-Hofstra and Roy Porter (eds), *Cultures of Psychiatry and Mental Health Care in Postwar Britain and the Netherlands* (Amsterdam and Atlanta, 1998), p. 290.

[55]     For a brief summary of the 1960s counter-culture, typically referred to as the Underground in the UK, see Roy Shuker, *Popular Music: The Key Concepts*, (London: Routledge, 2002) pp. 70–72.

[56]     Of those artists featured in the preceding chapters, the Beatles and Pink Floyd were most associated with the 1960s counter-culture, with both groups producing commercially successful psychedelic music on albums such as *Sgt. Pepper's Lonely Hearts Club Band* (1967) and *The Piper at the Gates of Dawn* (1967) respectively. To a lesser extent, Lou Reed was also enjoying commercial success at this time with The Velvet Underground, although they were not involved in the psychedelic scene and demonstrated more avant-garde influences. David Bowie's first real commercial success came in the form of *Space Oddity* (1969), but prior to this his first album, *David Bowie* (1967), contained discernible psychedelic elements. Elton John had been active since 1964 as a performer in the band Bluesology and released his first studio album, *Empty Sky*, with Bernie Taupin in 1969. Vincent Furnier's band Alice Cooper only adopted the name in 1968, but had been active since 1964, releasing their first album, *Pretties for You*, in 1969.

[57]     Sheila Whiteley, *The Space Between the Notes: Rock and the Counter-Culture* (London, 1992), p. 1.

it'.[58] He cites Laing and Goffman as two of the foremost and dynamic 'cultural heroes' alongside Herbert Marcuse and Gregory Bateson, claiming that the period's 'revolutionary stance proceeded in two directions, outwards towards social action and inwards towards psychological experience'.[59] Indeed, because of the exposure of anti-psychiatry concepts – particularly those espoused by Laing and Cooper – Henzell maintains that the 'mad' man/woman, in the form of the schizophrenic, was treated with uncommon reverence: 'The schizophrenic became a cultural hero [...] to be schizophrenic was to escape the inauthenticity society condemned most of us to, to embark on a "journey" [...] whose eventual destination might be existential integrity.'[60]

Colin Jones similarly argues that anti-psychiatry was part of a wider effort to challenge supposedly set archetypes of authority, explaining that while 'the youth movement in particular repudiated family norms, social and educational conventions and political orthodoxies [...] Anti-psychiatry proudly took a place within these wider struggles in the name of "anti-ness".'[61] He further maintains that, although challenges had been mounted against the medical model of psychiatry and the asylum system prior to the 1960s, the way in which anti-psychiatric ideas were articulated, and the receptiveness of the counter-culture to them, also assured its rise to prominence:

> In many ways it was less what anti-psychiatrists were saying which was new than the ways in which they were saying them and the nature of the audience they were addressing [...] The influence of anti-psychiatry in the culture of the 1960s and early 1970s owed less to proceedings of psychiatric conferences or to articles in medical and scientific journals or to intra-professional struggles than to general market publications. The paperback world (notably in the English speaking world, Penguin Books), the underground press, posters and popular visual imagery and an 'event'-seeking popular press all found grist for their mills in anti-psychiatry.[62]

---

[58]    John Henzell, 'Art, Madness and Anti-Psychiatry: A Memoir' in Katherine Killick and Joy Schaverien (eds), *Art, Psychotherapy and Psychosis* (London, 1997), p. 184.

[59]    Ibid.

[60]    Ibid., p. 185.

[61]    Jones, 'Raising the Anti', p. 285. In relation to anti-psychiatry's cultural significance, Jones also warns against underestimating the reasons for such: 'The movement's claims have been largely recuperated, distorted or made to look anodyne (or just plain silly) by later developments. Yet sometimes it is important not to let hindsight cloud our view. To do so in the case of anti-psychiatry is to miss one of the reasons for its cultural resonance in the late 1960s and early 1970s, namely its sense of belonging to and in some senses emblematising a more profound call for change' (p. 292).

[62]    Ibid., pp. 287–8. Jones's further claim that 'Anti-psychiatry presented a picture of the self ravaged by the technological fixations of late capitalism and the juggernaut of

In relation to Laing's addressees, Antonio Melechi equally notes that 'his politics of alterity found a ready audience in the psychedelic underground, who adopted Laing as a guide for their collective journey into inner consciousness';[63] and he claims that Kingsley Hall – Laing's attempt to establish a radical therapeutic community – 'was more than just a residential community. From the very beginning it staged exhibitions, conferences and lectures [...] Quickly establishing itself as an important centre of underground activity, Kingsley Hall came to embody a type of radical lifestyle and philosophy.'[64]

That Laing had an impact culturally as well as within the psychiatric profession is without doubt, and specific connections between him and the musical climate of the period were noted in an article by Albert Goldman for *Life* magazine in 1971:

> R.D. Laing and Arthur Janov share nearly equal time and prestige in Rolling Stone with the rock stars who are their most conspicuous patients [...] the insanity kick is rationalized as the only solution to living in a bad, mad world. When you flip, you get away from it all. You go, ideally, into an institution where the patients dictate the rules and the doctors are indulgent big brothers. You go off on a long voyage, comparable to an enormous acid trip, which carries you into the remotest recesses of human consciousness and raises you to the level of creative genius.[65]

While unmistakably sardonic, Goldman's observations nonetheless highlight many of the principal themes contained in the songs examined in the preceding chapters, suggesting they were, indeed, common currency at this time. What is more, he detected a noticeable shift in terms of what was deemed worthy of note within rock itself – a move away from discussing the actual music and its performance to an examination of the artists' internal psyche: 'The centre of interest in the rock world has shifted dramatically this year from the music, poetry and stage presence of the rockers to the case histories of their neuroses and psychoses and confessional outpourings in the press.'[66]

With respect to whether such an impact was possible or even intended, Ingleby suggests that 'Laing was not really interested in a showdown with the psychiatric profession. His message was aimed over their heads at the people who bought his

---

modernisation' (p. 290) is clearly pertinent to the anti-consumerism stance evident in Pink Floyd's *The Dark Side of the Moon*.

[63]    Antonio Melechi (ed.), *Psychedelia Britannica: Hallucinogenic Drugs in Britain* (London, 1997), p. 42.

[64]    Ibid., p. 44.

[65]    Albert Goldman, 'A Bad, Mad World: James and Livingston Taylor', in Albert Goldman, *Sound Bites* (New York, 1992), p. 198.

[66]    Ibid., p. 196.

books – the bearers of the new counter-culture';[67] and Melechi equally attests to the widespread recognition Laing's writing received: 'The publication of *The Politics of Experience* (1967) took Laing to new heights of popularity; his heady mixture of polemic and poetry fast becoming required reading for the counter-culture.'[68] There were also established links between Cooper and Laing and other so-called 'radical' writers and poets: Melechi, for example, details Laing's dealings with Beat writers William Burroughs and Allen Ginsberg[69] – this being significant in its own right, for the Beat writers may also have inadvertently influenced popular musicians' interest in madness at this time. The well-known passage from Jack Kerouac's *On The Road*, for example – 'the only people for me are the mad ones, the ones who are mad to live, mad to talk, mad to be saved, desirous of everything at the same time, the ones who never yawn or say a commonplace thing, but burn, burn, burn'[70] – clearly offers the possibility of a positive construal of the word 'mad', implying vitality, spontaneity and unconventionality of character; and, as Simon Warner identifies, the Beat poets and writers influenced many popular musicians keen to move rock lyrics beyond Tin Pan Alley 'moon and June' songs: 'while popular music since the rise of Elvis Presley in the mid-Fifties has drawn richly, from time to time, on literary sources […] it is the Beat era that provides the most fertile source for rock musicians who want to add substance, or at least the veneer of substance, to their work'.[71] Warner also suggests that Kerouac, Ginsberg and William Burroughs would have related to the concept of 'the artist against the world, the creative genius as the centre of a very personal universe';[72] and this is clearly relevant to the previous discussion of creativity and madness, and the apparent sense of individual endeavour that popular music's 'mad' songs of the 1960s and 1970s display.[73]

---

[67]    David Ingleby, 'The View from the North Sea', in Gijswijt-Hofstra and Porter, *Cultures of Psychiatry*, p. 301.

[68]    Melechi, p. 46.

[69]    For details see Melechi, pp. 42–3, and Henzell, p. 185.

[70]    Jack Kerouac, *On the Road* [1957] (London, 2000), p. 7.

[71]    Simon Warner, 'Beat Generation/Rock Generation: A Cultural Continuum', *Route* (May 2000).

[72]    Ibid.

[73]    Many of the artists featured in the preceding chapters either met with key Beat figures or have acknowledged their influence. Warner details how 'McCartney became closer to Ginsberg in the mid-sixties when he proposed a spoken word label called Zapple which was to feature the poet alongside other literary innovators such as Burroughs and Ken Kesey […] By the Middle of the Sixties, William Burroughs had made his home in London […] In England he spent some time with McCartney' (ibid.) According to George Tremlett, Bowie 'began devouring the Beat writers from San Francisco and soaking up the traditions of decadence from Paris and Berlin' (George Tremlett, *David Bowie Living on the Brink* (London, 1996), p. 21) and he includes quotes from Bowie indicating the role his half-brother Terry played in introducing him to such literature: 'Yes, it was Terry who started everything for me […] Terry was into all the Beat writers, Jack Kerouac, Allen Ginsberg,

In addition to the aforementioned literary influences, a number of books published in the 1970s aimed at a lay readership – Nicholas Kittrie's *The Right To Be Different*; Peter Schrag's *Mind Control*; Samuel Chavkin's *The Mind Stealers*; Alan Scheflin and Edward Opton's *The Mind Manipulators* – promoted the idea that society itself was becoming like a 'closed institution'.[74] In particular, they drew attention to the apparently growing and largely deceptive means by which the individual could be policed and, if necessary, reconditioned – the notion that medical means were increasingly being drawn upon to solve ostensibly social problems: 'It is no longer the cop or the schoolmaster telling the individual what to do; it is science. The individual is no longer being punished; he is being treated.'[75] While many of these books were published too late to have a direct influence on those popular musicians exhibiting anti-psychiatry ideas within their songs in the early 1970s, they nevertheless reveal a contemporaneous interest in, and concern regarding, techniques formulated to control and modify human behaviour. Alan Scheflin and Edward Opton's warning concerning the relentless escalation of such techniques is typical: 'Lobotomy, psychosurgery, electrical stimulation of the brain, castration, brainwashing, hypnosis, behaviour modification – the list of techniques for gaining control of the mind of another is quite substantial. Left unchecked, the list will continue to expand, and the techniques already on it will reach a higher degree of efficiency.'[76] There was also an unmistakable irony resulting from the way in which madness had – thanks to the publicity surrounding figures such as Laing – become in vogue, for it meant that more people were now susceptible to the notion of treatment, as Schrag observed:

> By whatever name, madness has always served a social function. The special
> significance of its current form is that while it loses some of its classic stigma,
> it becomes increasingly prevalent and fashionable, spawning more and more

---

Gregory Corso, Lawrence Ferlinghetti, William Burroughs (p. 19). With reference to Lou Reed's Beat associations, biographer Victor Bockris explains how, while studying music, philosophy and literature studies at Syracuse University, Reed 'wanted to make a point of being a writer more than a rock and roller [...] Lou preferred to be associated with writers like Jack Kerouac.' Victor Bockris, *Lou Reed the Biography* (London, 1994), p. 44.

[74]     Nicholas Kittrie, *The Right To Be Different: Deviance and Enforced Therapy* (London, 1971). According to Schrag, there appeared to be 'a growing tendency to employ new methods of intervention, to create wholly new systems of "treatment," and to promote a new ideology of control in which society itself becomes more and more like a closed institution'. Peter Schrag, *Mind Control* (New York, 1978), p. xiii.

[75]     Ibid., pp. xvii–xviii. Chavkin, whose work concentrates on the potential abuse of psychosurgery, makes a similar point: 'There is much concern about the growing acceptance of behaviourist and psychosurgical remedies for what basically are socioeconomic problems requiring political solutions.' Samuel Chavkin, *The Mind Stealers: Psychosurgery and Mind Control* (Boston, 1978), p. 2.

[76]     Alan W. Scheflin and Edward M. Opton, *The Mind Manipulators* (New York, 1978), p. 10.

marginal ailments and anticipatory symptoms [...] Historically, madness was usually a yes-or-no proposition – the individual was either a lunatic (or a heretic), or he wasn't. He was either in or out of an institution; he was one of us or one of them. Nowadays we are all supposed to be a little crazy.[77]

Added to this, a number of books emerged in the 1970s that focused their critique of psychiatry on specific treatments, with the express intention of raising public awareness concerning their potential harm – John Friedberg's *Shock Treatment Is Not Good For Your Brain* (1976) and Leonard Frank's *The History of Shock Treatment* (1978) being two such examples.

Thus it may be argued that the songs featured in the previous chapters (alongside the aforementioned publications) were part of a general desire to explore, and in some cases draw attention to, the way in which an individual might be contained and potentially damaged by organized psychiatry. The work of the anti-psychiatrists during the 1960s was arguably the principal catalyst for such widespread attention – and here the association of figures such as Laing, Cooper and Goffman with the counter-culture was a significant factor; but it was not until the end of that decade that such ideas began filtering through into popular song, whereupon the suitability of more overtly theatrical styles was undoubtedly important. As indicated in the preceding chapters, the fact that a number of other popular works (films, novels and autobiographies) emerged at this time espousing similar ideas – from literature such as Charles Willeford's *The Machine in Ward Eleven* (1963) and *One Flew Over the Cuckoo's Nest* through to films such as *Family Life* and autobiographies in the vein of Frances Farmer's *Will There Really Be A Morning* – suggests that this was a unique and, for a time, widespread event in the history of popular culture.

Having explored popular music's absorption and evocation of anti-psychiatry ideas in the late 1960s and 1970s, and the possible factors which may have prompted these, it is worth surmising why the presence of such views eventually diminished. As explained in the introduction, anti-psychiatry was never a united, univocal movement; however, it is fair to say that the fall in popularity of some of its principal figures, and the eventual criticism it received from both academic and popular media sources, signalled an end to its extensive cultural influence. While the reasons for anti-psychiatry's downfall are too numerous and complex to be extensively explored here, the principal ones are nevertheless relevant to an understanding of popular music's deviation from what may be termed more sympathetic and challenging representations of madness. In the case of the British anti-psychiatrists, the dissolving of the counter-culture had a notable impact on their future influence, a fact capitalized on by some commentators to imply a lack of substance and good policy: 'Its vague theories, its detachment from traditional politics, and its disregard to strategy all seem to have condemned it –

---

[77]     Schrag, pp. 58–9.

like flower power – to wilt when the good vibes faded away',[78] wrote Ingleby. At the same time, criticisms of Laing and his associates became more prevalent – the previously mentioned article by Goldman being one such example: 'The promises of cure from the curse of contemporary consciousness held out by the new witch doctors sound rather like variations on the now widely condemned illusion of truth through drugs.'[79] In short, Laing, in particular, was maligned for what Humphrey Osmond termed his 'psychedelic model of madness',[80] an accusation which Ann Claytor finds credible because 'Laing did produce material which encouraged the romanticization of psychosis as a prophetic spiritual state and linked psychosis by implication with the LSD "trip".'[81] Moreover, as Henzell observes: 'A criticism of Laing and others involved in anti-psychiatry is that they made schizophrenia too glamorous' – although, as previously indicated, this probably enhanced its appeal as a topic for exploration in popular music.

Further contributors to anti-psychiatry's demise[82] may be located in the individual paths its principal figures took during the 1970s, with Laing leaving Britain in 1971 only to return in 1976 showing few signs of his previous views; Cooper becoming increasingly political and detaching himself from his former colleagues; and Szasz publicly distancing himself from the British contingent. Added to this – as Pilgrim and Rogers observe with respect to the work of Goffman and Scheff – 'the 1980s witnessed sociological interest in health and illness turning more and more to mainstream topics of physical and chronic illness. Sociology's reputation for being an intellectual fellow traveller of, or contributor to, "anti-psychiatry" had diminished.'[83] Perhaps equally significant, the work of the anti-psychiatrists continued to attract criticism for the lack of workable solutions to the numerous problems within institutional psychiatry it identified, as exemplified by Ussher: 'whilst we may want to acknowledge the critiques of the dissenters [...] They offered very little other than (often poorly worked out) theoretical explanations, and vilifications of professional care.'[84] And here we see a further connection between anti-psychiatry and the representation of its ideas within

---

[78]     David Ingleby (ed.), *Critical Psychiatry: The Politics of Mental Health* (Harmondsworth: Penguin, 1981). Quoted in Lucy Johnstone, *Users and Abusers of Psychiatry: A Critical Look at Psychiatric Practice* (London, 2000), p. 239.

[79]     Goldman, p. 199.

[80]     Miriam Siegler, Humphrey Osmond and Harriet Mann, 'Laing's Models of Madness', in Robert Boyers and Robert Orrill (eds), *Laing and Anti-Psychiatry* (Harmondsworth, 1972), pp. 99–122. Sourced from Melechi, p. 48.

[81]     Ann Claytor, *A Changing Faith: A History of Developments in Radical Critiques of Psychiatry Since the 1960s* (Sheffield, 1993), p. 105.

[82]     Here I am referring specifically to the anti-psychiatry movement of the 1960s and the principal figures associated with it. Anti-psychiatry as a way of thinking clearly is not locked into this brief period of time.

[83]     Pilgrim and Rogers, p. xiii.

[84]     Ussher, p. 241.

popular music, for none of the songs examined in the previous chapters make any attempt to provide actual solutions to the evidently serious questions they raise concerning both psychiatric diagnosis and treatment, a fact that effectively illustrates John Street's belief that: 'Pop can capture what it is like to be oppressed; it cannot explain that oppression or remove it.'[85]

A further reason for the apparent disappearance of songs demonstrating an alignment with anti-psychiatric thinking by the close of the 1970s was that the new musical styles to emerge were arguably less suited to exploring such themes. The immediacy and upfront character of punk, for example, may have been able to adopt the delinquent stance evident in Reed's and Alice Cooper's 'mad' songs, but had neither the musical means nor aspiration to offer the kind of complex representations of madness and unmasking of constructs evident in the more theatrical styles of the early 1970s. In addition, the romantic notion of the undisputed link between creativity and madness, and the mystery and intrigue surrounding the figure of the 'mad' fool, were arguably more relevant to the thinking of the late 1960s counter-culture for which the day was undeniably gone. While an interest in the topic of madness was maintained within the genre of heavy metal (as previously identified) this took a different path, with many songs exploring men's madness and its assumed association with criminality and violence.

The evident exposure and popularity of anti-psychiatry ideas during the 1960s and 1970s has yet to be replicated, although many organizations critical of psychiatry exist today and most acknowledge the work and influence of its early proponents, Laing and Szasz. Opposing the biological model and emphasizing social factors as the root cause of people's emotional distress remains a common ethos (see, for example, the Critical Psychiatry Network), and most organizations stress a person's fundamental right to self-determination, opposing any form of psychiatric coercion (the International Association Against Psychiatric Assault; the Blue Panthers Party: Rage Against Psychiatry; and The Anti-Psychiatry Coalition being cases in point). The past decade has also witnessed renewed interest in the questioning of invasive psychiatric drug treatments from within the general media, as evidenced by the documentaries *Panorama: The Secrets of Seroxat* (2002); Louis Theroux's *America's Medicated Kids* (2010),[86] national newspaper articles 'Child's Ordeal Shows Risks of Psychosis Drugs for Young' (2010);[87] 'Doctors

---

[85]     John Street, *Rebel Rock: The Politics of Popular Music* (New York, 1986), p. 162.

[86]     Both these programmes were BBC productions broadcast on 13 October 2002 and 18 April 2010 respectively. Seroxat was alleged to be the second most prescribed anti-depressant in the UK in 2002.

[87]     Duff Wilson, 'Child's Ordeal Shows Risks of Psychosis Drugs for Young', *New York Times*, 1 September 2010.

Told to Curb Use of Ritalin in Hyperactive Children' (2008),[88] and Jon Ronson's investigative book *The Psychopath Test* (2011).

Since the late 1990s, controversy surrounding the medication of children diagnosed with the conditions depression, schizophrenia, attention deficit disorder (ADD) and attention deficit hyperactivity disorder (ADHD) has arguably prompted the occurrence of lyric references to this particular subject within a variety of popular music contexts: from a humorous ditty on *The Simpsons* – 'When I can't stop my fiddling I just takes me Ritalin, I'm popping and sailing, man'[89] (sung by Bart Simpson to the tune of 'Popeye the Sailor Man') – to Paolo Nutini's comment on the allure of a quick mental fix: 'Oh, take this pill because you're ill, I bet you didn't even know, Take one in a day and one in a night, And watch them problems go … And everybody's scuttling rattlin rizzin around' ('Ritalin', 2009). Songs bearing the direct title 'Medication' from prominent bands Queens of the Stone Age (2005), Garbage (1998) and Spiritualized (1995) also allude to the negative consequences of a progressively more medicated society.

Despite such occurrences, it appears more specific allusions to 'crazy' and 'insane' behaviour remain in evidence within popular music ostensibly as a means to engender or augment elements of quirkiness and nonconformity – see, for example, Cypress Hill's 'Insane in the Brain' (1993) and The Charlatans' 'Oh Vanity' (2008), both of which contain lyrical references to insanity but no apparent effort to question the implications and meaning of such. Thus, while artists such as Eels, Emilie Autumn, Amanda Palmer and Green Day have produced examples of post-1970s songs that retain a certain engagement with anti-psychiatry thinking, it is fair to say that such cases are now comparatively rare.

In his memoir 'Art, Madness and Anti-Psychiatry', Henzell reveals his desire to witness a return of the social and political climate that enabled the rise of anti-psychiatry in the 1960s and 1970s, primarily because he hopes that a further period of development may ensue in which 'those involved will, in their own fashion, create some of the exciting, sometimes foolish, but rewarding excesses that spiced those years'.[90] In many respects, the same sentiment may be applied to popular music's representations of madness, for as this study demonstrates, the absorption and evocation of anti-psychiatry ideas was characteristic of a number of songs written in the late 1960s and 1970s and has not been replicated to the same extent since. With reference to anti-psychiatry's achievements, Ingleby claims that 'Laing lost the battle with psychiatry. However, he won the war with "reality" […] for

---

[88]     Mark Henderson, 'Doctors Told to Curb Use of Ritalin in Hyperactive Children', *The Times*, 24 September 2008.

[89]     The song appears in the second episode of the eleventh season, titled 'Brother's Little Helper' (an allusion to the Rolling Stones' song 'Mother's Little Helper'), in which Bart is diagnosed with ADD and given 'Focusyn' to improve his academic performance. The original broadcast date was 3 October 1999. It was written by George Meyer and directed by Mark Kirkland.

[90]     Henzell, p. 194.

the counter-culture he contributed to ushered in the post-industrial, post-modern era [...] Gone was the belief in objective truths, the faith in scientists as impartial guardians of those truths'.[91] While the role of psychedelic and progressive rock has been largely documented in this regard (see, for example Whiteley 1992), the evidence herein suggests those songs expounding anti-psychiatry ideas in the 1970s made an equally vital contribution, effectively supporting Bart Moore-Gilbert's premise that 'the conception of the 1970s as a moment of cultural "closure" may well be misplaced'.[92] But perhaps of greatest importance, the songs examined in the previous chapters attest to popular music's ability to question general suppositions regarding madness, its identifying features and appropriate means of 'treatment'. In particular, they bring to the fore issues of men's madness that are all too often neglected, employing reversal strategies, humour and role play in a way that is both entertaining and ultimately thought-provoking.

---

[91]  Ingleby, 'The View from the North Sea', pp. 301–2.

[92]  Bart Moore-Gilbert (ed.), *The Arts in the 1970s: Cultural Closure?* (London, 1994), p. 15. Here Moore-Gilbert is counteracting the opinion of Christopher Booker, who describes the 1970s as 'a time when, in politics, in the arts or in almost any other field one considers, the prevailing mood was one of a somewhat weary, increasingly conservative, increasingly apprehensive disenchantment'. Christopher Booker, *The Seventies: Portrait of a Decade*, (London: Allen Lane, 1980), p. 5. Quoted in Moore-Gilbert, p. 1.

# Bibliography

Adame, Alexandra and Gail Hornstein, 'Representing Madness: How Are Subjective Experiences of Emotional Distress Presented in First-Person Accounts?' *The Humanist Psychologist*, 34/2 (2006): 135–58.

Artaud, Antonin, *Manifesto In Clear Language* (1925).

———, *The Theatre and Its Double*, Collected works, vol. 4, trans. Victor Corti (London: Calder & Boyars, 1974).

Auslander, Philip, *Performing Glam Rock: Gender and Theatricality in Popular Music* (Ann Arbor: The University of Michigan Press, 2006).

Bangs, Lester, 'Killer', *Rolling Stone* (6 January 1972).

Bayer, Ronald, *Homosexuality and American Psychiatry* (New Jersey: Princeton University Press, 1987).

Benjamin, Walter, 'The Author as Producer', in Peter Demetz (ed.), *Reflections: Essays, Aphorisms, Autobiographical Writings* (New York: Schocken Books, 1978).

Bernardin, Claude and Tom Stanton, *Rocket Man: Elton John from A–Z* (Westport, CT: Praeger, 1996).

Berrios, German and Roy Porter (eds), *A History of Clinical Psychiatry: The Origin and History of Psychiatric Disorders* (London: Athlone Press, 1995).

Black, Susan, *Elton John: In His own words* (London: Omnibus Press, 1993).

Bockris, Victor, *Lou Reed the Biography* (London: Hutchinson, 1994).

Boyers, Robert and Robert Orrill (eds), *Laing and Anti-Psychiatry* (Harmondsworth: Penguin, 1972).

Brackett, David, *Interpreting Popular Music* (Berkeley and Los Angeles: University of California Press, 2000).

Breggin, Peter, *The Crazy from the Sane* (New York: Lyle Stuart, 1970).

———, *Toxic Psychiatry* (London: Harper Collins, 1993).

Buckley, David, *The Complete Guide to the Music of David Bowie* (London: Omnibus Press, 1996).

Busfield, Joan, *Men, Women and Madness: Understanding Gender and Mental Disorder*, (Basingstoke: Palgrave Macmillan, 1996).

Cagle, Van M., *Reconstructing Pop/Subculture: Art, Rock and Andy Warhol* (Thousand Oaks, CA: Sage Publications, 1995).

Charters, Ann, *The Penguin Book of the Beats* (London: Penguin Books, 1993).

Chavkin, Samuel, *The Mind Stealers: Psychosurgery and Mind Control* (Boston: Houghton Mifflin, 1978).

Chekhov, Anton, *Ward No. 6.* [1892], in Anton Chekhov, *Ward No. 6 and Other Stories, 1892–1895*, trans. Ronald Wilks (London: Penguin, 2002).

Chesler, Phyllis, *Women and Madness* (New York: Avon Books, 1972).

Clarke, Eric F. and Nicola Dibben, 'Sex, Pulp and Critique', *Popular Music*, 19/2 (2000).

Claytor, Ann, *A Changing Faith: A History of Developments in Radical Critiques of Psychiatry Since the 1960s* (Thesis: The University of Sheffield, Jan 1993).

Clément, Catherine, *Opera, or the Undoing of Women*, trans. B. Wing (London: Virago Press, 1989).

Cooke, Deryck, *The Language of Music* (Oxford: Oxford University Press, 1959).

Cooper, David, *Psychiatry and Anti-Psychiatry* [1967] (London: Routledge, 2001).

———, *The Death of the Family* (London: Penguin, 1971).

Critchley, Macdonald and R.A. Henson (eds), *Music And The Brain* (London: Heinemann, 1978).

Cross, Simon, 'Visualizing Madness: Mental Illness and Public Representation', *Television New Media*, 5/3 (August 2004).

Davis, Derek R., *Scenes of Madness: A Psychiatrist at the Theatre* (London: Routledge, 1995).

Deleuze, Gilles and Felix Guattari, *Anti-Oedipus*, trans. R. Hurley, M. Seem and H.R. Lane (London: Athlone Press, 1984).

Doggett, Peter, *Lou Reed: Growing up in Public* (London: Omnibus Press, 1991).

Dollier, Trevor, 'Swing the Sword, Paint your Face, and Electrify the Stage, It's Alice Cooper Time', *Rock On* (13 August 1971).

Farber, Seth, *Madness, Heresy, and the Rumor of Angels: The Revolt Against the Mental Health System* (Chicago: Open Court, 1993).

Farmer, Frances, *Will There Really Be a Morning? An Autobiography by Frances Farmer* [1972] (Glasgow: Fontana/Collins, 1983).

Feder, Lillian, *Madness in Literature* (Princeton and Guildford: Princeton University Press, 1980).

Fleming, Michael and Roger Manvell, *Images of Madness: The Portrayal of Insanity in the Feature Film* (London: Associated University Presses, 1985).

Foucault, Michel, *Madness and Civilization: A History of Insanity in the Age of Reason*, trans. R. Howard (London: Routledge, 1997). Originally published in French in 1961 as *Histoire de la Folie*; first published in Great Britain in 1967 by Tavistock Publications.

Frame, Janet, *Faces in the Water* (New York: George Braziller, 1961).

Frank, Leonard (ed.), *The History of Shock Treatment* (San Francisco: L.R. Frank, 1978).

Friedberg, John, *Shock Treatment Is Not Good For Your Brain* (San Francisco: Glide, 1976).

Frith, Simon, *Performing Rites: On the Value of Popular Music* (Oxford: Oxford University Press, 1996).

Gijswijt-Hofstra, Marijke and Roy Porter (eds), *Cultures of Psychiatry and Mental Health Care in Postwar Britain and the Netherlands* (Amsterdam and Atlanta, GA: Rodopi, 1998).

Gilman, Sander, *Seeing the Insane* (New York: John Wiley, 1982).

————, *Difference and Pathology: Stereotypes of Sexuality, Race and Madness* (Ithaca and London: Cornell University Press, 1985).

Goffman, Erving, 'The Moral Career of the Mental Patient' [1959], in Thomas Szasz, *The Age of Madness* (London: Routledge & Kegan Paul, 1975), pp. 251–66.

————, *Asylums: Essays on the Social Situation of Mental Patients and Other Inmates* [1961] (London: Penguin, 1991).

Gogol, Nikolay, *Diary of a Madman and Other Stories* [1834] (London: Penguin, 1972).

Goldman, Albert, *Sound Bites* (New York: Random House, 1992).

Gotkin, Janet and Paul Gotkin, *Too Much Anger, Too Many Tears: A Personal Triumph Over Psychiatry* (New York: Quadrangle, 1975).

Gross, Elaine, 'Where Are the Chickens?' *Rolling Stone* (15 October 1970).

Hames, Annette and Ian Inglis, 'And I Will Lose My Mind … Images of Mental Illness in the Songs of the Beatles', *International Review of the Aesthetics and Sociology of Music (IRASM)*, 30/2 (1999): 173–88.

Harper, Stephen, 'Media, Madness and Misrepresentation: Critical Reflections on Anti-Stigma Discourse', *European Journal of Communication*, 20/4 (2005).

Harris, Thomas, *Red Dragon* (New York: Dell, 1981).

————, *The Silence of the Lambs* (New York: St Martin's Press, 1988).

Heller, Joseph, *Catch 22* [1962] (London: Vintage, 1994).

Henzell, John, 'Art, Madness and Anti-Psychiatry: A Memoir', in Katherine Killick and Joy Schaverien (eds), *Art, Psychotherapy and Psychosis* (London: Routledge, 1997).

Hoskyns, Barney, *Glam! Bowie, Bolan and the Glitter Rock Revolution* (London: Faber and Faber, 1998).

'How Pop Life Drives Stars Insane: The Psychic Dangers, and Mental Casualties', *Q* Magazine, 147 (December 1998), p. 88.

Ingleby, David, 'The Social Construction of Mental Illness', in Peter Wright and Andrew Treacher (eds), *The Problem of Medical Knowledge: Examining the Social Construction of Medicine* (Edinburgh: Edinburgh University Press, 1982).

————, 'The View from the North Sea', in Marijke Gijswijt-Hofstra and Roy Porter (eds), *Cultures of Psychiatry and Mental Health Care in Postwar Britain and the Netherlands* (Amsterdam and Atlanta, GA: Rodopi, 1998).

Johnstone, Lucy, *Users and Abusers of Psychiatry: A Critical Look at Psychiatric Practice* (2nd edn, London: Routledge, 2000).

Jones, Cliff, *Another Brick in the Wall: The Stories Behind Every Pink Floyd Song* (reprinted edn, London: Carlton, 1999).

Jones, Colin, 'Raising the Anti: Jan Foudraine, Ronald Laing and Anti-Psychiatry', in Marijke Gijswijt-Hofstra and Roy Porter (eds), *Cultures of Psychiatry and Mental Health Care in Postwar Britain and the Netherlands* (Amsterdam and Atlanta, GA: Rodopi, 1998).

Jones, David W., *Myths, Madness and the Family: The Impact of Mental Illness on Families* (Basingstoke: Palgrave Macmillan, 2002).

Jones, Kathleen, *Asylums and After: A Revised History of the Mental Health Services: From the Early 18th Century to the 1990s* (London: Athlone Press, 1993).

Kerouac, Jack, *On the Road* [1957] (London: Penguin, 2000).

Kesey, Ken, *One Flew Over the Cuckoo's Nest* (New York: Viking, 1962).

Kittrie, Nicholas N., *The Right To Be Different: Deviance and Enforced Therapy* (London: The Johns Hopkins Press, 1971).

Kosinski, Jerzy, *Being There* [1971] (London: Black Swan Books, 1983).

Kotowicz, Zbigniew, *R.D. Laing and the Paths of Anti-Psychiatry* (London: Routledge, 1997).

Laing, Ronald D., *The Divided Self: An Existential Study in Sanity And Madness* [1960] (Harmondsworth: Penguin, 1964).

————, *The Politics of Experience* [1967] (Harmondsworth: Penguin, 1978).

Laing, Ronald D. and Aaron Esterson, *Sanity, Madness and the Family* (Harmondsworth: Penguin, 1964).

Lemert, Edwin M., *Social Pathology* (New York: McGraw-Hill, 1951).

London, Jack, *The Star Rover* (New York: Macmillan, 1915).

Lynch, Kate, *David Bowie: A Rock'n'Roll Odyssey* (London: Proteus Books, 1984).

MacDonald, Ian, *Revolution in the Head: The Beatles' Records and the Sixties* (London: Fourth Estate, 1994).

Mackenzie, Henry, *The Man of Feeling* [1771] (Oxford: Oxford University Press, 1987).

McClary, Susan, *Feminine Endings: Music, Gender, and Sexuality* (Minneapolis: University of Minnesota Press, 1991).

Melechi, Antonio (ed.), *Psychedelia Britannica: Hallucinogenic Drugs in Britain* (London: Turnaround, 1997).

Mendelsohn, John, 'Love It to Death', *Rolling Stone* (15 April 1971).

Miles, Barry, *David Bowie Black Book* (London: Omnibus Press, 1980).

Moore, Allan F., *Rock – The Primary Text: Developing a Musicology of Rock* (Buckingham: Open University Press, 1993).

O'Grady, Terence J., *The Beatles: A Musical Evolution* (Boston, MA: Twayne, 1983).

Moore-Gilbert, Bart (ed.), *The Arts in the 1970s: Cultural Closure?* (London: Routledge, 1994).

Nuttall, Jeff, *Bomb Culture* [1968] (London: Paladin, 1970).

Otto, Beatrice K., *Fools Are Everywhere: The Court Jester Around The World* (Chicago and London: University of Chicago Press, 2001).

Parry-Jones, William L., *The Trade in Lunacy* (London: Routledge & Kegan Paul, 1972).

Pilgrim, David and Anne Rogers, *A Sociology of Mental Health and Illness* (2nd edn, Buckingham and Philadelphia: Open University Press, 1999).

Plath, Sylvia, *The Bell Jar* [1963] (reset edn, London: Faber and Faber, 1996).

Porter, Roy, *A Social History of Madness: Stories of the Insane* (London: Phoenix, 1996).

———, *Madness: A Brief History* (Oxford: Oxford University Press, 2003).

Prior, Lindsay, *The Social Organization of Mental Illness* (London: Sage Publications, 1993).

Roberts, Andrew, *Mental Health History Timeline*, A Middlesex University Resource at: <http://www.mdx.ac.uk/www/study/mhhtim.htm> (accessed 19 July 2005).

———, *American History Timeline*, A Middlesex University Resource at: <http://www.mdx.ac.uk/www/study/America.htm> (accessed 19 July 2005).

Ronson, Jon, *The Psychopath Test* (London: Picador, 2011).

Rose, Philip, Which One's Pink? An Analysis of Concept Albums of Roger Waters and 'Pink Floyd' (Burlington, Ontario: Collectors' Guide Publishing, 1998).

Ross, Alison, *The Language of Humour* (London: Routledge, 1998).

Roszak, Theodore, *The Making of a Counter Culture: Reflections on the Technocratic Society and Its Youthful Opposition* (London: Faber and Faber, 1970).

Rule, Ann, *The Stranger Beside Me* [1980] (New York: Time Warner, 1994).

Sandford, Christopher, *Bowie: Loving the Alien* (New York: Da Capo Press, 1998).

Scheff, Thomas J., *Being Mentally Ill: A Sociological Theory* (London: Weidenfeld & Nicolson, 1966).

Scheflin, Alan W. and Edward M. Opton, *The Mind Manipulators* (New York: Paddington, 1978).

Schrag, Peter, *Mind Control* (New York: Pantheon, 1978).

Schwarz, Ted, *The Hillside Strangler: A Murderer's Mind* (New York: Doubleday, 1981).

Scott, Derek B., *From the Erotic to the Demonic: On Critical Musicology* (Oxford: Oxford University Press, 2003).

Scull, Andrew, *Social Order/Mental Disorder: Anglo-American Psychiatry in Historical Perspective* (London: Routledge, 1989).

———, *The Most Solitary of Afflictions: Madness and Society in Britain, 1700–1900* (New Haven and London: Yale University Press, 1993).

Sedgwick, Peter, *Psycho Politics: Laing, Foucault, Goffman, Szasz, and the Future of Mass Psychiatry* (New York: Harper & Row, 1982).

Showalter, Elaine, *The Female Malady: Women, Madness, and English Culture, 1830–1980* (New York: Pantheon Books, 1985).

Shuker, Roy, *Popular Music: The Key Concepts* (London: Routledge, 2002).

Siegler, Miriam, Humphrey Osmond and Harriet Mann, 'Laing's Models of Madness', in Robert Boyers and Robert Orrill (eds), *Laing and Anti-Psychiatry* (Harmondsworth: Penguin, 1972).

Simonton, Dean K., 'Are Genius and Madness Related? Contemporary Answers to an Ancient Question', *Psychiatric Times*, 22/7 (31 May 2005).

Snelders, Stephen, 'LSD and the Dualism between Medical and Social Theories of Mental Illness', in Marijke Gijswijt-Hofstra and Roy Porter (eds), *Cultures of Psychiatry and Mental Health Care in Postwar Britain and the Netherlands* (Amsterdam and Atlanta, GA: Rodopi, 1998).

Storr, Anthony, *The Dynamics of Creation* [1972] (Harmondsworth: Penguin, 1991).

Street, John, *Rebel Rock: The Politics of Popular Music* (New York: Basil Blackwell, 1986).

Sullivan, Terry and Peter T. Maiken, *Killer Clown: The John Wayne Gacy Murders* (New York: Grosset & Dunlap, 1983).

Szasz, Thomas S., *The Myth of Mental Illness: Foundations of a Theory of Personal Conduct* [1961] (London: Paladin, 1972).

———, *Law, Liberty and Psychiatry* [1963] (London: Routledge & Kegan Paul, 1974).

———, *The Manufacture of Madness* [1970] (London: Paladin, 1973).

———, *Ideology and Insanity: Essays on the Psychiatric Dehumanization of Man* [1970] (London: Calder & Boyars, 1973).

———, *The Age of Madness* (London: Routledge & Kegan Paul, 1975).

———, *Psychiatric Slavery* (New York: Free Press/Macmillan, 1977).

———, *Insanity: The Idea and Its Consequences* (New York: John Wiley, 1987).

———, *Cruel Compassion: Psychiatric Control of Society's Unwanted* (New York: John Wiley, 1994).

———, 'The Mad-Genius Controversy', *The Freeman*, 55 (December 2006): 22–3.

Tarsis, Valeriy, *Ward 7: An Autobiographical Novel*, trans. K. Brown (London: Collins and Harvill Press, 1965).

Tepa Lupack, Barbara, *Insanity as Redemption in Contemporary American Fiction* (Gainesville: University Press of Florida, 1995).

Tremlett, George, *The David Bowie Story* (New York: Warner Paperback Library, 1975).

———, *David Bowie Living on the Brink* (London: Century Books, 1996).

Trethowan, William, 'Music and Mental Disorder', in Macdonald Critchley and R.A. Henson (eds), *Music and the Brain* (London: Heinemann, 1978).

Trilling, Lionel, *The Liberal Imagination* (New York: Doubleday, 1950).

Turner, Steve, *A Hard Day's Write: The Stories Behind Every Beatles Song* (London: Index Books, 2006).

Ussher, Jane, *Women's Madness: Misogyny or Mental Illness* (Hemel Hempstead: Harvester Wheatsheaf, 1991).

Valenstein, Elliot, *Brain Control: A Critical Examination of Brain Stimulation and Psychosurgery* (New York: John Wiley, 1973).

Vonnegut, Kurt, *Slaughterhouse-Five: or, The Children's Crusade, a Duty Dance with Death* (New York: Dell, 1969).

Wahl, Otto, *Media Madness: Public Images of Mental Illness* (New Brunswick, NJ: Rutgers University Press, 1995).

Walser, Robert, *Running with the Devil: Power, Gender and Madness in Heavy Metal Music* (Hanover, NH: Wesleyan University Press, 1993).

Warner, Simon, 'Beat Generation/Rock Generation: A Cultural Continuum', *Route* (May 2000).

Whiteley, Sheila, *The Space Between the Notes: Rock and the Counter-Culture* (London: Routledge, 1992).

Willeford, Charles, *The Machine in Ward Eleven* (New York: Belmont Books, 1963).

Wilshire, Bruce, *Role Playing and Identity: The Limits of Theatre as Metaphor* (Bloomington and Indianapolis: Indiana University Press, 1991).

Winick, Charles, 'The Image of Mental Illness in the Mass Media', in Walter R. Gove (ed.), *Deviance and Mental Illness* (London: Sage Publications, 1982).

Witkiewicz, Stanislaw I., *The Madman and the Nun/Wariat i zakonnica* (1923), in *The Madman and the Nun and the Crazy Locomotive: Three Plays by Stanislaw Ignacy Witkiewicz*, edited, translated and with an introduction by Daniel C. Gerould and C.S. Durer [1966] (New York: Theatre Book Publishers, 1989).

Yates, Richard, *Revolutionary Road* [1961] (London: Vintage, 2007).

## Additional Materials (Documentaries, Films, Plays, Comic Books)

*A Beautiful Mind* (2001) directed by Ron Howard, Dreamworks.

*Animal Man* #60 (DC comics/Vertigo, June 1993).

*Clive Barker's A–Z of Horror* (1997) directed by Ursula Macfarlane, BBC.

*Coogan's Bluff* (1968) directed by Don Siegel, Universal Pictures.

*Family Life* (1971) directed by Ken Loach, screenplay by David Mercer, EMI Films.

'How Mad Are You?' *Horizon*, BBC (broadcast 11 November 2008).

*King of Hearts* (1966) directed by Philippe de Broca, MGM United Artists.

*Law Breakers Always Lose* #4 (Marvel Comic Group, #1 Spring 1948–#10 October 1949).

*Louis Theroux: America's Medicated Kids*, (broadcast 18 April 2010), BBC.

*Marat-Sade* (1967) directed by Peter Brook, United Artists.

*Me, Myself and Irene* (2000) directed by Bobby Farrelly and Peter Farrelly, TCF/ Conundrum.

*Mr Deeds Goes to Town* (1936) directed by Frank Capra, Columbia.

*My Learned Friend* (1943) directed by Basil Dearden and Will Hay, Gainsborough Pictures.

*Peeping Tom* (1960) directed by Michael Powell, Anglo-Amalgamated.

*Pressure Point* (1962) directed by Hubert Cornfield, United Artists.

*Shine* (1996) directed by Scott Hicks, Fine Line Features.

*The Incredible Hulk* (Marvel, February 1995).

*The Madwoman of Chaillot* (1969) directed by Bryan Forbes, Warner.

*The Ruling Class* (1972) directed by Peter Medak, United Artists.

'The Secrets of Seroxat' *Panorama*, BBC (broadcast 13 October 2002).
*The Three Faces of Eve* (1957) directed by Nunnally Johnson, TCF.
*When the Clouds Roll By* (1919) directed by Victor Fleming and Theodore Reed, United Artists.

# Discography

Alice Cooper (1971) 'The Ballad of Dwight Fry', *Love It to Death*, Straight Records, Warner Bros.
——— (1978) *From the Inside*, Warner Bros.
Autopsy (1989) 'Critical Madness', Severed Survival, Peaceville.
Emilie Autumn (2006) 'Opheliac', *Opheliac*, Trisol Music Group.
Beatles (1965) *Help!* Parlophone.
——— (1966) *Revolver*, Parlophone.
——— (1967) *Sgt. Pepper's Lonely Hearts Club Band*, Parlophone.
——— (1967) 'The Fool on the Hill', *Magical Mystery Tour*, Parlophone.
Black Sabbath (1970) 'Paranoid', *Paranoid*, Vertigo.
——— (1975) 'Am I Going Insane (Radio)', *Sabotage*, NEMS.
James Blunt (2005) 'Out of My Mind', *Back to Bedlam*, Atlantic.
David Bowie (1967) *David Bowie*, Deram DML.
——— (1969) 'Space Oddity'/'Wild Eyed Boy From Freecloud', Philips.
——— (1971) 'All the Madmen', *The Man who Sold the World*, Mercury.
——— (1971) *Hunky Dory*, RCA.
——— (1972) *The Rise and Fall of Ziggy Stardust and the Spiders from Mars*, RCA.
——— (1974) *Diamond Dogs*, RCA, APL.
The Dead Weather (2010) 'I'm Mad', *Sea of Cowards*, Third Man.
Camel (1976) 'Lunar Sea', *Moon Madness*, Deram.
Charlatans (2008) 'Oh! Vanity', *You Cross My Path*, Cooking Vinyl.
Charlotte Church (2005) 'Crazy Chick', *Tissues and Issues*, Sony BMG.
Kasabian (2009) *West Ryder Pauper Lunatic Asylum*, RCA/Columbia.
Kevin Coyne (1972) 'Mad Boy', *Case History*, Dandelion.
——— (1972) 'Sand All Yellow', *Case History*, Dandelion.
——— (1973) 'House on the Hill', *Marjory Razorblade*, Virgin.
——— (1978) 'Lunatic', *Dynamite Daze*, Virgin.
Kevin Coyne and Siren (1969) 'Asylum', *Siren*, Dandelion.
——— (1970) 'Our Jack' on (1995) *Siren – The Club Rondo*, DJC.
Cradle of Filth (2003) 'Babalon A.D. (So Glad for the Madness)' *Damnation and a Day*, Sony.
Cypress Hill (1993) 'Insane in the Brain', *Black Sunday*, Ruff House.
Deceased (1995) 'The Blueprints for Madness', *The Blueprints for Madness*, Relapse.
Willie Dixon (1967) 'Insane Asylum', *Chess LP 1532*, Chess.
Doctors of Madness (1976) 'I Think We're Alone', *Late Night Movies All Night Brainstorms*, Polydor.

Doors (1970) 'Ship of Fools', *Morrison Hotel*, Elektra.

Eels (1996) 'Mental', *Beautiful Freak*, DreamWorks.

——— (1996) 'Novocaine for the Soul', *Beautiful Freak*, DreamWorks.

——— (1998) 'Electro-Shock Blues', *Electro-Shock Blues*, DreamWorks.

——— (1998) 'My Descent into Madness', *Electro-Shock Blues*, DreamWorks.

Marianne Faithful (1990) 'The Ballad of Lucy Jordan', *Blazing Away*, Island.

Fields of the Nephilim (1987) 'Vet for the Insane', *Dawn Razor*, Beggars Banquet.

Frank Zappa and The Mothers of Invention (1968) 'Mom & Dad', *We're Only In It for the Money*, Verve/MGM.

Fun Boy Three (1982) 'The Lunatics Have Taken Over the Asylum', *Fun Boy Three*, Chrysalis.

Diamanda Galás (1998) 'Insane Asylum', *Malediction and Prayer*, Asphodel.

Garbage (1998) 'Medication', *Version 2.0*, Mushroom.

Genesis (1976) 'Mad Man Moon', *A Trick of the Tail*, Charisma.

The Grateful Dead (1974) 'Ship of Fools', *From the Mars Hotel*, Grateful Dead Records.

Green Day (1994) 'Basket Case', *Dookie*, Reprise.

——— (2004) 'Jesus of Suburbia', *American Idiot*, Reprise.

Helloween (2000) 'The Madness of the Crowds', *The Dark Ride*, Nuclear Blast.

Iron Maiden (1988) 'Can I Play With Madness', *Seventh Son of a Seventh Son*, EMI.

Jimi Hendrix Experience (1967) 'Manic Depression', *Are You Experienced?*, Track.

Elton John (1971) 'Madman Across the Water', *Madman Across the Water*, DJM.

King Crimson (1969) '21st Century Schizoid Man', *In the Court of the Crimson King*, Atlantic.

Kinks (1971) 'Acute Schizophrenia Paranoia Blues', *Muswell Hillbillies*, Velvel.

Lambert, Hendricks & Ross (1960) 'Twisted', *Lambert, Hendricks, & Ross!* Columbia.

Macabre (1987) *Grim Reality*, Vinyl Solution.

——— (2003) 'Drill Bit Lobotomy' 7 inch

Madness (1982) 'Madness (Is All in the Mind)', *The Rise & Fall*, Stiff.

——— (1985) 'Mad Not Mad', *Mad Not Mad*, Zarjazz.

Mental Crypt (1999) 'Chemical Lobotomy', *Ground Zero* (promo recording).

Joni Mitchell (1974) 'Twisted', *Court and Spark*, Asylum.

Move (1968) 'Cherry Blossom Clinic', *The Move*, Regal Zonophone.

Murder Squad (2001) 'Unsane, Insane and Mentally Deranged', *Unsane, Insane and Mentally Deranged*, Crash Music.

Napalm Death (1992) 'Dementia Access', *Utopia Banished*, Earache.

——— (1991) 'Mass Appeal Madness', *Death by Manipulation*, Earache.

——— (1991) 'Mentally Murdered', *Death by Manipulation*, Earache.

——— (1991) 'Walls of Confinement', *Death by Manipulation*, Earache.

Napoleon XIV (1966) 'They're Coming To Take Me Away Ha Haaa!' Warner Bros.

Paolo Nutini (2009) 'Ritalin', Atlantic.

Ozzy Osbourne (1980) 'Crazy Train', *Blizzard of Oz*, Jet.

—— (1981) 'Diary of a Madman', *Diary of a Madman*, Jet.

Amanda Palmer (2008) 'Runs in the Family', *Who Killed Amanda Palmer*, Road Runner.

Tom Paxton (1970) 'Crazy John', *Tom Paxton 6*, Elektra.

Pink Floyd (1967) *The Piper at the Gates of Dawn*, Columbia/EMI.

—— (1973) *The Dark Side of the Moon*, Harvest.

Dory Previn (1970) 'Mr Whisper', *On My Way to Where*, Mediarts/United Artists.

Procol Harum (1968) 'In the Autumn of My Madness', *Shine on Brightly*, A&M.

Psycho Realm (1998) 'Psycho City Blocks/Psychic Interlude', *The Psycho Realm*, Ruff House.

Queen (1991) 'I'm Going Slightly Mad', *Innuendo*, Parlophone.

Queens of the Stone Age (2005) 'Medication', *Lullabies to Paralyze*, Interscope.

Ragnarok (2002) 'The Beast of Madness', *In Nomine Satanas*, Regain.

Ramones (1977) 'Teenage Lobotomy', *Rocket to Russia*, Sire.

—— (1977) 'Gimme Gimme Shock Treatment', *Leave Home*, Rhino.

—— (1978) 'Go Mental', *Road to Ruin*, Rhino.

—— (1983) 'Psycho Therapy', *Subterranean Jungle*, Warner Bros.

Lou Reed (1974) 'Kill Your Sons', *Sally Can't Dance*, RCA.

Melanie Safka (1970) 'What Have They Done to My Song, Ma', *Candles in the Rain*, Buddah.

—— (1970) 'Psychotherapy', *Leftover Wine*, Buddah.

Scent of Flesh (2003) 'Witness my Madness', *Roaring Depths of Insanity*, Blot.

Sepultura (1989) 'Lobotomy', *Beneath the Remains*, Roadrunner.

—— (1987) 'Septic Schizo', *Schizophrenia*, Roadrunner.

Slayer (1986) 'Criminally Insane', *Reign in Blood*, Def Jam.

Small Faces (1968) 'Mad John', *Ogden's Nut Gone Flake*, Immediate.

Spiritualized (1995) 'Medication', *Pure Phase*, Dedicated.

Rod Stewart (1977) 'You're Insane', *Foot Loose & Fancy Free*, Warner Bros.

Thin Lizzy (1971) 'Old Moon Madness', *Thin Lizzy*, Deram.

—— (1973) 'The Hero and the Madman', *Vagabonds of the Western World*, Deram.

Ugly Kid Joe (1992) 'Madman', *America's Least Wanted*, Mercury.

# Index